Understanding the .NET Framework

Tony Baer
Jan D. Narkiewicz
Kent Tegels
Chandu Thota
Neil Whitlow

Wrox Press Ltd. ®

Understanding the .NET Framework

© 2002 Wrox Press

wrox

Published by Wrox Press Ltd,
Arden House, 1102 Warwick Road, Acocks Green,
Birmingham, B27 6BH, UK
Printed in the USA
ISBN 1-861007-09-4

Trademark Acknowledgments

Credits

Authors
Tony Baer
Jan D. Narkiewicz
Kent Tegels
Chandu Thota
Neil Whitlow

Additional Material
Adam Cartwright
David Schultz
Julian Skinner

Commissioning Editor
Craig A. Berry

Technical Editors
David Barnes
Catherine Alexander

Managing Editor
Louay Fatoohi

Project Manager
Christianne Bailey

Author Agent
Charlotte Smith

Technical Reviewers
Slavomir Firman
Damien Foggon
Mark Horner
Shefali Kulkarni
David Schultz

Production Coordinator
Abbie Forletta

Production Assistant
Neil Lote

Proof Reader
Chris Smith

Cover
Chris Morris

Index
John Collin

About the Authors

Tony Baer

Tony Baer, the president of onStrategies (http://www.onstrategies.com), is a well-published IT analyst with over 15 years background in enterprise systems. A leading authority on J2EE and .NET platforms, Baer focuses on strategic technology utilization for the enterprise, specializing in distributed data management, application development, middleware architecture, data warehousing, and leading enterprise application areas including ERP, supply chain planning, and customer relationship management.

Baer has authored numerous books, white papers, media articles, and essays, and regularly publishes onStrategies Perspectives, periodic analyses of technology market trends available to qualified technology users and providers.

Jan D. Narkiewicz

Jan D. Narkiewicz is Chief Technical Officer at Software Pronto, Inc (jann@softwarepronto.com). In his spare time Jan is Academic Coordinator for the Windows curriculum at U.C. Berkeley Extension, teaches at U.C. Santa Cruz Extension, and writes for *ASP Today*.

Kent Tegels

Kent Tegels is a system developer and engineer working for HDR, Inc., a leading Engineering, Architecture and Consulting Firm. He is a Microsoft Certified Professional plus Site Builder, System Engineer (plus Internet), and Database Administrator.

Chandu Thota

Chandu Thota works as a Technical Lead for ClickCommerce Inc, a leading Channel Management Software Company. He spends a lot of time in researching and programming for Web Services and related technologies. He has published many articles on Web Services and .NET technologies for leading magazines including MSDN. He also founded an online .NET XML Web Services portal http://www.esynaps.com. You can reach him via his web site http://www.csthota.com or at csthota@att.net.

I would like to dedicate my work to my mom – Katyayani Devi and my dad - Ramachandra Rao for giving me everything that I need to be here today in my life.

Neil Whitlow

Neil's first experience with recreational programming was with Basic on a Commodore Vic 20, and as the years went by it became an addiction that grew into QuickBasic 4.5, Visual Basic 1.0 in DOS and Windows, and a course of study in college. After graduating, his first job was developing with MicroFocus PC-based COBOL for OS/2 and DOS. From there it was on to jobs using QuickBasic 4.5 and Visual Basic versions 3-6. He's also had his fingers into solutions with goodies such as Java, Perl, ASP, and SQL Server, to name a few. Currently, Neil is a Senior Systems Analyst developing rich-client software for pen-based mobile PCs with a large insurance company in Nashville, TN. When not programming or doing yardwork, Neil enjoys woodworking, watching football and hockey, and re-reading fiction from H. Beam Piper, J.R.R. Tolkien, Robert A. Heinlein, and the like.

I thank Jesus Christ for his unconditional love. I thank my wife, Lillian, for loving me despite my inner geek and for her patience with my profession. Thanks to my parents for buying their son a Commodore Vic 20 on that Christmas long ago. Thanks to all the Wrox folks for their patience and guidance. Finally, thanks to some friends at previous jobs who have been influential and inspirational in my professional programming career: Mac Gardner, Curt Nazor, Analiese Merrill, Becky Moore, and most of all Shane Russell.

Neil can be reached at authorwhitlow@comcast.net

.NET

Table of Contents

Table of Contents

Table of Contents

Table of Contents

vi

.NET

Introduction

Welcome to *Understanding the .NET Framework*. When it comes to the .NET Framework there is a great deal that can be learned and must be understood before you can effectively begin to develop applications. What's more, unlike previous new releases of Microsoft's development tools, .NET is such a radical shift that most developers (even seasoned Microsoft guys) have to virtually start from scratch. There is also the potential for a great deal of confusion given Microsoft's sudden predilection for trying to brand everything .NET.

The aim behind this book is to help clarify exactly what all the fuss regarding .NET is all about. The decision to starting working in .NET should not be undertaken lightly, so this book serves to provide an overview to whole .NET fandango so that you can better understand the decision you are about to take.

Along the way, we hope to answer several basic questions:

- ❑ What is .NET exactly?
- ❑ What advantages does .NET bring?
- ❑ Why should I choose .NET?
- ❑ How do I use .NET?
- ❑ What can I do with .NET?

By the end of the book you should have a clear idea of whether .NET is a worthwhile investment for your career and/or company, and be ready to start learning .NET development properly.

Who Is This Book For?

This book is for developers with experience in Java, C++, Visual Basic, or another modern general-purpose language who want to find out about .NET. It provides an overview of the technology for evaluating .NET's fit to your own business needs. It also gives a broad .NET grounding, enabling you to decide which areas on the .NET Framework to investigate further.

What You Need to Use This Book

You will learn a lot about .NET from simply reading this book. However to get the most from this book you will need to get your hands dirty with some .NET programming. To do this you will need:

❑   Windows 2000 or Windows XP

❑   The .NET Framework redistributable or SDK. Both of these are available for free download from MSDN at http://msdn.microsoft.com/netframework/prodinfo/getdotnet.asp.

Parts of the book also use the following products:

❑   Visual Studio .NET 1.0. We have tested the code for version 1.0, although most of the code should work in late pre-release versions.

❑   SQL Server 2000 – although most of the techniques we use could apply to any database system, including Access.

What Does This Book Cover?

The book starts with an introduction to .NET as a whole, followed by an overview of .NET's impact on developers. We then move on to look at some common development tasks, and how we'd carry them out using the .NET Framework. Finally we take a look back at what we've learned, and then look forward to the ways that .NET will change the world.

Here are the main points covered in each chapter:

Chapter 1, *.NET in Perspective* covers what .NET is, why it is here, and where it is going. We look at the components of Microsoft's .NET strategy, the circumstances that have caused Microsoft to create .NET, and some of its most likely effects.

Chapter 2, *Developing with .NET* examines the underlying infrastructure of the Framework including the runtime (Common Language Runtime, Common Type System, and Common Language Specification) and the basic class library. We will also cover some of the basics of .NET development from Visual Studio .NET to deployment.

Chapter 3, *Web Development* looks at the changes that ASP.NET makes to the way we build dynamic web sites. We will review how it builds on CGI and scripting languages such as ASP, and then see how to develop our own ASP.NET pages – in a text editor or Visual Studio .NET.

Chapter 4, *Windows Client Development* looks at Windows Forms, the .NET Framework's classes for creating Windows applications. We see how to create Windows applications using the built-in controls, and then how we can extend and combine controls to produce our own. We also see how to use visual inheritance to maintain common elements across several forms in an application.

Chapter 5, *Working with Data* explores different types of data, and how to process them using .NET. We cover relational databases, XML, and flat files, learning about ADO.NET, the .NET XML classes, and streams.

Chapter 6, *Legacy and Enterprise Systems* looks at integrating .NET with DLLs, COM components, and COM+ middle-tier services.

Chapter 7, *Web Services* are the new kid on the block in development possibilities and a big factor in the genesis of .NET itself. This chapter explores their significance, how they came about and how to develop them in .NET.

Chapter 8, *Where Do We Go From Here?* draws conclusions from everything we've learned, and then looks to the future. We look at the future of .NET – where it will lead, and what implications it will have. We also look at how to develop .NET skills and practices within your organization.

Conventions

We've used a number of different styles of text and layout in this book to help differentiate between the different kinds of information. Here are examples of the styles we used and an explanation of what they mean.

Code has several styles. If it's a word that we're talking about in the text – for example, when discussing a For...Next loop, it's in this font. If it's a block of code that can be typed as a program and run, then it's also in a gray box:

```
<?xml version 1.0?>
```

Sometimes we'll see code in a mixture of styles, like this:

```
<?xml version 1.0?>
<Invoice>
    <part>
        <name>Widget</name>
        <price>$10.00</price>
    </part>
</invoice>
```

In cases like this, the code with a white background is code we are already familiar with; the line highlighted in gray is a new addition to the code since we last looked at it.

Advice, hints, and background information comes in this type of font.

> **Important pieces of information come in boxes like this.**

Bullets appear indented, with each new bullet marked as follows:

- ❑ **Important Words** are in a bold type font
- ❑ Words that appear on the screen, or in menus like the File or Window, are in a similar font to the one you would see on a Windows desktop
- ❑ Keys that you press on the keyboard, such as *Ctrl* and *Enter*, are in italics

How to Download the Code from the Web Site

The code in this books tends to be short snippets do demonstrate concepts, rather than full applications. However, the code examples are available for download from the Wrox web site. To get the code, visit www.wrox.com and navigate to *Understanding the .NET Framework*. Click on Download in the Code column, or on Download Code on the book's detail page.

The files are in ZIP format. Windows XP recognizes these automatically, but Windows 2000 requires a de-compression program such as WinZip or PKUnzip.

Customer Support

We want to hear from you! We want to know what you think about this book: what you liked, what you didn't like, and what you think we can do better next time. Please send us your comments, either by returning the reply card in the back of the book, or by e-mailing feedback@wrox.com. Please mention the book title in your message.

We do listen to these comments, and we do take them into account on future books.

Errata

We've made every effort to make sure that there are no errors in the text or in the code. If you do find an error, such as a spelling mistake, faulty piece of code, or any inaccuracy, we would appreciate feedback. By sending in errata you may save another reader hours of frustration, and help us provide even higher quality information.

E-mail your comments to support@wrox.com. Your information will be checked and if correct, posted to the errata page for that title, and used in subsequent editions of the book.

To find errata for this title, go to www.wrox.com and locate *Understanding the .NET Framework*. Click on the Book Errata link, which is below the cover graphic on the book's detail page.

E-mail Support

If you wish to directly query a problem in the book with an expert who knows the book in detail then e-mail support@wrox.com, with the title of the book and the last four numbers of the ISBN in the subject field of the e-mail. Please include the following things in your e-mail:

❑ The **title of the book**, **last four digits of the ISBN**, and **page number** of the problem in the Subject field.

❑ Your **name**, **contact information**, and the **problem** in the body of the message.

We *won't* send you junk mail. We need the details to save your time and ours. When you send an e-mail message, it will go through the following chain of support:

❑ Customer Support – Your message is delivered to our customer support staff, who are the first people to read it. They have files on most frequently asked questions and will answer anything general about the book or the web site immediately.

❑ Editorial – Deeper queries are forwarded to the technical editor responsible for that book. They have experience with the programming language or particular product, and are able to answer detailed technical questions on the subject.

❑ The Authors – If even the editor cannot answer your problem, they will forward the request to the author. We do try to protect the author from any distractions to their writing, but we are happy to forward specific requests to them. All Wrox authors help with the support on their books. They will e-mail the customer and the editor with their response, and again all readers should benefit.

The Wrox support process can only offer support to issues that directly relate to the content of the book. Support for questions that fall outside the scope of normal book support is provided via the community lists of our http://p2p.wrox.com/ forum.

p2p.wrox.com

For author and peer discussion join the P2P mailing lists. Our unique system provides **programmer to programmer™** contact on mailing lists, forums, and newsgroups, all in addition to our one-to-one e-mail support system. If you post a query to P2P, you can be confident that the many Wrox authors and industry experts who use our mailing lists will examine it. At p2p.wrox.com you will find a number of different lists that will help you, not only while you read this book, but also as you develop your own applications.

To subscribe to a mailing list just follow these steps:

1. Go to http://p2p.wrox.com/.

2. Choose the appropriate category from the left menu bar.

3. Click on the mailing list you wish to join.

4. Follow the instructions to subscribe and fill in your e-mail address and password.

5. Reply to the confirmation e-mail you receive.

6. Use the subscription manager to join more lists and set your e-mail preferences.

Why This System Offers the Best Support

You can choose to join the mailing lists or you can receive them as a weekly digest. If you don't have the time, or facility, to receive the mailing list, then you can search our online archives. Junk and spam mails are deleted, and the unique Lyris system protects your e-mail address. Queries about joining or leaving lists, and any other general queries about lists, should be sent to listsupport@p2p.wrox.com.

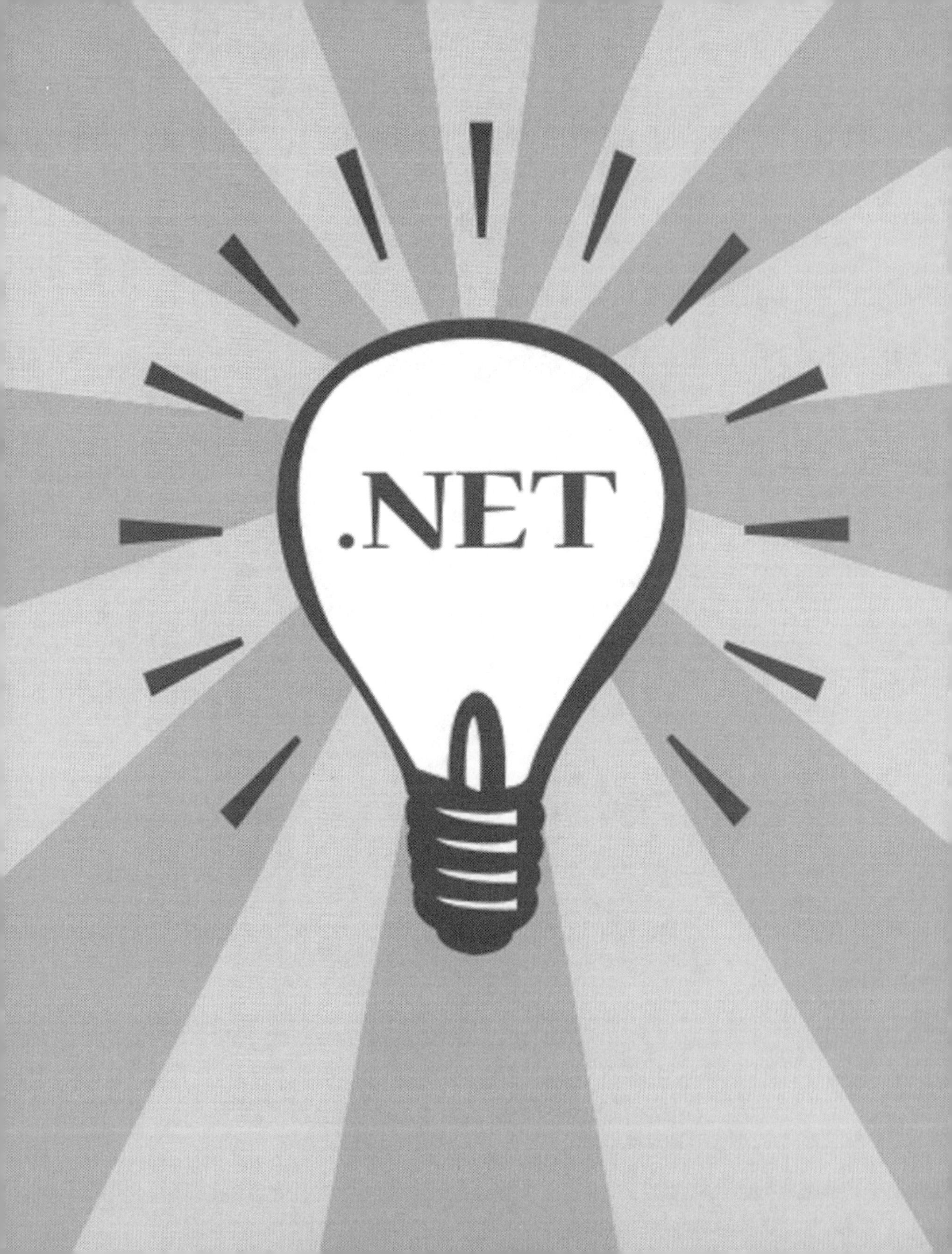
.NET

1

.NET in Perspective

The emergence of the **Microsoft .NET Framework** and Visual Studio .NET is just the latest chapter in Microsoft's quest to bring computing to the masses. For starters, the underlying technology provides several features that not only unify all of Microsoft's development languages, but tools and languages from many third parties as well. With Visual Studio .NET, it provides an IDE that standardizes development for all of Microsoft's languages. With the .NET Framework, it has similarly standardized the way .NET applications written in any compliant language are executed and deployed. Furthermore, .NET paves the way for software as services.

To take advantage of the new power and versatility of the .NET Framework, Windows developers must, to some extent, "re-invent themselves". VB programmers need to adopt object-oriented methodologies, C++ developers need to get used to VB style RAD capabilities and a high-level class library, and Java developers need to learn to love proprietary Microsoft environments – at least for the time being.

Welcome to the world of .NET. It's a world of opportunity – and tough love – for developers. And because of Microsoft's tendency to stretch its brands far and wide, .NET is potentially very confusing. Today Microsoft is using the .NET label to brand operating systems, servers, personalized web services, programming languages, component models, integrated development environments, and run-time deployment environments. As time passes, .NET will come to mean even more.

So what is .NET anyway, and why all the hype? *Understanding the .NET Framework* dissects the .NET Framework architecture enabling you to make a realistic appraisal of what it can offer and deliver to your needs. But before we tell you how to take advantage of the newest features in Microsoft's development technologies, we want to introduce you to .NET and describe its significance.

Specifically, this chapter introduces .NET by:

❑ Providing the historical background on the emergence of the .NET Framework

❑ Describing what .NET actually is and what it is supposed to deliver

❑ Providing a brief comparison of the .NET Framework with J2EE, the obvious alternative

❑ Outlining the challenges for .NET applications

Historical Background

Microsoft's mission has always been to penetrate – many say, dominate – enterprise computing from the ground up. For application developers, this crusade became especially clear with the 1991 release of Visual Basic, the first Integrated Development Environment (IDE) for Windows. VB liberated developers from relying on cryptic text editors to write code, graphics editors for developing GUI elements, and standalone C compilers to generate executable code. It provided developers with the power of developing the types of graphical, event-driven applications normally developed in C using a language that was much easier to learn.

VB combined code editing, graphics design, and a Just-in-Time (JIT) compiler all in one easy-to-use, drag-and-drop environment. For more advanced developers seeking to develop more powerful enterprise applications, Microsoft also offered Visual C++, followed several years later by its Java dialect, Visual J++. Microsoft offered these languages, both à la carte and as part of the Visual Studio bundle, which added supporting tools like Visual SourceSafe for version control and Visual Modeler for introductory UML design.

As Microsoft set its sights on the enterprise with NT, SQL Server, Exchange, and the other server products, its development environments became increasingly enterprise focused. The evolution of VB in many ways paralleled that of client-server technology in general. VB applications were initially simple, standalone affairs that provided the ability for power users to quickly learn application development and develop simple productivity applications.

However, VB's part in Microsoft's plans for world domination became clearer with VB 3's addition of database access and OLE (Object Linking and Embedding); VB 4's object-based class modules; VB 5's improved native code compilation and web-friendly ActiveX controls; and VB 6's addition of full ODBC database connectivity and other 'serious' features.

In so doing, Microsoft helped introduce legions of developers to component development techniques through the Component Object Model (COM) architecture. Over the years, COM and its successors DCOM (Distributed COM) and COM+ gradually added the middle tier necessary for developing web and enterprise applications that could scale more easily.

With the .NET Framework, Microsoft supersedes the COM model, not simply grafting on object-oriented features such as inheritance and overloading, but replacing the entire runtime with a modular environment that automates housekeeping functions such as memory and object management, reduces version conflicts, and extends support to non-Microsoft languages. While Visual C++ may have already had many of these features, they were new to VB.

Genesis of .NET

By 1990, Microsoft dominated the PC market. As we've seen above with its attitude to development products, Microsoft planned to dominate the server market by gradually moving up – starting by taking control of workgroup computing, and networks in small businesses, then setting its sights ever higher.

During the nineties, a couple of things happened that shook up this vision:

❑ The rise of the Internet – people realized that networks could work really well using platform-independent, non-proprietary standards on the server. You could even get your server's operating system for free! Suddenly Microsoft's desktop domination looked less valuable.

❑ The move to non-PC devices such as network computers, set-top-boxes, and WAP phones. This was driven even further by the Internet's killer app – the Web. You could put a web browser on any client platform, and then look at a site hosted on any server platform.

Enter Java. Its introduction in 1995 took the web development world by storm because it seemed built for the Web.

It had the robust, efficient 'feel' of a serious C-based language, but the high-level rapid-development capability of Visual Basic. It could run on any server; it could run on any client. At the time, Microsoft had just begun its 180-degree turn to embrace the Internet, and lacked a clear alternative. In fact one could argue that a significant factor in the emergence of the .NET Framework was the on-again, off-again Microsoft relationship with Java.

Microsoft hit back with some success. Attacking platform-independent clients, Microsoft set about producing the best web browser software – and focusing it on Windows. Internet support started appearing in Office and Windows, making Windows the clear platform for the web-enabled desktop. Then ASP (Active Server Pages) appeared as a means to dynamically produce web content through a simpler API than other tools and languages provided at the time.

However, Java had carved out a place for itself – and Microsoft's incremental approach to attacking enterprise computing started looking inadequate. With Java already out there and gaining popularity, Microsoft grudgingly licensed Java from Sun – adding Visual J++ to the stable of Visual Studio languages.

As uneasy bedfellows, Microsoft and Sun's Java coexistence couldn't last. Sun's crusade for platform-independence clashed with Microsoft's vision to optimize Java for Windows. Microsoft's embrace and extension of Java, enhancing Visual J++ with native Windows Foundation classes (WFCs) and other calls, ironically made Windows one of the fastest Java deployment platforms.

However, because Sun owned the intellectual property, Sun sued Microsoft for violating its Java license. Sun eventually prevailed in court, forcing Microsoft and Sun to go their separate ways, rendering Visual J++ a footnote in history. Anticipating the divorce decree, Microsoft was already busily developing a clean room Java replacement, code-named "COOL".

As history proved, COOL wasn't simply another Microsoft attempt to add its own Java, but a cornerstone of a broader strategy to make application development language-, rather than platform-independent. In so doing, Microsoft ended up, not with a modernized COM or COM+, but a complete replacement that turns the run-time environment upside down. When Microsoft announced the new .NET Platform in June 2000, the outlines of its response started becoming clear. With .NET, Microsoft devised a clever way to embrace the heterogeneous world on its own terms.

Java Killer or Natural Evolution?

To understand the origins of .NET, it is critical to know the technology that it was designed to leapfrog.

Java's "write once, run anywhere" tenet was initially construed as the ability to write smart clients that could run on any target platform without porting. Java's initial success came by deploying miniature bits of code (applets) over the Internet at run time, or through conventionally installed client-side software. However, where Java really found its home was on the server.

Java's fruition came with the 1999 release of the Java 2 Platform, Enterprise Edition (J2EE), a framework encompassing component definitions, web page generation, and object/relational data mapping, plus APIs to directory services, transaction management, messaging, and database access. J2EE quickly gained critical mass acceptance among application server vendors, who made it the de facto standard alternative to Microsoft's Windows-centric Distributed Network Architecture (DNA, which encompassed COM+). J2EE was considered more scalable than Windows DNA, not necessarily because of the deployment architecture, but owing to its ability to run on larger UNIX platforms.

> *Of course, J2EE wasn't without its problems. For one thing, the very richness of the framework made it difficult for many enterprise IT groups to implement. Compounding the problem was the fact that each application server vendor has different deployment semantics. J2EE vendors such as BEA are introducing tools to simplify deployment, a task that will get easier once application server deployment is standardized by the JCP (Java Community Process, the body charged with ratifying Java standards), probably sometime in 2003.*

The .NET architecture is Microsoft's answer to J2EE. However, because it emerged after Sun's framework, .NET learned from the rival platform's shortcomings. Although we'll go into the gory details a bit later, suffice it to say that Microsoft adapted Java concepts such as the elimination of multiple inheritance plus several other features, including memory management, garbage collection, and Just-in-Time compilers. .NET's trump cards, however, included a twist on Java's virtual machine concept, and a design that embraced XML web services support straight out of the box.

The results? The .NET Framework embraced XML technology from the start, simplifying deployment of software as web services and the repurposing of data objects to a variety of applications or client targets. A powerful common run-time environment handles plumbing functions that minimize coding requirements. As for that virtual machine-like concept, Microsoft uses an intervening layer between the computing language and the underlying platform to make .NET language-, not platform-independent. (Although some third parties are trying to adapt .NET technologies to other platforms like Linux.) With its strong support of web services and multiple computing languages, .NET provides Microsoft a Windows-centric approach to co-existing with the non-Windows world.

Web Services: The Concept

Here's what the fuss is all about. **Web services,** the latest in a string of concepts for cross-platform integration, takes the Web giant steps beyond its roots in static page display and dynamic database interactions. With web services, applications themselves can interact dynamically, using standard interfaces. Microsoft .NET relies on web services technologies to integrate with the rest of the world.

The web began with a few simple technologies: HTML, a markup language for page display; HTTP, a protocol for web navigation; and IP, the protocol for communications over global networks. At the dawn of the Internet, interactions were confined to static page displays. Later, innovations such as Dynamic HTML along with technologies such as Active Server Pages (ASP) from Microsoft and servlets from the Java community opened the way for database-driven interactivity.

Web services take that a huge step forward by turning online applications into interchangeable services that can dynamically interact with one another. In practice, web services provide a standard way for objects that encapsulate pieces of data and business logic to interoperate over the Internet. In so doing, they provide a simpler and less costly alternative to the custom interfaces traditionally required for linking applications.

To achieve the promise of interoperability, two things must happen. First, software applications must be chopped into pieces that are small enough to minimize the chance for mismatches in data structures, application logic, or syntax. Then, standards must be in place to enable web services to interoperate between different organizations and systems. These standards are largely based around XML, a markup language that shares common roots with HTML, which is used to communicate structured data.

While web services are an intrinsic part of the .NET platform, they are not exclusive to .NET. For instance, Sun's J2EE environment is rapidly adding web services support, with members of the Java community introducing their own tools for deploying applications as services. Web services are becoming the tangible piece that will link Microsoft and non-Microsoft environments alike, using platform-neutral XML-based technologies.

What is .NET?

So what is .NET exactly? Is it something that you buy, subscribe to, or find bundled in your new PC? Or is .NET simply an application development *philosophy* requiring moral support? Is .NET synonymous with web services? Does .NET spell the end of conventional Windows applications as we know them? And what pieces of .NET do you need to develop .NET applications?

Microsoft defines Microsoft.NET as its next-generation-commerce platform. In effect, .NET is a mix of products, frameworks, services, and concepts designed to provide the technology infrastructure for deploying software either conventionally or as web services.

To cut through the clutter, let's break Microsoft.NET down into several tangible pieces:

❏ **The .NET Framework**
This is the technology on which .NET applications are developed and deployed.

❏ **The .NET Products**
These are the .NET things that you can buy.

❏ **The .NET Services**
These are the supporting commerce and personalization services that Microsoft is promoting.

The .NET Framework

The .NET Framework is a programming model for building, deploying, and running XML web services and other applications. Although XML web services are the exciting new concept, and receiving a lot of the hype, you can use the .NET Framework to develop and deploy many kinds of conventional applications.

The Framework consists of two main components: the **Common Language Runtime (CLR)**, which provides the engine for developing, deploying, and executing applications; and the **Unified Classes**, which cover system functions, data access, component models, transaction processes, and other services.

Before we look at the two main components in more detail, here are a few useful factoids to know about the Framework:

- ❏   The Framework doesn't replace the COM+ middle tier services; it expands on them.

- ❏   The Framework introduces the new .NET component model, but also lets existing Visual Studio language developers deploy COM components.

- ❏   To offer language independence, the Framework provides a Common Language Infrastructure (CLI), which has been ratified by ECMA as an international standard. Language providers must support the CLI to be .NET-compliant.

- ❏   To design programs that can run against the .NET Framework, the code must meet the Common Language Specification (CLS), which in effect dictates object-oriented development practices.

- ❏   When it comes to CLS compliance, not all languages are created equal. They may have features or constructs that may not be compliant, which must be avoided if you want to have the program run in the .NET Framework.

The Common Language Runtime

The heart of the hub, the CLR is the execution engine for .NET programs. Although the CLR performs similar functions to the well-known runtimes for Java or C++, its unique feature is that it was designed to be *common* across many languages.

A key feature of the CLR is that it *manages* code – that is, it automatically provides the underlying services for code that is compliant. For developers, this eliminates the need to write calls or interface definitions that trigger run-time services. Some of the services provided by the CLR, both at development and at run time, encompass object creation and lifecycle management, dynamic binding, method calling, and component-level security enforcement, along with memory, process, and thread management. Significantly, the CLR's exception-handling capability is designed to run across multiple languages (obviously, those that comply with the Framework).

In general, the CLR provides a single run-time environment that uses an Intermediate Language (IL) that, in turn, natively compiles to the Windows OS and the underlying hardware. It enforces advanced object-oriented development practices by requiring self-describing (declarative) components – ones that identify what they are and how they behave. Similarly, it also specifies strong data typing. By requiring that logic, presentation, and data all be separated, declared, and typed, the CLR requires that traditional client-server developers accustomed to event-based programming change their ways. Combined, these features allow .NET programs to avoid the much-maligned Windows Registry, a frequent source of deployment and execution problems.

Finally, the CLR's security mechanism is flexible, using a combination of code-, role-, and evidence-based security measures. Ironically, the default setting steals a page from Java's secure sandbox, prohibiting code from touching any internal resources such as memory blocks. However, administrators can override this by specifying "unsafe code", terminology that makes us wonder whether Microsoft is trying to tell us something.

Unified Classes

This comprises all the services that are used by .NET applications. The key innovation of the .NET Framework is that all the classes are standardized for all .NET programs, a marked departure from past practice. Aside from the Framework's requirement for object-oriented design, this is the other major hoop that applications must jump through to work with .NET. Specifically, the languages that are used must map to the classes specified by the .NET Framework.

In general, the Framework provides classes covering collections, I/O, data types, numerals, and access to Windows services such as graphics, networking, application threading, cryptography, and data access. Additionally, just as the .NET Framework requires strong typing, it also provides naming conventions for class libraries that are created by developers.

Major technologies within the class framework include:

❑ **ASP.NET**
Provides controls, security, session, and configuration classes for dynamically generating web pages. Compared to previous versions of ASP, ASP.NET takes advantage of performance improvements from the .NET Framework's caching and JIT compiler features.

❑ **ADO.NET**
Provides classes supporting data access, and expands on the existing ActiveX Data Objects (ADO) model by adding XML as the intermediate data format, enabling data to be easily repurposed into different device targets or fed into other applications and databases. It supports a "loosely-connected" architecture (which assumes that database connections are intermittent) by persisting data in XML-based caches called datasets, which can be treated as intermediate data sources. For many developers, specifying datasets may be easier than having to know the actual structures of the underlying data sources.

❑ **Windows Forms**
For developing conventional desktop applications using Windows GUI metaphors.

❑ **Web Forms**
For developing server-side controls that are displayed to the user on HTML pages, which can detect the type of browser being used (such as standard desktop browser, WML, etc.).

❑ **XML Classes**
Encompassing style sheets, paths, and serialization.

❑ **Enterprise Services**
Covering transactions, messaging, and security.

❑ **System Classes**
Handles I/O, threading, serialization, reflection, collections, diagnostics, and other functions.

The .NET Products

OK, so you want to go out and buy something? Here are the tangible .NET products that cost real money:

❑   Development Tools

❑   .NET Servers

❑   Smart Client Devices

What Microsoft products do you need to develop or run .NET applications? Strictly speaking, you don't need any outside of the Windows platform if you are deploying your applications as web services that comply with W3C standards, because by nature, they are supposed to be completely platform-independent. Since that begs the question, however, we'll give more specific answers while describing each product category below.

As to what versions of Windows are required for .NET applications, you will need NT4 or later to develop applications, and Windows 98 or later to run them. In each case, you will have to download the .NET Framework, which is freely available from Microsoft via an MSDN download. (For more information on how to get the .NET Framework, point your browser to http://msdn.microsoft.com/netframework/prodinfo/getdotnet.asp.) In the future, the .NET Framework will also come bundled with future versions of Windows.

Development Tools

Following a prolonged public beta, Microsoft officially released its .NET family of integrated development tools in February 2002. For over a decade, Microsoft has offered a family of tools covering the complete application lifecycle, from design to development, version control, and component reuse. Microsoft's tools have covered VB and C++. Of course, for a while, Java (Visual J++) was also included. After the court settlement with Sun, Microsoft replaced Visual J++ with C#, a new language that is sort of a clean-room Java. It also released a transitional upgrade to Visual J++ called Visual J#, which is meant to be a bridge to .NET for Visual J++ developers.

Visual Studio .NET (VS.NET) includes Visual Basic .NET, Visual C++, and C#, and as with past Microsoft IDE releases, the .NET languages are also available individually. It includes several key enhancements that could promote team collaboration. First, it unifies the IDE for all Microsoft languages. By contrast, VB 6 and earlier versions had separate IDEs for each language that were similar, but not identical. VS.NET changes all that, by having the same IDE for VB.NET, Visual C++.NET, and C#. Additionally, Microsoft has published APIs to VS.NET enabling third-party tools to integrate tightly as plug-ins that appear within the IDE itself. These front-end features are complemented by new standard back-ends that are provided by the .NET Framework, which is described in more detail below.

The result is that developers have a common front-end that provides a common look and feel to the VS.NET languages, and a back-end that standardizes how applications developed in VS.NET are deployed.

Backwards compatibility is provided with several features. First, VS.NET is bundled with tools to migrate older VB and Visual J++ applications to the .NET environment. Additionally, for developers preferring to create or modify applications based on Microsoft's previous technologies, VS.NET supports interoperability between .NET and classic COM components, so VB developers (whose language underwent the most changes to get to .NET) can still produce COM components written in VB 6.

Requirements

All of Microsoft's .NET development tools, including all Visual Studio .NET editions and the various single language packages, require Windows NT4 or later, running on a Pentium-class system of 450 MHz or better. But as mentioned earlier, you can develop .NET applications with other tools, if Microsoft certifies them as compliant with the framework.

In fact you can develop .NET applications just using Notepad and the compilers that ship with the Framework for no additional cost. Of course, this hardly compares to the benefits that Visual Studio .NET can bring.

.NET Development Tools FAQ

Q: Is VS.NET only useful for web services applications?
A: No, the VS.NET generation of tools also supports development of conventional Windows applications thanks to its "Windows Forms" and "Web Forms" features. This leads to another rather interesting possibility. Thanks to the .NET Framework's Common Language Runtime (CLR), developers could conceivably generate Windows forms with CLR-compliant non-Microsoft languages, including some not normally associated with Windows clients.

Q: Will old-style VB applications still be supported?
A: Developers who haven't learned the new .NET Framework will still be able to do things the old way for a while.

Q: Is VB 6 still available?
A: Yes, VB 6 will continue to be sold and supported for now, since Microsoft usually keeps the most recent previous version in the catalog. (Of course, the release of VB.NET means curtains for VB 5 users.)

Q: Will .NET applications interoperate or coexist with COM applications?
A: Yes, COM components and .NET components can interoperate. And, because .NET isn't built on COM, VS 6 and VS.NET can reside on the same developmental machine.

Q: Do you need to buy Visual Studio.NET to develop .NET-compliant applications?
A: Absolutely not. Thanks to the multi-language support of the framework's CLR, you can develop .NET applications without buying Microsoft tools, as long as the third-party language or tool has received Microsoft certification for support of the Common Language Interface (CLI). Conceivably you might also be able to do so with tools that have not been certified by Microsoft if you are willing to take more risks. In addition, you can use a combination of basic text editors with the language compilers. However, regardless of the tool, you must develop your programs correctly. Programs written in .NET-compliant languages must be fully object-oriented "managed code" that supports CLR's standard classes.

Q: Do you need the .NET Framework to run .NET applications?
A: OK, here's the first bit of "bad" news. If you develop a .NET application as a standard Windows application, it requires the services of the Framework's Common Language Runtime (CLR), meaning, it has to be installed on the client. And for that, you'll need Windows 98 or later. If your copy of the OS doesn't have the Framework yet, you can freely download it from the Microsoft Software Developer Network (MSDN). Of course, if the application deploys as a web service, it can run in any environment that supports XML web service standards, assuming that the syntax is understood by the receiving application.

.NET Servers

Microsoft defines these as the middleware used for delivering software as services, covering functions related to application deployment, integration, and data storage. This is where branding gets confusing, because Microsoft's next versions of Windows 2000, called Windows .NET, is not part of this narrow definition. For now, the same is true for many products in Microsoft's .NET enterprise servers family, which officially include:

❑   Microsoft Application Center 2000, which is used for deploying application clusters

❑   Microsoft BizTalk Server 2000, providing an XML-based server for integrating business processes and applications

❑   Microsoft Host Integration Server 2000, the successor to Microsoft SNA Server, providing access to legacy platforms

❑   Microsoft Mobile Information 2001 Server, providing access to PDAs, cell phones, and other mobile devices

❑   Microsoft SQL Server 2000, Microsoft's enterprise SQL database (.NET applications also support rival databases that can act as ODBC sources, such as Oracle)

Although at first glance, the notion of branding all of these products .NET servers might be confusing in the short run, as Microsoft adds XML support into all of these products, the tie-in with the .NET Framework will become more real.

Requirements

You will need Windows NT4 or later to run any of the .NET server products. But you won't necessarily need any or all of these middleware products themselves unless you require specific capabilities (for example, unless you have mainframe hosts or mobile device clients), or your organization is committed to being a 100% Microsoft shop.

For instance, you won't need SQL Server, because .NET applications can run against Oracle, DB2 or other SQL relational databases. Furthermore, even if you need any of this type of middleware, it doesn't have to be Microsoft-branded if your .NET applications are deployed as web services, or if the third-party products in question directly support the .NET Framework. On the other hand, it won't hurt to have Microsoft middleware since Visual Studio .NET easily deploys to those targets.

What about Windows .NET? The .NET branding implies that you'll need this OS if you are running .NET applications. Don't be misled. Windows .NET is simply an upgrade of the Windows 2000 Server product family. However, it will be the first version of Windows to come with the .NET Framework bundled in. Surprisingly, the early versions of the bleeding-edge 64-bit edition do *not* yet support the .NET Framework (something that's obviously going to change).

Smart Client Devices

Microsoft has always bet its fate on smart clients, an evolution that began in the dark old days of standalone PCs. Eventually, those machines began hooking up to local file and print servers, followed by more elaborate enterprise client-server applications, and culminating with a more nuanced architecture that includes a mix of server- and client-deployed data, presentation, and business logic. In each scenario, the PC usually contained at least some local application logic and data such as standard-issue desktop word processors or spreadsheet programs, and in many cases, the data files that accompanied them. While the Sun/Java world has emphasized fat servers and thin clients, Microsoft says, in effect, deploy resources wherever it is most practical for that particular application.

Consequently, .NET clients can range from embedded devices and appliances to full-blown PCs. Microsoft's belief in local intelligence is reflected in its PocketPC product line, which sports far richer functionality than rival PalmOS devices. Web services are used to provide a flow of intelligence between servers and clients, which could have their own local logic to, in effect, make local, client-deployed applications "smarter".

Requirements

The Microsoft products involved here include their client-side OS, such as Windows XP or Pocket PC. Of course, if your .NET programs are deployed as web services, Microsoft OS clients are strictly optional.

The .NET Services

This is Microsoft's proposed commercial implementation of personalized web services that are designed using .NET technologies, including the Framework and the e-business server products such as BizTalk Server and the SQL Server database.

.NET My Services, formerly known as "Hailstorm", consists of specific consumer-oriented web services that use Microsoft's Passport and .NET Alerts services (enterprise versions are planned). Specifically, Passport is a Microsoft membership-based service that provides single sign-in and related personal identification, authentication, and access control, while Alerts are the mechanisms through which merchants could send messages to Passport members.

The goal is to provide a convenient means for consumers using the web to manage and store information about themselves, which could include passwords, authentication, digital signatures, contact lists, personal schedules or calendaring, web page preferences, and electronic wallets storing credit card numbers and related data. For instance, a healthcare system could enable a patient to create a calendaring web service that reminds the patient of doctor appointments or when to renew a prescription, or provide alerts of new healthcare services that might be of personal interest. If clients decide to buy a product or service, their electronic wallets could be used to secure the commerce transaction.

As such, .NET My Services is far more than cookies on steroids. For consumers, personalization services should make web surfing and online shopping much easier, not just because they eliminate the need to memorize a confusing array of passwords, but because preferences can be much more easily managed compared to editing cookies. Businesses in turn could benefit by gaining access to consumer data (legally on a permission basis) to better target products and services.

And maybe there's more. With Microsoft building the middleware infrastructure with the .NET servers, plus a growing stable of .NET-enabled vertical applications such as Great Plains back office and a new CRM offering, .NET My Services could become the customer touch point of a broad business solution suite. Furthermore, if .NET My Services becomes the de facto standard for personalized commerce, it will draw support from a critical mass of other enterprise software vendors.

Not surprisingly, the idea of one company controlling the technology for digital personalization has raised a lot of eyebrows, and not just from Microsoft's usual technology rivals. Consequently, when Sun, Oracle, and other members of the Anyone-but-Microsoft (ABM) camp formed the Liberty Alliance to push for open standards in web personalization, it attracted support from many leading financial services players who were concerned about the idea of a single company controlling what could be direct access to consumer wallets. In October 2001, Microsoft sent olive branches indicating its openness to supporting some form of standards-based "federation" between web authentication systems.

So, what does all this have to do with .NET technology itself? Microsoft's strategy is to make .NET My Services a – or "the", depending on your viewpoint – de facto standard for online commerce personalization. Of course, .NET My Services would be built on the .NET Framework. Furthermore, Microsoft's growing stable of back-office applications, which would use .NET My Services as the customer touch point, would also rely on .NET technology. Logically, if your organization buys these applications, it would develop extensions or tie-ins using .NET languages.

But, if Passport and Liberty ever decide to interoperate, that means that these same entities would not necessarily be locked into .NET, or Java technologies for that matter, to build the personalized web of the future.

.NET Deliverables

Now we've been introduced to what .NET actually "is", let's examine if it lives up to the hype.

What .NET is Supposed to Deliver

To recap, Microsoft .NET is supposed to help transition your application portfolio to a new form called software as services – although of course, it will still give you several options for deploying software conventionally as well. In practice, .NET technology won't necessarily require organizations to rewrite their code bases, but to link them using the .NET Framework and Windows as the application servers, and Internet-standard XML web services as the glue.

That encompasses:

❑ Providing a common run-time environment and common classes to make the platform language-independent

❑ Standardizing the way languages and tools interface with the common runtime

❑ Delivering a more robust application deployment environment

❑ Automating the deployment of software as web services through simple checkboxes that command the runtime to deploy the necessary headers and APIs to generate the building blocks of web services

❑ Embracing more robust development practices, specifying a rigorous, object-oriented component model and strong data typing guidelines

❑ Providing backwards compatibility for earlier COM-based applications

In turn, Microsoft has developed supporting tools and servers for developing and deploying .NET applications, and, using the Common Language Infrastructure (CLI), providing paths for non-Microsoft products to support development and deployment to the .NET Framework. And of course, all this is being promoted to compete head-on with the Java platform.

What .NET Actually Delivers

So how well has Microsoft met these goals?

The Common Run-time Environment

Microsoft has pulled a rabbit out of its hat, designing a platform that can seriously compete for the non-Java world, while still keeping customers on the Windows platform. Ironically, Microsoft can thank the Java community for many of the concepts that it is using to insulate languages from the runtime. The ultimate success of this strategy, however, rests in execution. How well will developers of non-object-oriented languages like Perl or COBOL adapt to the new environment. More importantly, how well will VB 6 developers adapt?

Standard Language Interfaces

Microsoft's Common Language Infrastructure (CLI) has become an official international standard, thanks to approval by ECMA. In practice, the formal ratification was primarily for propaganda purposes to counter Sun's claims that Java technologies are open. Given Microsoft's obvious market clout, CLI would have become a de facto standard even without ECMA's ratification. Either way, it gives third-party product developers a stable target against which to design or extend their tools and languages, and Microsoft a formal means for certifying compliance with CLI. So far, Microsoft claims to have roughly a couple dozen languages certified for the .NET Framework.

However, the CLI standard in place does not guarantee that programs developed using certified compliant tools will necessarily deploy successfully. That part is up to developers. As one consultant recently said, "The Java programming language's object-oriented structure didn't prevent errant developers from writing event-based code." Developers will have to pay especially close attention to architectural issues when working in many legacy languages, even if the tools are .NET-compliant.

Robustness

The .NET Framework combines the middle-tier services of the COM+ architecture with a component architecture that enforces object-oriented design practices. Among the byproducts of this architecture are self-describing components that eliminate the need for the Windows Registry, which yields several key benefits:

- **No more "DLL Hell"**
  OK, never say never, but the new system should eliminate most of the problems when applications call up shared libraries that were previously changed by other programs. For instance, if one application overwrites a shared library, the internal metadata of the second application could interrogate the CLR to see if a compatible one still exists, and use that instead.

- **Side-by-Side copies**
  The strong internal naming standards for libraries means that multiple versions of the same libraries can coexist, thereby increasing the likelihood that applications can find the right library.

- **"No-touch" Deployment**
  Since the CLR bypasses the Windows Registry, you no longer have to register the file on a remote machine –you can just copy the relevant files and directories onto the filing system to deploy.

XML Support

The .NET Framework has a clear, although not impregnable advantage here because of the standardized web services APIs and the fact that .NET was designed for XML and web services from the ground up. The benefits show in the simplified deployment for web services, and the use of XML as the de facto standard intermediate, data format for the Framework's ADO.NET.

However, the Java community is fast catching up (remember, Java came around before there ever was XML). Most Java IDEs and application servers have some form of simplified web services deployment feature, and the Java community is busily finalizing all the relevant web services standards. By 2003, the XML web services disparity between .NET and J2EE should be a non-issue.

Backwards Compatibility

When watching vendors demonstrate the tricks of their latest technologies on the exhibit floor of a conference, one should keep in mind the disclaimer shown before automotive commercials on TV, "This demonstration was filmed on a closed course with professional drivers."

With those caveats in mind, the .NET Framework provides as much backwards compatibility as practicable for a new technology platform. Also keep in mind that, in developing a platform that supports multiple languages, Microsoft has bitten off an extremely ambitious agenda.

Microsoft has developed several methods for bridging technology generations:

❑ **From Old to New**
Microsoft is rebranding tools from ArtinSoft, a Costa Rican software tools developer, that migrate programs developed in VB6 to VB.NET, and from Java (any flavor, including Visual J++) to C#.

❑ **From New to Old**
The .NET Framework provides developers several choices on how they want to deploy applications. In addition to .NET components and XML web services, the Framework provides the option to deploy as a classic COM component. It can also recognize COM components and have .NET components interoperate with them.

❑ **From Everywhere Else to New**
The .NET Framework's CLI provides an API that developers of nearly two dozen non-Microsoft languages are supporting. Conceivably, this could provide a path to .NET, not only for new programs, but also for new extensions to existing programs.

The results are likely to be mixed. Not surprisingly, it is usually easier to start with newer applications than to retrofit new features to make older applications more robust. In this case, the .NET architecture's more rigorous development practices should make that especially easy; deploying a VS.NET-based application as a COM component should be relatively straightforward.

Conversely, migrating older VS 6 generation applications is likely to encounter more mixed results. Migrating from any of the Java flavors or C++ should create relatively few surprises, assuming that they were already developed using OO principles. However, converting VB 6 applications could be more problematic, especially if they are based in traditional event-based programming mode.

As for deploying old or new applications from any of the two dozen or so .NET-compliant non-Microsoft languages, prospects will vary depending on the structure and syntax of the original language, and of course, the practices of the developer.

.NET vs. J2EE

The .NET architecture benefited from the lessons of Java, adapting many of its principles, but with a twist. The frameworks sport similar features (see table), although obviously, they come from different code bases and implement their bells and whistles differently. While Java (and Enterprise JavaBeans in particular) borrows some technologies from CORBA, Microsoft has stuck to its own COM+ knitting.

Feature	.NET Framework	Java/J2EE Framework
Current Version	1.0 (Feb '02)	1.3 (Aug '01)
Component Architectures	.NET, COM+	Enterprise JavaBeans, JavaBeans, Servlets
Database Access	ADO.NET (encompasses ODBC and OLEDB)	JDBC
Web Services	WebMethod (SOAP), WebServiceUtil.exe (WSDL)	Java XML Pack including JAXP (parsing), JAXM (messaging), JAXR (registries), JAX-RPC (remote procedure calls)
Web Page Generation	ASP.NET	JSP, and servlets
Languages	Multiple Languages (certified for CLI)	Java
Platforms	Windows (although third parties are working to port the framework to Linux)	Multiple

Application Server Philosophies

Obviously, both .NET and J2EE have middle tiers; however, a major differentiator is that Microsoft has traditionally embedded much of the functionality in Windows, whereas with Java, those services are handled inside the J2EE framework. The result, of course, is that in the Microsoft world, "application server" is a foreign term.

Microsoft buttresses its argument by claiming that in reality, J2EE application servers are dissolving into the underlying platform, citing the fact that Sun, HP, and IBM bundle them with their hardware. In reality, the bundling is based on marketing, not technology, because J2EE does not tolerate the idea of making anything native (that's why Sun sued Microsoft). On the other hand, as a product category, J2EE application servers are slowly dissolving into integration servers, commerce servers, portal servers, databases, and applications that are optimized for those respective applications or functions.

Runtimes

The similarities and differences begin with the run-time environments. Microsoft's CLR and Java's JVM (Java Virtual Machine) both operate on the premise that a middle layer is needed to provide some form of interoperability. .NET compiles to an Intermediate Language (IL) and Java compiles to a machine-neutral byte code. This intermediate format is then compiled to a machine-native binary. Both employ Just-in-Time (JIT) compilers that pre-compile frequently used code to enhance performance. In all, similar approaches, opposite results: NET's write (almost) any language, run on Windows vs. Java's write once, run (almost) anywhere.

For instance, both enforce object-oriented design practices, such as declarative components and strong data typing. Both specify similar forms of internal component management housekeeping functions, such as lifecycle management, but implement them differently: Java focuses these processes in application server middleware while .NET splits the housekeeping between the runtime and the underlying Windows platform.

For now, there is a tactical difference in the way that .NET and Java components are deployed. For .NET, there is one target (the CLR), whereas with Java, there are many different application server vendors, each of which have different APIs for deployment. That gives .NET a temporary advantage, but by 2003, the Java community will likely standardize deployment.

Related to the deployment issue is development. Many point to the Visual Studio IDE as being the grand unifier of all .NET development environments, and claim that Microsoft has an advantage here, because the Java world has so many different IDEs. In fact, this advantage is partially illusory. First of all, VS.NET will not be the only .NET IDE, although it will be far and away the most dominant. Secondly, in the Java world, all the IDEs support the same language, which makes them easily replaceable. However, the varieties of Java IDEs are not of the same quality as VS.NET, which contains many productivity features that should improve developers' efficiency.

Security

In this area the two are similar, but different. As mentioned earlier, the default setting for .NET security looks just like the Java sandbox, where code interactions with underlying resources are verboten. But then, Microsoft lets you override this with "unsafe code".

Does Standard = Open?

For most observers, the words "open" and "standard" should be synonymous, because they both imply technology that is not controlled by any single vendor.

Not surprisingly, this has become one of the chief points of contention between Microsoft and Sun.

Microsoft claims .NET is open because it has gained ECMA ratification of the Common Language Infrastructure (CLI) and the C# language as international standards. Sun claims Java is open because it is designed to work on multiple platforms.

So who's right? No one and everyone.

Microsoft has scored a few propaganda points through the ECMA ratifications. However, its technologies would have become de facto standards even if the technologies were submitted through the standards process.

By contrast, Sun shunned ECMA and other standards bodies by forming the Java Community Process. Although Sun set the rules, in practice, the JCP has functioned as a quasi-public standards body because its membership is open, and Sun does not have veto power over its deliberations. In effect, Java has become a de facto standard.

Does that make both frameworks open? The answer is in the eyes of the beholder. The .NET platform is open to multiple languages that comply with its APIs, but currently runs only on Windows. You don't have to license the .NET Framework, but you'll have to obtain a Windows license to run it. Conversely, the Java platform supports only the Java language, but it runs on practically any OS. While you won't have to buy a Solaris license, your tool or application provider must buy a Java license from Sun.

Web Services

Some of the most publicized – and the most temporary – differences stem from the rival frameworks support for XML web services. Stated simply, Java came before anybody knew how to spell XML, whereas .NET came well after and provided Microsoft the opportunity to design its new framework around XML. Consequently, Microsoft incorporated a standard API that automatically exposes functionality as web services. Using the keyword "WebMethod", a SOAP message containing all the necessary headers can be generated from an application object or method. Additionally, the Framework contains the utility WebServiceUtil.exe that exposes specific methods as a web service using WSDL that is capable of receiving SOAP messages from external sources.

> *SOAP is a standard for communicating XML documents over standard HTTP. In effect, HTTP provides the Internet "envelope" for inserting XML documents.*

By contrast, Sun has the Java "XML Pack" release (updated every quarter), which encompasses APIs for XML messaging, parsing, registries, and remote procedure calls (RPCs). Currently this is an add-on and not part of the main J2EE specification so vendors are not required to support it, but it is planned to become part of J2EE 1.4, which should be released early 2003. In contrast to Microsoft's approach, where the APIs focus on a specific standard (such as SOAP), the JCP took a more generalized strategy. For instance, instead of designing a specific API for SOAP, it used an umbrella approach that encompassed SOAP as one of many options (for example ebXML, and provision for other XML messaging protocols that might emerge). The same was true for registries and synchronous RPCs.

The .NET Framework benefits from another use of XML: ADO.NET, which uses XML as the intermediate data format. The practical effect of this is that the data, once retrieved from the data source, can be easily repurposed because it is in a neutral format. The .NET Framework provides the option to create interim "datasets" that can send the data to another component without having to maintain connections back to the source database(s). Although interim XML documents can be created with the Java platform, currently, the process requires additional coding.

The Challenges for .NET

Although the .NET Framework supports conventional application deployment, the real story focuses on the evolution of web-based applications. As a young medium, the Web has been a fast-moving deployment target since it burst into popularity in the nineties. Since that time, it has undergone three generations of change:

- ❏ From static to active pages embellished with ActiveX controls or Java applets (more recently, hassles with browser support have largely replaced these controls with Dynamic HTML) that provided splashier graphics, and in some cases, enhanced web page intelligence.

- ❏ From document-sharing applications to database-driven applications that consisted of web front ends to transaction applications or database-driven page generation. Database-driven applications currently dominate enterprise intranet or extranet applications, along with many B2C consumer web commerce applications.

- ❏ From web applications to software as services. Still in its infancy, this transition promises to take matters to the next level, as applications dynamically interact with each other through standard protocols, rather than custom-built interfaces or remote deployment of business logic.

The prospect of web services adds new opportunities for loosely-coupling different applications both inside and outside the enterprise. And we can further muddy the waters with a whole new generation of non-PC clients such as smart phones or pagers, PDAs, set-top boxes, and telematics systems in cars, to name a few.

So how does this impact on application architecture, and what requirements will .NET have to fill?

The Client

Ever since the dawn of client-server computing, deploying applications with smart clients has continually proved challenging. The "fat" clients that emerged with client-server in the long run proved huge maintenance burdens because of the varying hardware and software configurations of enterprise desktops, not to mention the noted instability of the Windows OS itself.

Therefore, when the web evolved from static, document-serving to dynamic, database-driven applications, the way was opened up, not only for making web sites more compelling, but also for migrating many enterprise applications to more reliable intranet, thin-client architectures that could support thousands of clients. However, even here there were client-side deployment issues, because browser versions became the latest addition to desktop configuration hassles. The result is that web clients have tended to dispense with fancier bells and whistles, such as ActiveX Controls, Java applets, or even Dynamic HTML (DHTML), in favor of plain vanilla HTML and JavaScript.

Today, the emergence of web services and new target client devices promises to open up new horizons for client-side deployment. All that is needed is XML support, which most version 5 browsers already accommodate. Additionally, the .NET Framework's remote deployment features could eliminate many software maintenance hassles traditionally associated with fat clients.

Let's start with web services. The .NET Framework addresses this, not only with direct support of web services, but through its extensive internal use of XML and object-oriented architectures (that abstract the presentation layer), which should make multi-client deployment much simpler. .NET's use of object technology, plus a new Compact Framework that provides a subset of core .NET Framework functions, should further facilitate development of applications for non-PC devices. However, while Microsoft's compact device extensions (which will be supported in VS.NET) will enable applications to extend the same core business logic towards new targets, headaches will remain because there are few if any form factor standards for mobile devices and appliances. Tools can't solve everything.

As to the revival of fat clients, .NET supports a capability that began development under Microsoft's old 1997 Zero Administration Workstation (ZAW) initiative (which itself was a response to Java thin clients) for central management of client workstations. One of the measures was automated software deployment – a technology that in practice has been challenging to implement. With .NET, there is a new approach to this: maintaining a cache on the client that is updated automatically when the server version changes (Java has had a similar capability for several years). With this new feature, software versions can synchronized, eliminating a major administrative headache of fat clients.

The Enterprise

Web services are the latest step in the evolution of enterprise applications to inter-enterprise. Traditionally, enterprise systems were focused on internal operations. Prior to the web, enterprises applications communicated outside the enterprise through Electronic Data Interchange (EDI), file transfers, or in some cases, e-mail. With the Web, organizations erected portals or HTML –enabled user interfaces to enterprise applications, in many cases using Microsoft or Java-based application servers. In each case, enterprises were typically separated by database transactions because of the sheer impossibility of getting outside organizations to install copies of the same application software.

But web services are different. While they aren't likely to replace existing enterprise transaction systems, they will supplement them with more flexible front ends that, in effect, deconstruct applications as services. That means several things:

❑ **Web applications are driven, not just by database transactions, but the interplay of multiple applications**
Applications must be designed to support web services standards, or interface with middleware that can convert or bundle transactions as services.

❑ **Interactions are less predictable**
You may not always know which applications will answer your request, especially if web services registries, such as UDDI, enter common use. This reinforces the need to adhere to standards.

❑ **Monolithic applications are deconstructed into services that are available on demand**
Traditionally, applications functioned by processing one or more discrete transactions. When deployed as services, however, the result is likely to disaggregate conventional transaction processes because services may bundle varying combinations of transactions from one, or more, back-end systems. Or, conversely, services may abstract a single transaction from an established transaction process. This dictates flexible interfaces to established back-end systems.

❑   **Clients are redefined**
With the emergence of smart mobile clients, services may have to be deployed flexibly to enable them to display on multiple form factors, including PCs and mobile devices alike.

❑   **Client and server metaphors are transformed**
In the world of web services, the system requesting a service may not be a conventional end-user client machine, but another enterprise server that must complete a business process by asking for a service from another server, inside or outside the organization.

The role of the .NET Framework (and J2EE for that matter) will be to provide the core middleware services that generate actions such as SOAP messages or web service definitions. It will provide those services to existing packages and internally developed applications (or extensions to off-the-shelf applications) alike. In the long run, the platform-independence of XML-based web services should ensure that requestors and service providers on both platforms should be able to communicate.

Although .NET is a half step ahead of J2EE in supporting XML web services, the real gap here isn't technology, but knowledge. As yet, the best practices for developing or deploying software as services have yet to emerge. Few if any IT organizations have deployed XML web services except as pilot applications. Furthermore, the core technologies for everyday use are just beginning to fall into place, and as yet, there is little consensus as to which web services standards will achieve critical mass adoption. Eventually, as IT organizations get up to speed and the technology community consolidates the standards base, .NET and J2EE platforms should each provide the necessary tools.

Web Services

As mentioned just above, web services technology is a work in progress. As envisioned, web services are supposed to leverage the universal reach of the web to enable software to deploy as self-contained business services. The goal is loosely-coupled logic that deploys and interacts at run time, without the need to know what applications or technologies are used at the receiving end.

But the standards and knowledge are still falling into place. Today, the web services world only has a handful of core standards, including:

❑   SOAP: The "message envelope" for transporting XML documents via HTTP

❑   WSDL: A standard protocol for describing a web service

❑   UDDI: A standard directory or registry that would list available web services

Obviously, these foundation standards are not the last word, and it is not certain that they will all remain the definitive standards in the long run.

So far, the W3C has taken the lead in ratifying web services standards. However, in the long run, multiple standards organizations are likely to get involved, ranging from technology organizations to vertical industry groups such as the electronics industry's RosettaNet. Recently, a new quasi-standards group, the Web Services Interoperability Consortium (WS-I) was formed just to check on the activities of standards groups, devise compatibility test regimens, and help decipher which standards are gaining critical mass support to become, not only formal standards, but de facto ones as well.

Of course, at this point, it is far from certain which standards will prevail. For instance, although SOAP has gained mind share as the best-known communications protocol for web services, it is by no means assured that it will remain the de facto standard. For instance, critics dismiss SOAP as a lowest common denominator, tactical alternative that, in the long run, won't scale because of its lack of an object model base. Significantly, the ebXML framework makes provision for other possible messaging protocols, as does J2EE.

For technology providers such as Microsoft, keeping up with standards activity is a tall order. Microsoft itself has responded by taking a driving role behind much of the standards work, having already authored SOAP and co-authored UDDI with IBM and Ariba. And Microsoft itself has proposed the "Global XML Architecture" (GXA) that adds features that are taken for granted in the transaction world, such as acknowledgement, rollback and recovery, message prioritization, encryption, and authentication. And Microsoft isn't the only player offering proposals in this area. Furthermore, standards work is also underway for devising standard protocols for web services to identify themselves.

On the developer side there are a number of guidelines that should be considered:

❑ **Objects, Objects, Objects**
There is an easy one-sentence answer to the question, "How can you adapt your applications to web services technologies?" Namely, embrace component-based development techniques because they are easier to enhance and update, compared to traditional event-driven applications. If your development team maintains strong object-oriented design disciplines, then modifying web services to accommodate new or evolving standards could be as simple as changing a single object. Towards that end, the .NET Framework's reliance on objects will encourage teams to maintain proper discipline – but even the strictest rules cannot prevent developers from straying from proper OO techniques!

❑ **Loosely-Coupled Applications**
In contrast to traditional approaches for integrating applications, web services are designed for loosely-coupled interoperability. This starts with the self-contained nature of the transactions themselves. Designed with declarative headers, transactions should be self-explanatory to the right recipients. Furthermore, if web service requests and responses travel the Internet, applications must accommodate the latency and interrupted connections that characterize the Internet.

❑ **Keep It Simple, Stupid**
Other guidelines include keeping it simple, stupid. Don't design overly complex web services, especially while you are just learning how to develop them. Developing successful web services requires command, not only of technology, but business requirements and syntax. In most cases, business managers will make the business decisions regarding what to offer as web services. However, like any IT projects, development professionals are responsible for determining whether the bells and whistles demanded by the business folks can easily be implemented and maintained. As web services are new technology, development professionals should initially tread cautiously. In an ideal world, devoid of outside business pressures, you should keep the web services as simple as possible, and gradually add new bells and whistles over time. Of course, when are things ever ideal?

❏ **Allow Room for Growth**
Web services technologies are in their infancy. New standards will emerge that eventually fill the gaps. Therefore, applications that deploy functionality as web services should be designed for future enhancements that may add new features, or replace interim proprietary technologies that may be used for necessary processes such as authentication. And, as developers of the first generation of dot-com applications learned the hard way, traffic patterns on the 'net can be unpredictable, especially if the web service is made available to consumers at large. Therefore, when designing the back end, scalability is paramount.

❏ **Don't reinvent the Wheel**
Languages and development tools should provide the means for deploying software as web services. Don't waste your time developing essentials like headers for SOAP messages or WSDL service definitions. The .NET Framework and .NET-compatible tools, not to mention rival Java technology tools, should perform the legwork for you. As mentioned earlier, when this book went to press, Visual Studio .NET had a 6-month lead over the Java community when it came to interfaces for SOAP, WSDL, and UDDI. Over the long haul, both camps will furnish the basics for developing web services.

Summary

Over the course of this chapter you've had your first taster as to what the .NET Framework is all about. As you should be beginning to realize, Microsoft has not just added some new bells and whistles to its old development and run-time technologies but completely reinvented them from the base level, and for good reasons too.

The .NET Framework represents the culmination of several years of development work by Microsoft to produce a platform that can be a real "player" in enterprise computing. What it has produced has one foot in the present and past (learning from and building on current successful platforms such as Java and J2EE) and one looking to the future (with the Framework being constructed with XML and web services very much at its core).

Over the remaining chapters, this book will explore the features of the .NET Framework more closely so that you can decide for yourself whether it lives up to its promise, starting with a closer look at the underlying infrastructure upon which we build our .NET applications.

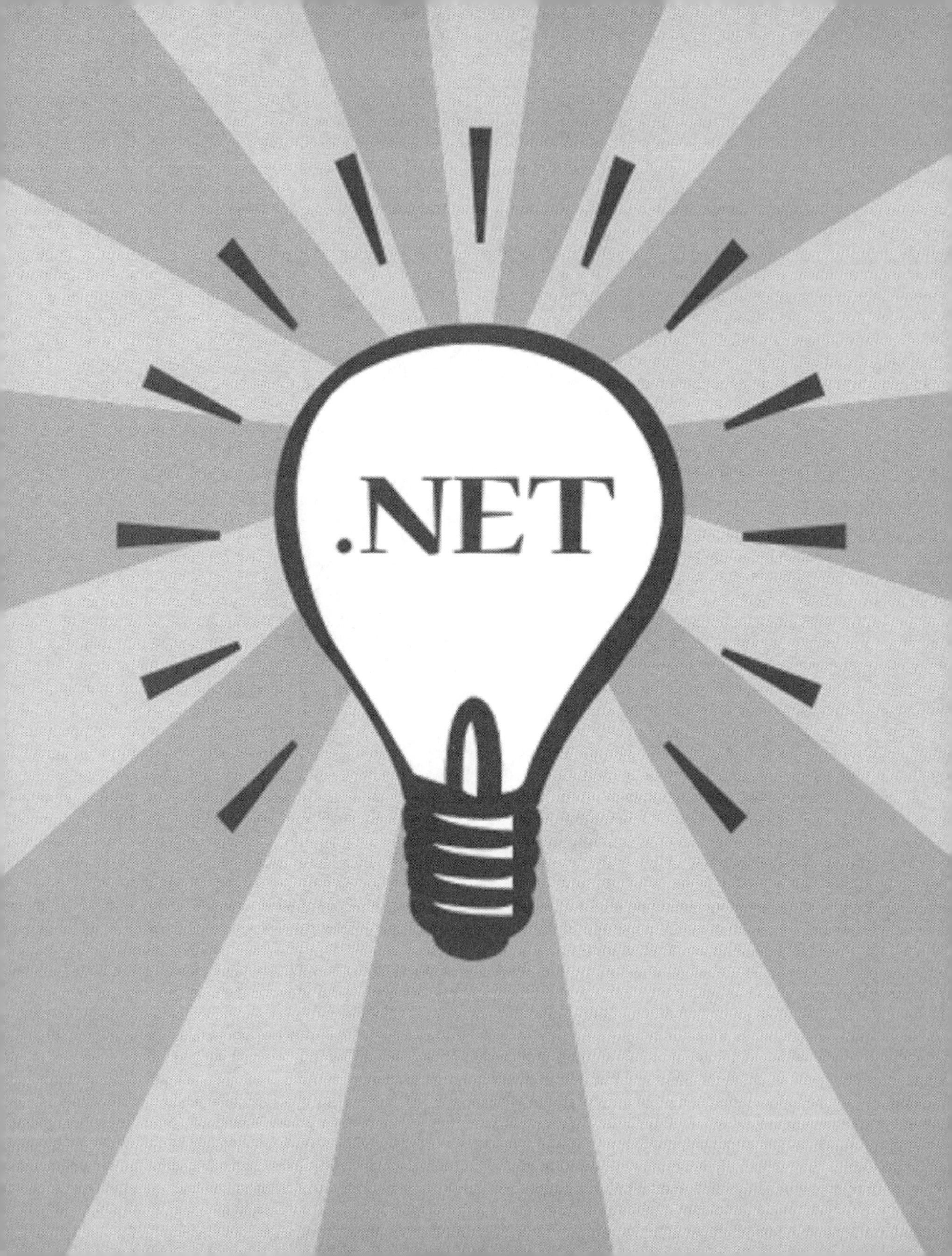
.NET

2

Developing with .NET

This chapter presents an overview of the infrastructure provided by .NET upon which we develop our applications. These applications can range from web applications generating HTML, through desktop Windows applications, to backend server components (Windows services, web services, etc.). The tool of choice used to develop these applications is **Visual Studio .NET**. Development under .NET is a departure from the old style COM programming in that code running under .NET is **managed** (controlled by a runtime, which provides services to the code being executed). It is still possible to develop legacy applications that do not use the runtime (legacy MFC applications, ATL applications, etc.), but these lack the advantages provided by .NET (multi-language support, common error handling, unified memory management and cleanup, etc.).

The .NET Framework infrastructure includes support for developing applications written in multiple languages. In order to achieve interoperability, these languages must agree to behave in a certain manner such that they can all run within the .NET-managed environment. Developing managed applications is more than just using high-level languages though. When compiled such high-level languages generate a binary that contains code not in native form (x86) but in an **Intermediate Language (IL)** binary representation. The purpose of IL is to allow an application to be distributed on any platform. Each platform will provide a Just-in-Time compiler that translates the compiled code (an **assembly**) into native format.

There is bit more infrastructure in place in order to enable an assembly to be compiled into native code or for an assembly to be run within a managed application. Languages that produce managed code must be implemented in a certain way dictated by the .NET Framework. By adhering to these constraints an application can run as a managed application, which means it will execute within .NET's **Common Language Runtime (CLR)**. The CLR provides a variety of services to an application including, but not limited to, memory management and garbage collection.

Gone are the days where C++ developers have to allocate and then explicitly free memory. Gone are the days where VB developers allocate and free memory one way, while C++ developers use an entirely different mechanism that makes it difficult to optimize the memory managed process for an application. The .NET Framework provides memory management as a service thus letting us developers focus on developing functionality rather than tracking down memory leaks or solving memory-related performance issues. At the same time the common memory-management scheme (including garbage collection) is designed to enhance an application's performance by keeping related data in close memory proximity.

So the .NET Framework is made of layered parts that provide the services, classes, and tools that work together to provide the development platform for .NET applications:

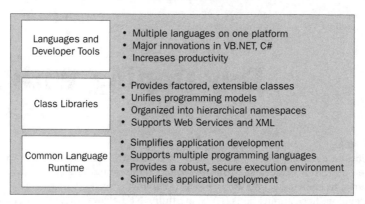

Once these topics have been reviewed, the basic infrastructure of .NET should be clear. More import than how .NET works should be why .NET works. This radical shift in development architecture is designed to *simply* development rather than adding to its complexity. The services provided are designed to let developers write new features for products rather than getting bogged down in debugging, deployment issues, or developing infrastructure services.

.NET Development Basics

Application types that can be developed with .NET (as defined by Visual Studio .NET's solution types) include, but are not limited to:

❑ **Class Library**
In legacy terms this can be thought as a DLL in that it provides a set of classes to be used by other applications.

❑ **Console Application**
A command-line application that displays a console window (often miscalled a "DOS Box" since there is no DOS in Windows NT/2000/XP).

❑ **Windows Application**
Desktop GUI application using the Windows OS interface.

❑ **ASP.NET Web Application**
A web server-side application that generates a GUI within a browser. ASP.NET is the replacement technology for Active Server Pages.

❑ **ASP NET Web Service**
A web server-side application that exposes an application interface (API) that can be called by web clients. The idea is to expose a set of objects and methods. This is as opposed to generating web pages to display in a browser.

❑ **Windows Service**
An executable that runs in the background on a Windows machine. Such an application can run even when no user is logged in.

Visual Studio .NET

Visual Studio .NET is a fully integrated development environment. It is designed to make the process of writing your code, debugging it, and compiling it to an assembly to be shipped, as easy as possible. What this means in practice is that Visual Studio .NET gives you a very sophisticated multiple-document-interface application in which you can do just about everything related to developing your code. It offers:

❑ **A text editor**
In which you can write your code be it VB.NET, C#, or C++. This text editor is quite sophisticated, and it is also aware of the syntax of the languages. This means that as you type, it can automatically lay out your code, for example by indenting lines, matching start and end brackets of code blocks, and color-coding keywords. It will also perform some syntax checks as you type, and will underline code that will cause compilation errors. Also, it features IntelliSense, which as you start typing names of classes, fields or methods will automatically display small listboxes detailing the possible ways to complete the names. As you start typing parameters to methods, it will also show you the parameter lists for the available overloads.

❑ **A design-view editor of your code**
This allows you to visually place user-interface and data-access controls in your project. When you do this, Visual Studio .NET will automatically add the necessary code to your source files to instantiate these controls in your project. (This is possible as, under .NET, all the controls are actually just instances of particular base classes.)

❑ **Supporting windows**
These allow you to view and modify aspects of your project. For example, there are windows available that show you the classes in your source code as well as the available properties (and their startup values) for Windows Forms and Web Forms classes. You can also use these windows to specify compilation options, such as which assemblies your code needs to reference.

❑ **Compilation from within the environment**
Instead of having to run the language compiler from the command line, you can simply select a menu option to compile the project and Visual Studio .NET will call the compiler for you. It will pass all the relevant command-line parameters to the compiler detailing such things as which assemblies to reference and what type of assembly you want to be emitted (executable or library DLL, for example). If you so wish, it will even run the compiled executable for you straight away so you can see whether it runs satisfactorily, and you can choose between different build configurations – for example, a release or debug build.

❑ **An integrated debugger**
It's in the nature of programming that you can virtually guarantee that your code won't run correctly the first time you try it, or the second time, or the third, etc. Visual Studio .NET will seamlessly link up to a debugger for you, allowing you to set breakpoints and watches on variables all from within the environment.

❑ **Integrated MSDN Help**
Visual Studio .NET can call up the MSDN documentation for you. For example, this means that in the text editor if you're not sure of the meaning of a keyword, you can select it, hit the *F1* key, and Visual Studio .NET will then bring up MSDN to show you related topics. Similarly, if you're not sure what a certain compilation error means, you can bring up the documentation for that error by selecting the error message and hitting *F1*.

❑ **Access to Other Programs**
And if all that wasn't enough, Visual Studio .NET is also able to call on a number of other utilities that allow you to examine and modify aspects of your computer or network, without you having to leave the developer environment. Using the tools available, you can check running services, database connections, and there's even an Internet Explorer window that lets you browse the Web.

Of course, assuming you are experienced in C++ or VB, you will already be familiar with the relevant Visual Studio 6 version of the developer environment for your particular language – so you will know that many of the features listed above are not new – you're probably already used to doing much the same things in Visual Studio 6. However, what's new in Visual Studio .NET is that it combines all the features that were previously available across all VS 6 developer environments. This means that, whatever language you used in VS 6, you'll find some new features in Visual Studio .NET. For example, in Visual Basic, you could not compile separate debug and release builds. On the other hand, if you are coming to C# from a background of C++, much of the support for data access and the ability to drop controls into your application with a click of the mouse, which has long been part of the Visual Basic developer's experience, will be new to you. The C++ developer environment did include some support for this, but it was very limited, and was restricted to the most common user-interface controls.

> *We should point out to people coming from a C++ background that you will find two things from VS 6 missing in VS.NET: Edit-and-continue debugging, and an integrated profiler. Microsoft was apparently unable to get edit-and-continue debugging for .NET working in time and has hinted that that facility will appear with a future service pack. MS is also not shipping any full profiler application with .NET. Instead, there are a number of .NET classes to assist with profiling in the* System.Diagnostics *namespace. The* perfmon *profiling tool is available from the command line (just type* perfmon*) and has a number of new .NET-related performance monitors. At the time of writing, Microsoft is also working with a number of partner companies who are developing performance profilers.*

Whatever your background, you will find the overall look of the developer environment has changed to accommodate the new features, the single cross-language IDE and the integration with .NET. There are new menu options and toolbar options, and many of the existing ones from VS 6 have been renamed. So you'll need to spend some time familiarizing yourself with the layout and commands available in Visual Studio .NET.

In order to demonstrate how Visual Studio .NET differs from Visual Studio 6.0, let's look at the development of a simple application. From within Visual Studio .NET select File | New | New Project, which displays the New Project dialog:

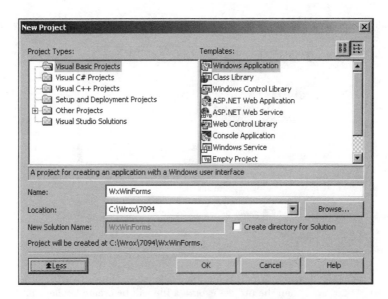

In this dialog, the language selected (under **Project Types**) is **VB.NET**. Actually, exactly the same list of project types to create would be displayed had **Visual C#** been selected as the project type. The application template selected is **Windows Application** and we've named the project WxWinForms.

When the **OK** button is clicked a new desktop-style GUI application is born:

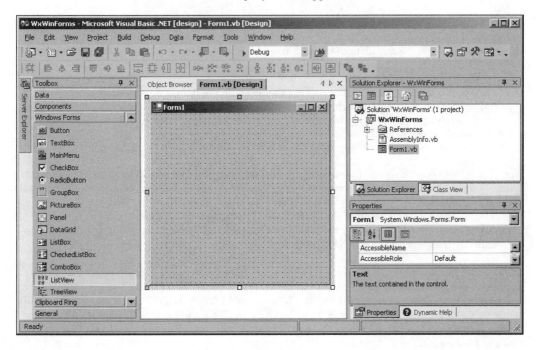

Take a look at the Solution Explorer for the new project (if it's not visible use the View menu):

Actually quite a bit can be learned from this humble screenshot. Notice that the project contains a file called AssemblyInfo.vb. When the project is built a file will be created called, WxWinForms.exe, but in actuality this file is an assembly. Executables files and DLLs under .NET are references to assemblies (more on this later). How do assemblies differ from Win32 DLLs or in-process COM servers (COM DLLs)? Assemblies are self-describing. Everything an application needs to use the assembly (types, methods, protection level, security, custom attributes, etc.) is contained in the assembly. In COM terms the metadata is like a super type library. In C/C++ terms, the metadata is a super header file.

Notice also that the previous project contained a folder, References. This is not a real folder on disk, but a virtual folder within the project. These references refer to other assemblies. The **types** exposed by these assemblies (via the metadata of the said assemblies) can be used in the WxWinForms project.

> **A type is a template used to describe the encapsulation of data and associated behaviors. Unlike COM, which is scoped at the machine level (via the registry), .NET types are scoped at the assembly level. There are two kinds of type:** *by-reference* **(generally classes) and** *by-value* **(structures and primitive data).**

The idea is that types of similar functionality are grouped together into an assembly. As you might guess, System.XML contains types used to manipulate XML, while System.Windows.Forms contains types that contribute to developing graphical user interfaces (classes like Button, TextBox, and CheckBox). There is one assembly not listed in the References virtual folder, mscorlib.dll. This assembly is the core .NET assembly that contains types so crucial to development that they are automatically referenced in every .NET project.

Types within an assembly are not referred to directly. In fact every type is prefixed by a **namespace** (the logical grouping of types by name). For example there is a class called Random that is unsurprisingly used to generate random numbers. This class is found in the System namespace so the **fully qualified name** for this class is System.Random. System also contains a namespace called IO that contains classes such a TextWriter and TextReader. Thus, the fully qualified name for TextReader is actually System.IO.TextReader.

Quite often the name of the assembly corresponds to the name of the namespace. For example the `System.Windows.Forms.dll` assembly contains the `System.Windows.Forms` namespace. In fact, an assembly can contain multiple namespaces. These namespaces serve to further refine the categorization of types within an assembly. The namespaces of the `System.Xml.dll` assembly reflect this philosophy:

- ❑ `System.Xml` – contains types for the general manipulation of XML

- ❑ `System.Xml.Schema` – contain types that handle XML Schemas

- ❑ `System.Xml.Serialization` – contains types that handle serializing objects to and deserializing them from XML

- ❑ `System.Xml.XPath` – contains types that access an XPATH parse

- ❑ `System.Xml.Xsl` – contains types that work and play with Extensible Stylesheet Transformation (XSLT) transforms

Do not worry if you do not know XPATH from XSLT. The point is that a namespace is a *categorization*. So a web page and a Windows GUI can each contain an instance of a `Button` class, but because of namespaces it is possible to have two types of `Button` class (or indeed a million types of `Button` class):

- ❑ `System.Web.UI.WebControls.Button` – the ASP.NET style (web) `Button` class

- ❑ `System.Windows.Forms.Button` – the Windows GUI-style (desktop application) `Button` class

There is one more musing to be made with respect to the `WxWinForms` application, namely that this application was a VB.NET application. The .NET Framework including the referenced assemblies (`System.dll`, `System.Xml.dll`, etc.) was written in C#. There is absolutely no work to be done in order to have a VB.NET application call into C#. Multi-language development within .NET works seamlessly but it is important to note there is a bit of plumbing under the covers in order to make the seamlessness happen.

Developing .NET Applications FAQ

Q: When deploying .NET applications is there anything extra required?
A: Aside from installing the Common Language Runtime it is becoming more and more important that you applications be signed. Signing is a way of identifying the author of the code (authenticating). Microsoft is being extremely security conscious and administrators will very easily be able to only allow signed applications (EXEs and DLLs) to run. To obtain a certificate that can be used to sign code, take a look at www.verisign.com or www.thawte.com.

Q: On what platforms can .NET applications be run on?
A: The Common Language Runtime can be installed on Windows 98, ME, NT 4.0, 2000, and XP. Windows 95 is not supported.

Q: Is every class in the .NET Frameworks class library available on every operating system?
A: No, but the fundamental classes are common to every operating system on which .NET can be deployed. The classes related to developing Windows services for example are not available under Windows 98 and ME since these operating systems do not permit services to be run. The classes related to developing COM+ applications (serviced components) are only available on Windows 2000 or later (including Windows XP).

Q: Do I need Visual Studio .NET in order to develop applications for .NET?
A: The tool (Visual Studio .NET) is technically separate from the .NET Framework. It would be possible to use a third-party development environment (when one becomes available) or to use the command-line versions of the compilers vbc.exe (VB.NET compiler) and csc.exe (C# compiler).

Q: What operating systems does Visual Studio .NET run on?
A: Visual Studio .NET will not run on Windows 98 and ME. Applications on these environments will have to be debugged remotely. All other operating systems on which the CLR can be installed are supported with respect to Visual Studio .NET.

Q: I'm just a poor developer looking to learn .NET, is there a way to buy an academic version of Visual Studio .NET?
A: For less that a $100 U.S. dollars you can pick up Visual Studio .NET Academic, provided you are enrolled at least one class at a qualified academic institution (there are a lot of these). The following URL specifies what learning institutes qualify for the discount:
http://www.microsoft.com/education/default.asp?ID=academicdiscounts
The following URL provides locations where academic software can be purchased (hint: shop around – they are not all priced the same):
http://www.microsoft.com/education/default.asp?ID=AERFIND

Q: Since Visual Studio .NET only runs on Windows NT, 2000, XP, and above, can I also use an academic version of the operating system and save some money?
A: Yes. The URLs from the previous question should let you know if where you are studying qualifies and where to purchase.

Multi-Language Support

Play ball! These are the word uttered at the start of a baseball game but they are also the words for managed languages to live by. In order for a language to run on .NET, that language must agree to "play ball" with the .NET Framework. This means that the language must adhere to set of predefined types, a common memory allocation/cleanup model, and common error handling. A major perk of adhering to a standard is that Visual Studio .NET can seamlessly debug from one language (say VB.NET) to another (say C#) to another (even Visual Perl from www.activeperl.com). This also means that VB.NET can create a class derived from a base class implemented in C#; that a C# application can implement an interface declared in a managed C++ class library. The language an assembly is developed in is *irrelevant* to the developer using the assembly's components.

Before applications could "play ball" (adhere to a common language standard exposed by the .NET Framework), there was chaos. VB allocated memory using one approach while C and C++ allocated and freed memory using alternative approaches. Even a single C++ application could support several different versions of the C run-time library, which meant each version of the C run-time library maintained its own heap. Error handling was an even larger minefield of development. In the era of Visual Studio 6.0, different flavors of Visual Basic could not even agree on a common error handling approach. Within C++ applications, MFC, STL, Win32 functions, Win32 system exceptions, and COM/DCOM all handled errors differently. Even among Win32 functions errors were indicated using an inconsistent approach (function returns FALSE or zero or 0xFFFFFF or a positive number or a negative number).

In the past technologies such as COM promised language independence. For example, it was possible using COM to let VBScript applications (such as ASP applications) talk to C++ DLLs (in-process COM servers). Language interoperability was possible but it was not possible to debug from within one language into another language. Additionally it was often difficult to develop in one language using types common to both languages. C++ developers who've had to work with VB types such BSTR, VARIANT, and SAFEARRAY know all too well the complexities of alleged language independence. Language independence meant accessing a wide variety of Win32 functions (SysAllString, VariantInit, SafeArrayCreate, etc.) in conjunction with helper classes (CComBSTR, CComVariant, _bstr_t, _variant_t, etc.). These types were certainly not native C++ types.

There is nothing alleged about the language interoperability of .NET. Demonstrating this is this rather simple C# DLL (a.k.a. .NET assembly of type class library), WxCommonCode:

```
using System;

namespace WxCommonCode
{
    public class WxSharedCode
    {
        public static int WxAnyMethod()
        {
            int a = 10, b = 0;

            return a/b; // this will raise an exception
        }
    }
}
```

The previous code does not do a heck of a lot except expose a method that generates an exception (a divide by zero exception). This code can be called from a VB.NET console application (WxApplication) defined as follows:

```
Imports WxCommonCode

Module WxMain

    Sub Main()
        Try
            WxSharedCode.WxAnyMethod()
        Catch ex As DivideByZeroException
            Console.Error.WriteLine(ex)
        End Try
    End Sub

End Module
```

The previous VB.NET code snippet simply calls a C# method (WxAnyMethod) and of course handles any exception thrown by that C# method. The VB.NET code is blissfully ignorant that it is calling a C# method versus a VB.NET method versus any other .NET language method. Part of what is also being demonstrated is that VB.NET, C# and any managed language share common error handling (the Try...Catch construct in the previous code snippet).

What also needs to be demonstrated is that it does not take a major effort to make managed languages work and play well together. The steps to make the VB.NET console application WxApplication talk to the C# class library WxCommonCode are:

❑ Right-click the **References** folder of the Wxapplication solution as it is displayed in the Solution Explorer:

❑ From the pop-up menu, select the **Add Reference** menu item.

❑ From the **Add Reference** dialog select the assembly to reference. In this example the assembly to reference is accessed under the **Projects** tab (the WxCommonCode assembly).

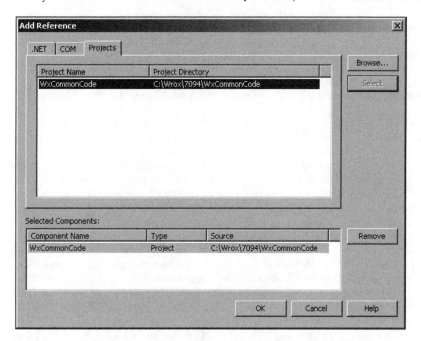

Even if the previous example was centered on Visual Studio .NET, it is the .NET Framework and not a particular version of Visual Studio that supports multi-language development. The previous code could have been compiled using the command-line C# (csc.exe) and VB.NET (vbc.exe) compilers shipped with the .NET Framework. It is the .NET environment that allows the languages work together.

The sum total of the effort required to utilize the .NET Framework's multi-language features using Visual Studio .NET is three mouse clicks. Closer inspection of the previous screenshot reveals that the WxMultiLanguage solution contains two projects WxApplication (VB.NET console application) and WxCommonCode (C# class library).

For developers who simple must execute the code:

❑ Open the WxMultiLanguage solution file in Visual Studio .NET from the downloaded source code for this chapter. Alternatively create two separate projects, one C# Class Library and one VB.NET Console Application, and write the above code modules into them, naming them as appropriate, and adding the reference as described a moment ago.

❑ From the **Build** menu select the **Build Solution** and build the solution (all projects in the solution).

❑ In the **Solution Explorer** window, right-click on the WxApplication project and from the pop-up menu select, **Set as Startup Project**. This means that when we debug the console application will be the project the debugger launches.

❑ From the **Debug** menu select the **Step Over** menu item repeatedly (or use the keyboard shortcut) until you have stepped through the entire program. After the code inside `Console.Error.WriteLine` method has been executed, the fun is basically over with (the error handled and displayed).

The output from running this application will certainly not win a Nobel Prize for literature:

```
System.DivideByZeroException: Attempted to divide by zero.
   at WxCommonCode.WxSharedCode.WxAnyMethod() in
C:\Wrox\7094\WxMultiLanguage\WxCommonCode\WxSharedCode.cs:line 11
   at WxApplication.WxMain.Main() in C:\Wrox\7094\WxMultiLanguage\WxApplication\WxMain.vb:line 6
```

Visual Studio 6.0 developers should recognize just how much work it would have taken to make the previous code work without .NET. The error handling alone would have been horrific.

> *To catch a divide by zero exception meant using the `__try` and `__exception` extension to the C++ language or the little know `_set_se_translator` function (a function that maps a Win32 exception into a C++ exception). Even after the Win32 exception was caught, it still had to be converted into HRESULT form so the value could be returned to VB and then we had to write the appropriate VB code to handle the error. Three separate error handling mechanisms were required.*

In this example, one type of error handling was required – catching the `DivideByZeroException` class using a `Try` in conjunction with `Catch`. The mechanism that handles this was the Common Language Runtime (CLR) in which our managed applications run. The CLR automatically passed the exception across language boundaries (more on the CLR later).

Supporting multiple languages means that an application can be constructed out of components that are basically agnostic with respect to language. It would be possible for a C# Windows Form to use a VB.NET base class. A C# application could therefore seamlessly use the functionality exposed by a different language. This seamless use applies to the calling of methods and properties, accessing fields, using events, and working types exposed through another language.

Disadvantages of Multi-Language Support

In searching for the disadvantages of multi-language support, one presentation from a Microsoft rival stood out. The basic premises against multi-language support were:

❑ Maintaining multiple languages on a single application will be difficult

❑ In an mixed-language environment it will be complicated for teams to interact

❑ In a mixed-language environment it will be difficult to generate common best development practices

❑ If an engineer leaves, code might be unreadable to co-workers

These criticisms were leveled against .NET's support for multiple languages, but to be honest multi-language development has gone on for decades. Obviously, you should have a good reason to support more than a single language. The reason for supporting multiple languages should still outweigh the disadvantages irrelevant of how swish .NET makes it.

For example on a recent project, the original SDK code base was a series of ASP applications written in VBScript. A scripting language was the only option when it came to writing ASP code. This ASP code in turn called internal code in the form of COM servers written in C++ (for reasons of multi-threaded performance).

The next generation of the product required an ASP.NET control be developed (a .NET web control). The project was broken down as follows:

❑ SDK – written in VB.NET since the legacy SDK (VBScript) was still applicable. It was considered that most ASP developers (the customers using the control) would migrate from VB to VB.NET so VB.NET was the logical choice.

❑ Legacy COM servers – remained unchanged (unmanaged C++).

❑ ASP.NET control – written in C# since the code was internal to the project (not viewed by the customers). C++ was not considered viable because it is too complicated to develop managed code in C++. C# was viewed as the language closest to C++ (the language of the application's unmanaged code).

The point is that the multiple languages where not chosen on an arbitrary whim of temperamental developers. The team's make up, future development directions, and time to market were all factored into the decision. All the previous criticisms are technically valid. The point is that they are only issues if a poorly planned approach is taken to development. Use multiple languages if, and only if, there is reason to do so.

The .NET Languages

Microsoft is providing a variety of language choice when it comes to .NET. In fact at the time of writing, there are potentially over two dozen languages that you can use to write .NET applications, including:

❑ Visual Basic. NET (VB.NET)

❑ Visual C# .NET

❑ Visual C++ .NET

❑ Visual J# .NET

❑ JScript .NET

❑ COBOL for Microsoft .NET

❑ Perl for Microsoft .NET

❑ Eiffel for Microsoft .NET

❑ Python for Microsoft .NET

❑ Pascal for Microsoft .NET

❑ Mercury for Microsoft .NET

❑ Mondrian for Microsoft .NET

❑ Oberon for Microsoft .NET

❑ Salford FTN95 (Fortran) for Microsoft .NET

- ❑ SmallTalk for Microsoft .NET
- ❑ Standard ML for Microsoft .NET
- ❑ Dyalog APL for Microsoft .NET

However, of these only a few are likely to become the dominant languages for .NET development, primarily determined by what Visual Studio .NET supports out the box.

C# is the migration path for C++ developers moving to .NET. VB.NET is the migration path for VB, VBScript and VBA developers under .NET. J# is supposedly the migration path for Java developers moving to .NET but is more likely that such developers will simply use C#. Managed .NET code can be developed with C++ (a complicated process) but again is it is more likely that legacy C++ developers will simply move to C#.

C# – Why a New Language?

The .NET Framework is for the most part written in a newcomer to the world of software development, **C#**. With respect to ancestry, C# is closely related to C++, just as Java is closely related to C++. C# (just like Java) is designed to take advantage of a C++ developer's knowledge of inheritance and object-oriented development.

For decades software developers have suffered from ELPS (Excessive Language Proliferation Syndrome). A classic example of ELPS is the fact that before .NET there were three flavors of Visual Basic (Visual Basic 6.0, VBA, and VBScript). Given the prevalence of developers suffering from ELPS, why invent a whole new language?

A better question to ask would be, "Why not C++?" since in its day Visual C++ 6.0 was the most popular development tool in the world. C++ is a spectacular language. It was designed in the late 1980's and was state-of-the-art at the time, but that was a while ago now. A case in point is exception handling. Early versions of C++ did not support exception handling. Once exception handling was implemented there were no built-in mechanisms for determining where the exception was thrown (file name and line number) and no built-in mechanisms to get a stack trace at the time the exception was thrown. On the other hand, Java (a more contemporary language) has the ability to generate a stack trace but C++ does not expose this more contemporary technology. Consequently C++ developers do not use exception handling because if an exception is thrown from within a million lines of code, there is no mechanism built into the language that readily tracks down the offending line of code that caused the exception to be raised.

C++ is also a complicated language. Although C++ experts might disagree, most developers use only a small subset of the language. As a Windows instructor at U.C. Berkeley in the Silicon Valley, these conclusions are not mere conjecture. Templates are rarely used, and the same can be said for the standard template library (STL), new-style casts (`const_cast`, `static_cast`, etc.), and exception handling. Additionally every C++ project was developed using the same scheduling paradigm: eighty percent of the time in development and twenty of the time in finding memory leaks. Maybe twenty percent is an exaggeration, but most large-scale projects set aside significant time for cleaning up memory leaks.

The C++ heritage comes in handy in other ways. On occasion (the exception and not the norm) C# code must handle pointers (when working with legacy types). Since C# is a close relative of C++, there are constructs that can be readily used in order to access pointers.

Other features of C# include support for single inheritance. This means a C# object can have only a single base class (just like Java). There was a great deal of complexity and ambiguity in the world of C++ surrounding multiple inheritance.

Inheritance provides a way for a class to derive implementation and API from a base class.

Also added to C# is support for interfaces. An interface is directly analogous to a C++ pure virtual base class. The idea is that an interface mandates functionality that must be implemented by a class. If a class is derived from `IComparable` then the class must implement the `CompareTo` method. This is the only method exposed by the `IComparable` interface and when a class is derived from an interface it agrees to implement every construct exposed by the interface.

It should be recognized that an interface does not provide implementation.

An alternative to C# would have been to have C++ developers migrate to VB.NET. However, most C++ developers desire a syntax that they are comfortable with. C# provides this level of comfort while VB.NET (although simple to pick up) is a bit foreign.

Certain pundits will point to the rift between Microsoft and Sun with regards to Java in order to explain the origins of C#. This is somewhat true. For legal reasons Java is Sun's language; that left Microsoft looking for a successor to C++. A language (Cool) had been developed in house and this evolved into what is now know as C#.

Both C# and Java are excellent examples of contemporary languages. There are minor differences but they are fairly trivial details. For example it's possible to change the reference value of a parameter passed to a C# method while in Java a reference value can only be changed using the return value of a method.

The true differences are not really technical but are instead political. C# has been accepted as a standard by the ECMA General Assembly. Furthermore the infrastructure used to support languages under .NET (the common language interfaces) has been accepted as a standard by the ECMA General Assembly: http://msdn.microsoft.com/net/ecma/. However, merely being accepted by a standards board does not mean Microsoft will give up control of C#. Java is controlled by Sun, but in recent times Sun has expressed an interest in being open to extending the language. Any claim by Sun or Microsoft that they are "open" should be met with skepticism.

There is no right or wrong in the C# versus Java debate. It is a matter of corporate giants bickering both in and out of court. The languages are mostly equal from a feature standpoint. Clearly in a pure Windows environment, it is hoped that C# running inside the .NET Framework will out-perform Java and it is hoped that C# will also be more reliable. There are efforts underway to have C# run on a Unix-based operating system including FreeBSD, Linux, and Solaris. Microsoft is even behind one of these, a shared source version of a portion of the .NET Framework that will allow C# to run on FreeBSD. Would you bet your career and your company's future on these efforts? Java is still language of choice in Unix-style environments.

There is one factor in whether to solve a problem using C# (Microsoft infrastructure) or Java (non-Microsoft infrastructure) where a winner can be determined – development tools. Microsoft makes the best development tool, Visual Studio .NET. Still, even if Visual Studio .NET is the greatest development environment in the universe (which it is), a tool is not the only reason to pick a language.

VB.NET

VB.NET is an excellent choice for VB 6.0 developers looking to embrace .NET. However, Visual Basic 6.0 developers might get a shock when they first see the changes that the language has undergone to make it a .NET compatible language. VB.NET has additional constructs designed to take advantage of the features exposed by .NET: classes, structures, inheritance, use of namespaces, interfaces, delegates (type safe callbacks), and exceptions.

VB.NET also represents a unification. There will be no more VB, VB Script, and VBA. This is now just one language. There is no script in ASP.NET development, whereas a scripting language such as VBScript is the only option when developing classic ASP code.

Legacy VB code will not work in the .NET environment – or rather it will function perfectly happily on the Windows platform but you cannot take advantage of anything .NET provides. Visual Studio .NET does provide a wizard to upgrade existing VB 6 code to VB.NET, but it is by no means perfect as the differences in the language are so extensive. Fortunately, because of the interoperability features built into .NET it is relatively easy to use your old VB 6 components from new VB.NET code so there is no essential need to upgrade all your old VB 6 code.

VB.NET vs. C#

Developers not migrating from VB to VB.NET or C++ to C# will actually need to choose their .NET language. Is there a compelling feature in one language over the other? In Visual Studio .NET VB.NET has one feature C# does not:

❑   When a compilation error is displayed in the tools it is highlighted by a squiggly underline. When the error is fixed in VB.NET the line goes away. When the error is fixed in C#, the code must be compiled before the error goes away.

On the other hand, C# does support certain features that VB.NET does not:

❑   **Operator overloading**
In C# it is possible to overload operators. An example of this is that in C# you can subtract (-) one DateTime structure from another in order to determine how long something took to run. In VB.NET the Subtract() method must be used since there is no subtraction operator. Most experts view operator overloading as a way to add complexity to a language rather than a must-have feature. For this reason C# support of operator overloading is far from a compelling reason to make the decision.

❑   **Pointer support**
Most .NET code will never see, hear, or smell a pointer. When legacy functions are accessed there is a need at times to manipulate pointers to data. This is the domain of C# rather than VB.NET. Since most developers will not be developing pointers, again this is not a compelling reason to pick C# over VB.NET.

There are some somewhat more important reasons to pick C# over VB.NET. One reason is that when calling a method in C# the directions in which the parameters are passed (into the method, out of the method, and both into and out of the method) are specified as part of the method. To understand this, consider the following snippets of code written in C# calling methods:

❑   Class.Method1(a1) – would pass the variable a1 to Method1 (an input parameter).

- ❑ Class.Method2(out b1) – Method2 would be responsible for setting the underling value of b1 and returning it to the caller (an out-only parameter). The out keyword is what indicates this behavior.

- ❑ Class.Method3(ref c1) – the c1 parameter would be passed into Method3 and Method3 could set the underlying value of c1 (an in/out parameter). The ref keyword is what indicates this behavior.

Another reason to pick C# over VB.NET is based on how Visual Studio .NET supports events. To understand this consider an ASP.NET or Windows Form application that contains a Button class referenced by the name buttonPuch. This Button is associated with a Click event. If the Button's name is corrected to buttonPush using Visual Studio .NET then under C#, the Button will still correctly handle the Click event. However, if the Button was renamed in Visual Studio .NET for a VB.NET application then the Click event would no longer be handled. This difference in behavior is not a difference in languages but reflects a difference in how Visual Studio .NET handles languages.

Despite all this there really isn't any real compelling reason in the difference between the languages to pick one over the other. Maybe a small percentage of the time (maybe 0.1%) where access to legacy pointers is needed will the differences matter. In reality, the choice is more likely going to come down to which language you are more comfortable with, and truth be told once one of them has been learned there really isn't much work to be done to learn the other.

Managed and Unmanaged C++

Under .NET it is still possible to develop C++ code that does not run under .NET. Such code is referred to as **unmanaged code**. Despite the benefits that the CLR brings, there are still reasons to develop unmanaged code. For example the APIs that allow the settings of network cards to be manipulated are shipped as part of static library under Windows. In order to link with a static library (unmanaged code) then an unmanaged project is need. C++ in its unmanaged form could link with this static library and therefore set the IP address, gateway, and subnet mask associated with a specific network card.

C++ can also be used to develop code that runs under .NET (managed code). Developing managed code takes a bit of effort. This is because .NET is extremely explicit when it comes to passing by value or by reference. Structures and simple types (integer, char, Boolean, float, etc.) are stored by value on the stack while classes (including strings and arrays) are stored by reference with the actual data being stored in the managed heap. C++ predates .NET by a good decade. For this reason C++ has its own ways of storing data on the stack or on the C++ heap. It is possible to refer to data on the stack as a value, a pointer, or a reference. It is possible to refer to data on the heap by pointer or by reference. Structures can be placed on the stack or in the heap. Classes can be placed on the stack or on the heap.

The way managed C++ specifies which data goes where is by using extensions to the C++ language:

- ❑ __nogc – specifies that the type declared is unmanaged (does not use garbage collection)

- ❑ __value – the type is managed but is contained on the stack and not in the managed heap

- ❑ __gc – the type is contained in the managed heap

To understand the significance of the complexities of developing with C++ using .NET simply go to any site that sells books. At www.fatbrain.com (a site dedicated to technical books) there are eleven books available for developing with C++ and .NET, eighty-five books on C# and sixty-eight books on VB.NET. These numbers are an indication that managed code under C++ is not likely to be undertaken by most of the industry. Managed application development under C++ is clumsy and the direction most C++ developers will go in is C#.

One place where managed C++ may make sense is in porting unmanaged C++ code to managed code. Even so, simply migrating the unmanaged code to C# is also a viable option.

J#

As my mother always said, "If you can't say anything nice about a programming language, then don't say anything at all." J# is a version of the Java language based on the same version released with Visual J++ (based on JDK 1.1 whereas the current version is JDK 1.4). The purpose of J# is to facilitate Java developers moving to .NET. However, as a language, J# only allows development using the .NET Framework's class library and not Java's class library. The reasons for these restrictions/limitations are based on the legal disputes that have taken place, are taking place, and will take place between Sun and Microsoft.

The complexity of Java is not the language since the language is fundamentally a derivative of C++. What makes Java difficult to learn from scratch is the class library required to work in Java. This is exactly what makes .NET difficult to learn for any .NET developer. For Java developers, C# is a trivial language to pick up (and vice-versa). Language is not the barrier keeping Java developers from .NET. The reasons are political, legacy, and platform-specific. Since language is not the issue keeping Java developers from .NET, developing a language based on an older version of Java (J#) is not going to start a mass migration from Java to .NET.

The .NET Framework

The .NET Framework is composed of a variety of components that support the development and execution of a managed application. Each managed application when executed runs within the **Common Language Runtime (CLR)**. The CLR in turn provides managed applications with improved security, memory management, versioning, and a variety of other runtime-specific features.

In order for an application to be managed, it must make certain concessions with respect to the data types it declares and the method in which it will run. The **Common Type System (CTS)** provides a suite of common types that are implemented by managed types. The most crucial distinction in this area is the difference by between by-value types (data types stored on the stack) and by-reference types (data types stored on the CLR's managed heap).

Each language that can be used to develop .NET applications (managed applications) agrees to implement (at the very least) a set of types referred to as the **Common Language System (CLS)**. The CLS is a subset of the CTS. In fact there is a precise mapping between the specific types exposed by a managed language (int, bool, float, etc.) and types implemented by the .NET Framework's **Base Common Library (BCL)**, which includes the following structures within the System namespace: Int32, Boolean, and Single.

Each managed application can take advantage of an extensive class library made available as part of the .NET Framework. The functionality in this class library ranges from handling relational data access, through generating and working with XML, via file I/O, by way of GUI development to web page development and web service development. This list is just a smidgeon of the functionality exposed by the .NET class library.

The Common Language Runtime

The Common Language Runtime (CLR) provides services to managed code. For those familiar with Java, the CLR is roughly equivalent to Java's Virtual Machine (JVM). The CLR ultimately supports the ability to integrate code written in multiple languages. Versioning, security, common error handling (cross-language exceptions), memory management, debugging services, and profiling services are all provided by the CLR. Specific services provided by the Common Language Runtime include:

❑ The CLR enforces rigorous type safety. This means that a rogue managed application *cannot* overwrite critical sections of memory thus causing an application to become corrupted and crash. This should not happen in a .NET application due to inherent type safety.

❑ Components can be developed in one language and used from any .NET-compliant language.

❑ Components can be developed in one language and be accessed using inheritance in any .NET-compliant language.

❑ Types within the .NET class hierarchy can be extended by applications developing managed code.

❑ Code compiled for .NET is generated in an intermediate form (Intermediate Language). This code can be distributed on any CPU architecture or operating system that supports .NET. Basically such code is not platform specific.

❑ Common memory management – all applications take advantage of the same common heap, and memory cleanup is standardized between languages (garbage collection).

❑ The CLR provides a form of type safe function callbacks called delegates. This flavor of callback (delegates), like all compliant types in .NET, can be used by multiple languages. So a delegate specified in VB.NET can be used by a C# or managed C++ application.

❑ Complete support for the objected-oriented developer – the .NET Framework supports all the bells and whistles required to develop object-oriented applications: interfaces, inheritance (single), base classes that can be overridden, and abstract base classes.

The basic idea is to have a single engine providing these services to any compliant language. Managed code can subsequently be deployed in any environment containing the .NET Framework thus allowing applications to take advantages of these numerous features without having to know the specifics of the underlying operating system.

The Common Type System

The .NET Framework exposes a Common Type System (CTS) that dictates that managed code implements specific by-value types (simple types, structures) and by-reference types (classes including strings and arrays).

In object-oriented programming, a **type** is something that holds a value and supports an interface for describing the type. When most non-C++ programmers think of data types, they think only of values. However, in .NET, all types are object-oriented (and by-value types may be converted into by-reference types using a boxing conversion). This means that, in addition to storing values, they also exhibit a behavior that is defined by their interface. Types are reliable, because you can expect them to behave in a certain way.

By-value types are simple data types that roughly correspond to simple bit patterns like integers and floats. In .NET, a by-value type derives from the System.Object namespace, and supports an interface that provides information about the kind of data that is stored, as well as the data value. By-value types are useful for representing simple data types, and any non-object user-defined type, including enumerations. By-value types are known as **exact types**, which means that they fully describe the value they hold.

By-reference types are derived from the System.Object namespace, and may hold object references derived from classes. Reference types are self-typing, which means that they describe their own interface. This is not so different from the object references that we already use today. Object references are obviously very specific to the type of object you are assigning. Once the reference is assigned, you expect to query the object reference according to what its interface provides.

This diagram shows the breakdown of types:

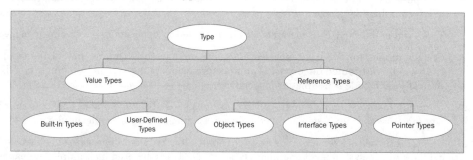

By-value types are contained on the stack while by-reference types are contained in the managed heap. Basically when by-value data (such as an integer) is declared *data* is placed on the thread's stack (4 bytes for an integer). Each thread contains a stack. As a thread executes its stack grows with each method called (parameters and return value are pushed on the stack) and with each variable declared in the methods data is placed on the stack. When a by-reference type is created a *reference* is placed on the stack pointing to data residing in a managed heap (a heap provided by .NET accessible by all threads in an application). Why bother with two schemes for memory management? First of all stacks are limited in the size in which they can grow – only a finite of memory can be consumed by a single thread (one megabyte is the default under Win32). Heaps can grow until all memory available to an application is exhausted. If multiple threads need to access the same data, it should not reside on a single thread. If that thread terminates then so does the thread's stack. For this reason all data shared between multiple threads should reside in a single repository (the managed heap).

From a coding standing to understand storage on the heap versus on the stack, consider the following lines of code:

```
int abc = 123;
Point p = new Point();
Random r = new Random();
```

The integer variable, abc, is a simple by-value type and is therefore stored on the stack. The Point type is a structure (declared as struct Point in C# terms) and is hence considered a by-value type (on the stack) by the CTS. This mean that the new operator calls a constructor associated with the Point structure but the new operator does not allocate any memory. Even if new was called a billion times it would allocate no memory since the memory for Point p is on the stack in a fixed location. The new operator does not allocate more memory on the stack it simple reuses the same location (a billion times if that is how many times new is called for the same by-value variable).

However, the Random type in the code snippet is a class. When new Random is called memory in the managed heap is allocated, the constructor for the Random class is called, and a reference to the allocated memory is added to the stack.

A diagram demonstrating the storage differences between the abc, p, and r variables is as follows where the arrows indicate a reference residing on the stack but referring to data contained in the managed heap:

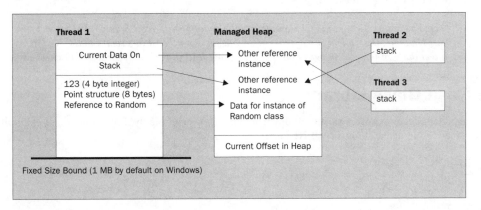

When a by-value type is passed as a parameter to a method, a complete copy of the type is placed on the stack. When a by-reference type is passed as a parameter, a reference to the type is placed on the stack. On the plus side, this ensures that even extremely large by-reference types only consume a small amount of space when passed as a parameter to a method. This means that a programmer is not required to specify what types should be passed by copying the data completely onto the stack and what data should be passed by reference.

In unmanaged C++, developers can actually pick and chose passing by-value and by-reference thus increasing the chance of exceeding the permissible stack size (the more data passed on the stack, the larger it gets) and thus generating an exception.

The Common Language Specification

Developing code using multiple languages is predicated on exploiting a subset of the CTS known as the Common Language Specification (CLS). A language which is CLS-compliant implements the following types found in the System namespace:

❑   Boolean

❑   Byte

- ❑ Char
- ❑ Decimal
- ❑ Double
- ❑ IntPtr
- ❑ Int16
- ❑ Int32
- ❑ Int64
- ❑ Single
- ❑ String

The names used, type declarations, type members, methods, properties, events, interfaces, and pointers all adhere to the CLS specification.

> *All languages that implement the CLS are potentially accessible to Visual Studio .NET. Remember it is the .NET Framework that supports multiple languages via the CLS. Visual Studio .NET is just a tool that can take advantage of the multi-language feature exposed by the .NET Framework.*

The Base Class Library

Managed languages expose a variety of intrinsic types. For example the following are all examples of intrinsic variable declarations in VB.NET:

```
Dim i As Integer = 0
Dim c As Char = "c"
Dim b As Boolean = True
```

The same variables specified above in VB.NET could also be specified in C# using C#'s intrinsic types:

```
int i = 0;
char c = 'c';
bool b = true;
```

Each such intrinsic (primitive) type implemented in a managed language corresponds to a type specified in the .NET class hierarchy. The specific region of the .NET Framework where these types are found is referred to as the Base Class Library (BCL). In fact the previous code snippet could be rewritten (rather tediously) using each language-intrinsic type's corresponding BCL type:

```
System.Int32 i = 0;          //Maps to C#'s int or VB.NET's Integer
System.Char c = 'c';         //Maps to C#'s char or VB.NET's Char
System.Boolean b = true;     //Maps to C#'s bool or VB.NET's Boolean
```

Be aware also that the System namespace implements a String and an Array class. The String class corresponds to the string type used in both VB.NET (type, String) and C# (type, string). The Array class is the underpinning for when an array is implemented natively in VB.NET, C# or any managed language. Below is a snippet demonstrating using a string in C# intrinsically versus exposing the same functionality using the corresponding BCL type:

```
string strIntrinsic = "Just assign it a value";
System.String strBCL = "More verbose way to assign a value";
```

The above code snippet demonstrates that languages provide a series of syntactic shortcuts when it comes to the manipulation of intrinsic types. In a similar fashion C# and VB.NET have language-specific mechanisms for manipulating intrinsic arrays (BCL type, `System.Array`) that are vastly simpler than manipulating an array in its BCL type form.

The basic mapping between BCL types and language-intrinsic types for VB.NET and C# is as follows where each BCL type corresponds to structure in the `System` namespace:

BCL Type	C# Type	VB.NET Type	Description	CLS Compliant
Boolean	bool	Boolean	Boolean value containing true or false	Yes
Byte	byte	Byte	8-bit unsigned integer	Yes
Char	char	Char	16-bit Unicode character	Yes
Decimal	decimal	Decimal	96-bit decimal number (currency)	Yes
Double	double	Double	64-bit floating point number	Yes
Int16	short	Short	16-bit signed integer	Yes
Int32	int	Integer	32-bit signed integer	Yes
Int64	long	Long	64-bit signed integer	Yes
SByte	sbyte	None, so use BCL type	8-bit signed integer	No
Single	float	Single	32-bit (single precision) floating point number	Yes
UInt16	ushort	None, so use BCL type	16-bit unsigned integer	No
UInt32	uint	None, so use BCL type	32-bit unsigned integer	No
UInt64	ulong	None, so use BCL type	64-bit unsigned integer	No

C++ developers migrating to C# should make note of one tidbit in the previous table: C#'s `long` type is an eight-byte signed integer and not a four-byte signed integer.

The .NET Class Library

Each .NET language uses a common framework (a common hierarchy of class objects). This means that a C# developer joining the VB.NET team to "to help out for a few weeks" can easily handle diverse tasks such as manipulating dates and times (the `System` namespace's `DataTime` and `TimeSpan` structures), developing user interfaces (elements of the `System.Windows.Forms` namespace) and processing XML using the `System.Xml` namespace. This is because irrespective of the syntactic difference between the languages, the way that each language uses the above namespaces is intrinsically the same.

The .NET Framework exposes an extensive hierarchy of **namespaces**. Each namespace in turn contains types that include enumerations, classes, structures, interfaces, and events. The Common Language Runtime is not cognizant of namespaces. A namespace is just part of the name and the CLR requires a name to be *fully qualified*. For example `Int32` is not the fully qualified name of the BCL type representing a 32-bit integer. The CLR requires the name be fully qualified (namespace plus data type name): `System.Int32`.

One of the easiest ways of getting started in understanding this massive class hierarchy is to take a look at the reference section of MSDN that pertains specifically to namespaces (the root level organization construct for the library): ms-help://MS.VSCC/MS.MSDNVS/cpref/html/cpref_start.htm.

A snippet of MSDN for the aforementioned URL is as follows:

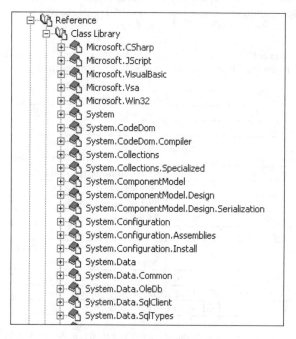

There are actually dozens and dozens of namespaces. All namespaces pertaining to the .NET Framework are stored in the form System.restofnamepace. Vendor specific namespaces contain the company name following a more specific indication as to the nature of what is contained in the namespace. An example of this is Microsoft.Win32. This namespace is used by the corporation Microsoft in order to expose functionality that directly accesses the legacy API it exposes for its operating systems (the Win32 API). This Microsoft is the same company as produces .NET but in the context of the Microsoft.Win32 namespace, Microsoft is exposing a product that is not specifically part of the .NET class library and hence the namespace starts with the company name (Microsoft.*).

> *Yes, the .NET Framework's* System.* *namespaces do access Win32, but remember that there is actually a FreeBSD version of the .NET Framework, which means that the framework is not required to access Win32 (a vendor-specific API).*

When working with the class library there are few things to understand. First of all, applications must reference the assembly in which a namespace resides. For example, by default every application built with Visual Studio .NET references the assembly, mscorlib.dll. Within this assembly there are multiple namespaces (System, System.IO, System.Collections, etc.). Determining if a class contained in a namespace must be referenced is a matter of checking MSDN. Demonstrating this, consider the following snippet from the documentation for the System.Collections SortedList class (taken from the root level documentation for this class found within MSDN):

Requirements

Namespace: System.Collections

Platforms: Windows 98, Windows NT 4.0, Windows Millennium Edition, Windows 2000, Windows XP Home Edition, Windows XP Professional, Windows .NET Server family

Assembly: Mscorlib (in Mscorlib.dll)

From this MSDN excerpt it should be clear that no reference is required for an application to access this class since each Visual Studio .NET application references `mscorlib.dll`. Had the assembly been different then a reference to this assembly would have to be set up (as the project did not already have such a reference). The previous discussion of `System.Collections` demonstrated one thing, namely that one assembly may contain multiple namespaces.

Actually the `mscorlib.dll` and `System.dll` assemblies share the implementation of certain namespaces such as `System.IO`. Normally each namespace is implemented in a single assembly. `System.dll` and `mscorlib.dll` are special because they are the foundation on which .NET is implemented. Demonstrating the overlap between these assemblies and the classes exposed by a variety of namespaces are the following two screenshots generated using the `ildasm.exe` utility (a utility provided with the .NET Framework that can view the contents of assemblies – more on this later):

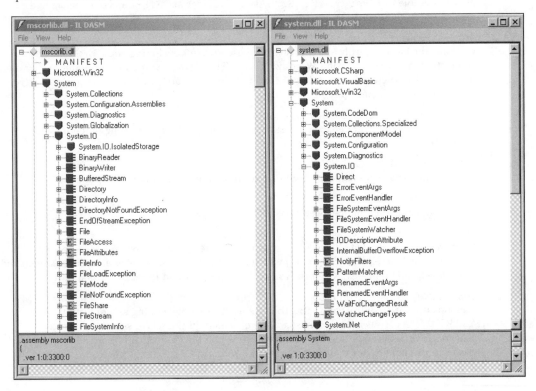

The easiest way to get a handle on which namespace exposes which functionality is to peruse the previously cited MSDN reference on namespaces. Overleaf is a list of ten namespaces that are commonly used in .NET development:

❑ System
Contains most of the basic types used by .NET. These types range from those categorized as BCL to a class for generating random numbers (Random), a structure for manipulating GUID's (Guid), and classes that allows access to console input and output (Console).

❑ System.Collections
Contains containers that hold data (sorted list, hash tables, stacks queues, etc.) and mechanisms for sorting such data (case-sensitive sort, case-insensitive sort, etc.).

❑ System.IO
Contains classes used in manipulating input and output. This namespace is logically broken down into entities such as the File class that contains methods related to file manipulation, Directory that contains directory manipulation methods, and Path that contains path-related manipulation methods. Also included are streams of various types (read-only, write-only, and read/write) including text and binary streams.

❑ System.Data, System.Data.OleDbClient, System.Data.SqlClient
Contains types required in order to use ADO.NET. As an API, ADO.NET is a conduit to data stores including relational (SQL-based) data stores. The System.Data.OleDbClient namespace provides access to the .NET managed data provider that accesses OLE DB providers while the System.Data.SqlClient provides access to the .NET managed data provider to SQL Server.

❑ System.Windows.Forms
Contains the basic controls and infrastructure used when developing client desktop applications and controls using Windows Forms. The classes exposed in this namespace reflect the basic infrastructure for a GUI application: TextBox, RadioButton, Button, TreeView, ListView, Label, and OpenFileDialog.

❑ System.Runtime.InteropServices
Supports interfacing with legacy code such as unmanaged DLLs exposing functions and COM objects.

❑ System.Threads
Contains the data types associated with supporting multi-threading in an application.

❑ System.Web.Services
Exposes functionality that lets web services be developed quickly.

❑ System.Xml
Exposes functionality that allows XML to be manipulated. The features of XML exposed by this namespace include XML 1.0 support (including DTD), XML namespaces at both the stream and DOM level, XSD schemas, XPATH, XSLT, DOM (Level 1 and Level 2 Core support).

❑ System.Web.UI.WebControls
Contains the basic controls and infrastructure used when developing an application using ASP.NET. The classes in this namespace are executed on the server side but ultimately generate HTML based on the browser flavor in which the control will be rendered. The classes in this namespace include AdRotator, Button, Calendar, CheckBox, CustomValidator, DataList, Image, Label, and ListBox.

One trick that is quite useful in understanding how classes work and fit into the .NET class library is to understand how to read the documentation. For example, in MSDN every class will present its entire class hierarchy. This class hierarchy is useful in understanding what functionality a class inherits from its base classes and what functionality a class must implement (dictated by the interfaces a class or its base classes implement). An example of this for the `System.IO` namespace's `StreamReader` class is as follows:

```
System.Object
    System.MarshalByRefObject
        System.IO.TextReader
            System.IO.StreamReader
```

The index entry for the `StreamReader` class found in MSDN demonstrates quite simply how to interpret what a class implements on its own versus what it inherits:

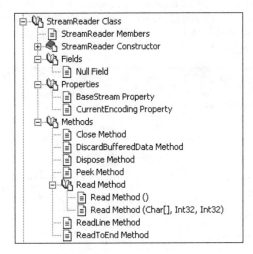

The screenshot above demonstrates the basic elements exposed by a .NET class (save for one):

❑ **Constructor**
Each class or structure is initialized using a constructor method. The constructor is called when the new operator is used to construct an object. Multiple constructors with different signatures are permissible. For example the `StreamReader` class contains several constructors including one that creates a `StreamReader` using a single string parameter that indicates the file to be associated with the `StreamReader`. Another flavor of `StreamReader` constructor takes a string (file name) and parameter indicating how the stream is encoded (ASCII, Unicode, etc.).

❑ **Fields**
Data for a class or object is exposed using fields.

❑ **Properties**
A class or structure can expose what looks like data but is actually code using a property. For a class that contains the data members `decimal price` and `int quantity` it might make sense to expose a `TotalCost` property (computed as `price * quantity`) which is a read-only property. Properties can be thought of the adjectives associated with an object.

❑   **Methods**
    Each class or structure exposes methods that can be thought as verbs, which take action
    against an object.

❑   **Events**
    The `StreamReader` class does not expose events. The `System.Windows.Forms Button`
    class does, including the `Click` event. The `Click` event is "fired" by .NET when a user clicks
    on the `Button` in a Windows Forms application. An event is data type that can be associated
    with zero or more callback functions. In .NET terms such callbacks are type safe and are
    referred to as **delegate instances**. Clicking a button (or firing any other kind of event) will call
    all delegate instances associated with that event.

In the previous screenshot demonstrating the MSDN index of the `StreamReader` class it appears that
the class only exposes two properties and seven methods. Actually each item contained in the index
(field, property, method, etc.) reflects an implementation specific to the class. So the `Close()` method is
expressly implemented by `StreamReader`. Clicking on the **Methods** folder for the `StreamReader` will
expose dozens of methods available to `StreamReader`. These methods will be displayed in MSDN's
result window and not in the index view:

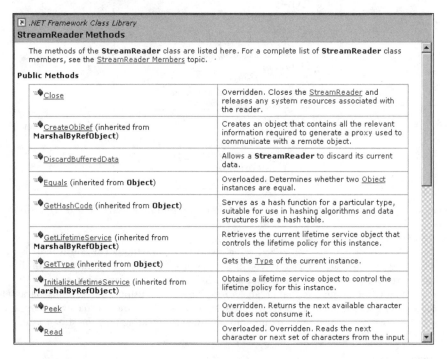

In the screenshot above the `CreateObjRef()` and `Equals()` methods are implemented by base
classes (`MarshalByRefObject` and `Object` respectively). These inherited items do not show up in the
`StreamReader` class's MSDN index entry. The methods implemented directly by `StreamReader` are
shown in the screenshot to be `Close()` and `DiscardBufferedData()`. The screenshot shows just a
small portion of the many methods available to an instance of the `StreamReader` class.

Intermediate Language

When managed code is compiled it does not generate native binaries (intrinsically x86 binaries). In other words, the assemblies (although valid Portable Execution (PE) executables) contain code that cannot be directly executed on the target processor. Instead the code generates assemblies (DLLs or EXEs) that contain **Intermediate Language (IL)**. Every managed language (C#, VB.NET, etc.) produces Intermediate Language assemblies. The purpose of IL is to provide a generic representation of compiled code that could be distributed on any underlying operating system using any processor – provided the .NET Framework is available on said operating system and processor, and also provided the processor or operating system data types have not been used by the assemblies generated.

How IL is converted to native code is discussed in the following section of this chapter on Just-in-Time compilation. Suffice it to say that an assembly containing IL could readily run on Windows 98 or Windows ME where the underlying operating system API uses ANSI characters. The same assembly containing IL could run on Windows NT, 2000, and XP, which are operating systems whose underlying system API is exposed natively as Unicode. In the past code had to be explicitly compiled as ANSI or Unicode because the binaries were specific to both processing and operating system. IL is basically equivalent in purpose to the byte format produced by Java (a generic format that can be used in a cross platform manner).

Most books take the tack of developing a "Hello world" application and then displaying it using the `ildasm.exe` utility. This chapter will buck this trend and instead demonstrate `ildasm.exe` being used with standard assemblies shipped with the .NET Framework. The `ildasm.exe` utility can generate raw IL given an assembly. This utility can also be used to display the contents of an assembly graphically. Demonstrating this usage of `ildasm.exe` is the following command:

```
%WinDir%\Microsoft.NET\Framework\v1.0.3705>ildasm System.XML.dll
```

The previous invocation of `ildasm.exe` displays the following:

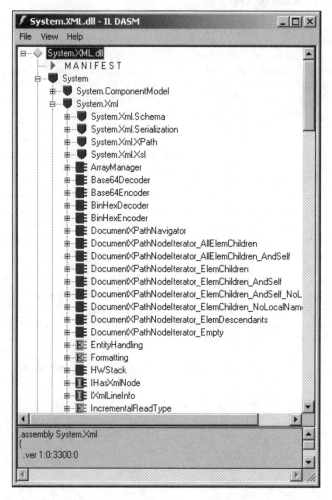

Basically the screenshot shows that `ildasm.exe` provides the way to view the entire contents of an assembly; in this case `System.Xml.Dll`. Traversing the hierarchy using `ildasm.exe`, it is possible to ultimately double-click on a specific method that in turn generates the Intermediate Language assembly code associated with that method. Following is an example generated by double-clicking on the `XmlAttribute` class's `getName()` property:

```
XmlAttribute::get_Name : string()                                    _ |□| x|
.method public hidebysig specialname virtual
        instance string  get_Name() cil managed
{
  // Code size       12 (0xc)
  .maxstack  2
  IL_0000:  ldarg.0
  IL_0001:  ldfld      class System.Xml.XmlName System.Xml.XmlAttribute::name
  IL_0006:  callvirt   instance string System.Xml.XmlName::get_Name()
  IL_000b:  ret
} // end of method XmlAttribute::get_Name
```

Without going into gross detail, IL is not assembly language as was taught in college (PDP 11 and x86 for my school). As an assembly language, IL is cognizant of constructs such as namespaces, classes, structures, methods, properties, and interfaces. The basic idea is to produce a binary format that is generic enough to generate native code at a later time but is specific enough to .NET to readily take advantage of how managed applications interface with the .NET Framework.

Using ildasm.exe and specific command-line options it is possible to generate reams and reams of disassembled code. Unless you are expressly developing a compiler for .NET, intimate knowledge of IL is a "nice to have" rather than a requirement.

Just-in-Time Compilation

Those of us who have worked in the Java world building on Windows but then copying over to Linux, can appreciate **Just-in-Time (JIT) compilation**. As an assembly is not machine-specific, it means that code can simply be copied from one machine to another and it gets JIT compiled to the native format. In order to demonstrate why this greatly simplifies development, consider the following mechanism used in a great many of the Windows SDK's include files:

```
#ifdef _WIN64
// 64-bit Windows prototypes/definitions here
#else
// 32-bit Windows prototypes/definitions here
#endif
```

When C or C++ code is compiled using a header file (such as the one shown), the behavior of the code is determined at compile time. If _WIN64 is defined then the functions used will only run on versions of Windows built to run on 64-bit platforms. This is because the code is built to run natively (x86 code running on a 64-bit CPU). If _WIN64 is not defined then the code is built to run on 32-bit Windows (what we have traditionally seen under Windows 95/98/ME/NT/2000/XP), since the code is build for a 32-bit x86 processor.

This example serves to demonstrate the potential of JIT compilation. Develop the code once and it will work on a 32-bit or 64-bit processor natively (courtesy of the processor-specific compilation). This processor-specific compilation takes place at run time rather than compile time as was the case with #ifdef _WIN64. JIT compilation could easily encompass more than just processor-specific issues. It could address operating system-specific issues. Should a version the .NET Framework be released for Linux, JIT compilation would ensure that the code ran natively on Linux.

To be specific, JIT compilation is performed on a per-method basis. To understand why, consider an application such as Microsoft Word. This application is humungous. If the JIT compiler converted Word from a .NET version of Word to native code, the start time of the application would be unbearably slow. Instead of JIT-ing the entire application, methods are JIT compiled on a per-method basis. When a method is called for the first time it is compiled to native format.

There is nothing magical about assemblies and JIT. Such files are simple Windows Portable Execution (PE) format files just like native x86 executables and dynamically linked libraries are PE format files. Each PE file is broken up into sections. Developers have long since recognized these sections as where thread-local storage is specified, data is placed, etc. For the case of a .NET assembly, each PE format file contains section in which metadata, attribute information, and intermediate language are contained. The term used for assemblies is *self-contained* since they hold all the type information and code required to be executed. When a .NET assembly is "run", the .NET Framework utilizes these other sections in order to run the assembly as managed code. This includes the process of performing JIT compilation so the managed code can ultimately be run as native code.

Garbage Collection

In the past a language tended to be closely tied to its memory management. For example it was possible to deploy a Windows application that contained VB, C++, and Java, but each of these languages would handle memory cleanup in its own way. The VB and Java runtimes would perform their own clean up (garbage collection) while C++ relied on the developers to perform the cleanup. For optimal performance it is better to have all the languages use the same approach to memory allocation and cleanup. A single memory manager can clearly do a better job because it sees the entire application rather than just any one piece created in a single language. The managed heap of the CLR acts as a common memory repository for a managed application in .NET.

A traditional heap contains a data structure in which free space is stored. Every time memory must be allocated the data structure is locked, free space is removed from the data structure and the data structure is unlocked. The lock is placed on the free space in order to allow multiple threads to access the heap. Clearly this presents quite a bottleneck. At the same time this model does not exploit data locality in order to improve performance. To understand this concept, consider the following two variables:

```
Employee employee1 = new Employee("Gates");
Employee employee2 = new Employee("Balmer");
```

If the previous code was executed on a traditional heap there is no guarantee that employee1 and employee2 are going to reside near each other in memory. From a CPU caching standpoint it makes a great deal of sense for employee1 to reside in memory near employee2 since if the variable employee1 is being used it is highly likely that the variable employee2 will also be used. Variables created near each other have a tendency to be used together. A better design for a heap would be to encourage data allocated at a particular time in the program's execution to reside near other such data in memory. At the same time, locking contention should be minimized.

This is precisely what the managed heap in .NET provides. The heap has a current offset pointer. If memory is to be allocated, it is allocated at the current offset and then this pointer is then incremented so it points to the next location in memory. Under this scenario employee1 would exist right next to employee2 within the heap (see the diagram which follows). At the same time, the only locking contention would be for the length of time it takes to increment the current offset:

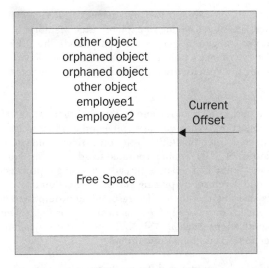

This scheme is fine and dandy provided that a machine has infinite memory. At some stage in the execution process, memory will run low. This is when **garbage collection** kicks in. Basically all pointers that are currently in use must reside in a global variable, a variable associated with a thread's stack or in a CPU register. Any pointer that is not referenced is **orphaned** and is therefore subject to cleanup.

At this stage, it important to note that .NET variables are accessed *by-reference* and not *by-pointer*. A pointer is considered to be *unsafe* in a .NET application. This lack of safety is because during garbage collection, valid pointers are moved to the bottom of the heap thus leaving space at the top of the heap into which new objects can be allocated. If an object is moved, the pointer hence becomes invalid. This is as opposed to references that are automatically maintained by the managed heap and are updated as part of garbage collection.

At this stage of the garbage collection process employee1 and employee2 might no longer reside next to one another. Still they were packed at the bottom of the heap. If these two variables exist for a long period of time they will be stored near each in the heap since they are placed near the bottom (see the diagram which follows). This means that a managed heap exploits data locality both before and after garbage collection is initiated:

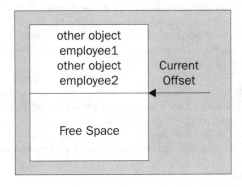

Speed of allocation and data locality are just two advantages of garbage collection. The other major advantage is that of applications never having to explicitly free memory. Since the variables in a .NET application are strongly typed (no generic pointers are permitted), the .NET runtime has knowledge of every pointer type and the size of every pointer. The .NET runtime as part of garbage collection ensures that data is freed. Not having to explicitly free data means that developers are freed from the tedium of tracking down memory leaks.

Garbage collection is not a perfect technology and in actuality there are a variety algorithms that can be used to perform garbage collection. When garbage collection is initiated, processing in other areas of the applications can be affected. Spending CPU cycles on garbage collection means that other tasks may get neglected. Certain features of .NET are incorporated to address this. For example, in a GUI application garbage collection runs in a separate thread. On a single-processor machine it is slower to run two threads than it is one. Even so, by placing garbage collection in a background thread, a primary thread is left running thus ensuring that the GUI is responding promptly to user input. In order to improve the user's experience, a more costly (yet practical) approach is taken (running multiple threads). In server style applications (such as ASP.NET applications) where overall performance is paramount, garbage collection is run in the same thread.

Running garbage collection in the same or a different thread is a bit more involved. When the .NET runtime is initiated, it can run as either a workstation or a server. When executing a client application, the .NET runtime runs in workstation mode and therefore garbage collection is performed in a separate thread. ASP.NET applications are used in conjunction with a .NET runtime that runs in server mode. This means that garbage collection is performed in the same thread as the application.

On systems with multiple CPUs, garbage collection is further enhanced. Each object initially created is placed in a separate per-thread heap. Actually, there is a specific term for objects that have yet to be compacted, via garbage collection: **Generation 0**. The reason Generation 0 objects are placed in separate per-thread heaps is to reduce contention for the ever popular (shared by every thread running managed code) managed heap. After garbage collection is initiated, all objects compacted are moved from their per-thread heap to a heap common to all threads. Actually, such objects are now Generation 1, so Generation 0 is in a per-thread heap while Generation 1 and the subsequent Generation 2 are placed in the standard (shared) managed heap. The basic idea here is that most objects are created for a short duration of time. There is no point in letting objects with a short lifetime contend for a critical resource such as a heap global to all threads. Only objects that survive the first round of garbage collection are therefore moved.

Per-thread heaps are not the end to the intricacies of garbage collection aimed at improving performance. For example there is a separate heap for large objects (memory allocations greater that 20k). Data in the large object heap is never compacted. This is because it costs too much to move around 20K of data in order to hope for better performance. Cleary 20K represents the exception rather than the norm when it comes to memory allocation.

There are even more intricacies to garbage collection than those presented thus far: object cleanup methods (finalization), categorizing objects into groups for improved locality (generations) and marking objects as candidates for cleanup in case memory resources run low (weak references). Those seeking more intricate knowledge of the garbage-collection process should take a look at the methods exposed by the System namespace's GC class (the class that manages garbage collection) and the .NET CLR Memory performance counters, which display information pertaining to garbage collection and managed memory in general.

Although only mentioned in passing in the previous paragraph, garbage collection provides object finalization. This is performed by calling the `Object.Finalize()` method. This is analogous to a C++ destructor. We pointed out earlier in the chapter that structures resided on the heap and were therefore not privy to the finalization provided by garbage collection.

Remember that garbage collection provides object-level clean up to types that reside on the managed heap. Such types are by-reference types in .NET. This cleanup is the equivalent in functionality to a legacy C++ destructor. In legacy C++ destructors could be associated with both classes and structures. In the .NET world structures are by-value types and are hence not subject to object finalization courtesy of garbage collection.

Assemblies

As we've learned, code under .NET (executables and dynamically linked libraries) is deployed as **assemblies**. Each assembly contains metadata that describes the types exported by the assembly and other critical piece of information such as the specific identify of the assembly (version number, cultural information, public key, etc.).

Demonstrating how this information is specified as part of development is the `AssemlbyInfo.cs` file in C# and the `AssemblyInfo.vb` file in VB.NET. The attributes inside these file specify an assembly's version number, cultural information, etc. To understand this consider the following excerpt from `AssemblyInfo.vb` for the `WxApplication` console application:

```
<Assembly: AssemblyTitle("WxApplication")>
<Assembly: AssemblyDescription("Demo application for show multi-language")>
<Assembly: AssemblyCompany("Anh Ngyen Software, Inc.")>
<Assembly: AssemblyProduct("WxMultiLanguage")>
<Assembly: AssemblyCopyright("Copy Right ANS, Inc 2002")>
<Assembly: CLSCompliant(True)>
<Assembly: AssemblyVersion("1.0.*")>
' paths are relative to the solutions directory which is one directory
' level above the *.snk file.
<Assembly: AssemblyKeyFile("WxApplication\WxApplication.snk")>
```

The previous metadata snippet supports the idea that the metadata of an assembly uniquely identifies that assembly. The final line of the assembly is significant from a deployment standpoint. The assembly name and version number do not precisely identify an assembly. For this reason a public/private key file is referenced inside `AssemblyInfo.vb` using the `AssemblyKeyFile` attribute.

The term that was used before for assemblies and their metadata is "self describing". An assembly contains all information needed for it to run. Recall that previously the `ildasm.exe` utility was used to display the contents of an assembly. This utility was actually displaying the metadata read from an assembly.

With an assembly, there is no type library in a separate file (as was the case in COM). With an assembly, there is no need to use the registry in order to describe how to marshal interfaces, where the type library resides, or where the code resides. The registry is not needed in the world of assemblies.

One way to put metadata in perspective is to consider the case of a .NET application accessing a COM server. Under this scenario, the type library of the COM server is used to generate metadata for a DLL that acts as a bridge between the .NET application and the COM server. This does not mean a type library is as complete as metadata, but they contain similar information and serve a similar purpose. Both a type library and metadata describe objects in order to support marshaling between applications.

Metadata enforces how applications are called and ensures that invalid data regions are not accessed. Metadata also contains information with regards to the security required for the assembly to run. Also contained within the metadata is the information associated with attributes placed in the code.

Attributes are a mechanism provided in order to extend the run-time behavior of an application. Each attribute is actually a class derived from the System namespace Attribute class. In order to demonstrate the power of attributes consider the following class definition, which uses an attribute specified as [WebMethod] in C# terms or <webmethod> is VB.NET terms:

```
public class Service1 : System.Web.Services.WebService
{
    // code removed here for brevity

    [WebMethod]
    public string RetrieveGreeting()
    {
        return "How are you?";
    }
}
```

This half line of code (the [WebMethod] attribute) seems to magically let the method RetrieveGreeting() be viewed externally as part of a web service. In actuality this attribute corresponds to a class named WebMethodAttribute. The significance of this is that the information provided by the attribute's class is contained in the assembly's metadata.

Attributes provide a variety of extensions to a language. They can be used to specify which methods are locked (synchronized); if data is serialized to XML (as attribute, as element); and the threading model used by .NET applications that call legacy COM objects. Of all the features of .NET, attributes can be the most intimidating because they appear to work magic. Actually they are just classes derived from a common base class. These attributes simply add extra functionality to an assembly's metadata.

Application Installation and Assemblies

The phrase Microsoft keeps using with respect to installing a .NET application is **XCOPY install**. XCOPY is a command-line utility that copies files and directory trees. When a .NET application runs (say an EXE file), it searches for the assemblies it references inside its current directory and all subdirectories. Since assemblies are self-describing simply placing them in the application's current directory or a subdirectory completes the installation process. OK, there may be a need to perform some other installation steps but applications should try to limit whatever these steps are.

When a .NET application accesses an assembly in its own directory or in a subdirectory, the assembly accessed is referred to as a **private assembly**. This assembly is not shared with other applications that are not installed in the same file and directory hierarchy.

The whole idea behind using XCOPY for installation means that there is no central repository (such as the registry) tracking what DLL is placed where, what version is placed where and how many applications are referencing which DLL. Each application maintains its own copies of its DLLs. Does this mean that there would be wasted space due to the same DLL residing on multiple locations on a hard drive? Of course, but who cares? Right now DLL conflicts (missing, incorrect version, etc.) are a vastly more serious problem than disk space.

It is possible to share an assembly with other applications. This might come as a shock to some of you but such an assembly is referred to as a **shared assembly**. Such an assembly must be *strongly named* and in order to be a strongly named assembly it must be associated with a public-private key file. Recall the use of the AssemblyKeyFile attribute in the previously demonstrated AssemblyInfo.vb file:

```
<Assembly: AssemblyKeyFile("WxApplication\WxApplication.snk")>
```

The previous snippet from AssemblyInfo.vb associated a public-private key file with the assembly; hence it is strongly named. Once an assembly is strongly named it can be placed in the **Global Assembly Cache (GAC)** using the GacUtil.exe utility. This process is straightforward:

```
GacUtil.exe AssemblyName
```

Once inside the GAC an assembly can be shared by multiple applications, but then again this just adds to the complexity of the installation process. The benefit of this complexity is disk space and memory savings. When assemblies are shared then only one copy of an assembly's read-only data (code) needs to be contained in the memory of the operating system. This increases performance. Additionally multiple applications will incur the minimal overhead of JIT compiling the application.

It is possible to view the assemblies in the GAC by running GacUtil.exe –l or by selecting the Windows shell extension found under the operating system directory's assembly subdirectory:

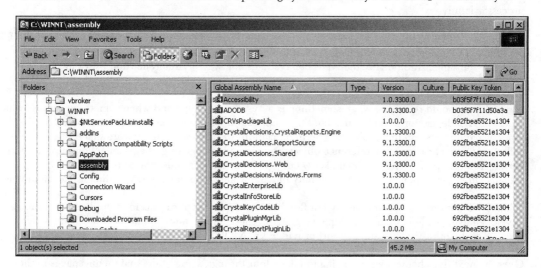

Chapter 6 also discusses the GAC and shared assemblies for reasons ranging from explaining how unmanaged applications access managed assemblies to how serviced components are run as Windows services.

Summary

After reading all of the complexities behind .NET development, it is important to recognize that these are complexities in how the technology is *implemented* rather than how you develop application with it. For example the process of developing code in multiple languages is dramatically simplified. The infrastructure to support multi-language development requires the .NET Framework to expose a potpourri of three letter combinations (BCL, CTS, CLS, etc.). The developers at Microsoft had to be aware of these specifics, as do the developers of high-level languages. A VB developer for example might recognize that the CLS is why VB.NET was suddenly bestowed with the Char type where previous incarnations of the language did not have a character type.

We also discussed how applications are deployed as assemblies. These assemblies are superior to legacy DLLs and COM servers because they contain a detailed accounting of what is contained in the assembly and how it is to be used (metadata). Installation is radically simplified because each assembly contains enough information for the assembly to be run. For this reason installation is a matter of just copying locations to a machine (XCOPY installation as Microsoft calls it) or assemblies can (in a more complicated way) be installed as shared assemblies.

Each assembly is composed of metadata and code. The later is in the form of Intermediate Language (IL). A .NET developer needs to know that IL is why code can be deployed on any system exposing the .NET Framework (regardless of operating system or processor) while a compiler developer would have to be aware of the intricacies of IL. This applies to compiler developers using high-level languages to generated IL and compiler developers translating IL into code native to an operating system and processor family.

The point of the infrastructure is *simplicity* and not complexity. The types exposed and used by VB.NET mean that a C# developer should feel comfortable working in VB.NET (and vice versa) because the types are the same. Additionally the types behave the same way (by-reference and by-value). Developers regardless of language can utilize the same extensive class library deployed with .NET.

A developer should recognize when something is a by-reference type and when something is a by-value type. A .NET developer should understand the implication when passing by-value and by-reference types as parameters and the implication on initialization (structures do not allocate space when new is called) and object cleanup (by-reference objects can take advantage of garbage collection in performing per-object cleanup). Developers should know enough about garbage collection to realize that it can actually aid in performance (location proximity of data) while at the same time speeding up development.

What .NET provides is not complexity but flexibility to deploy applications in multiple environments developed using code written in multiple languages. These applications should be more feature-rich because of the infrastructure and support provided by .NET.

Over the next five chapters we are going to take a tour through some of the main namespaces in the class library and look more specifically at how to develop different types of applications in .NET, starting with web applications.

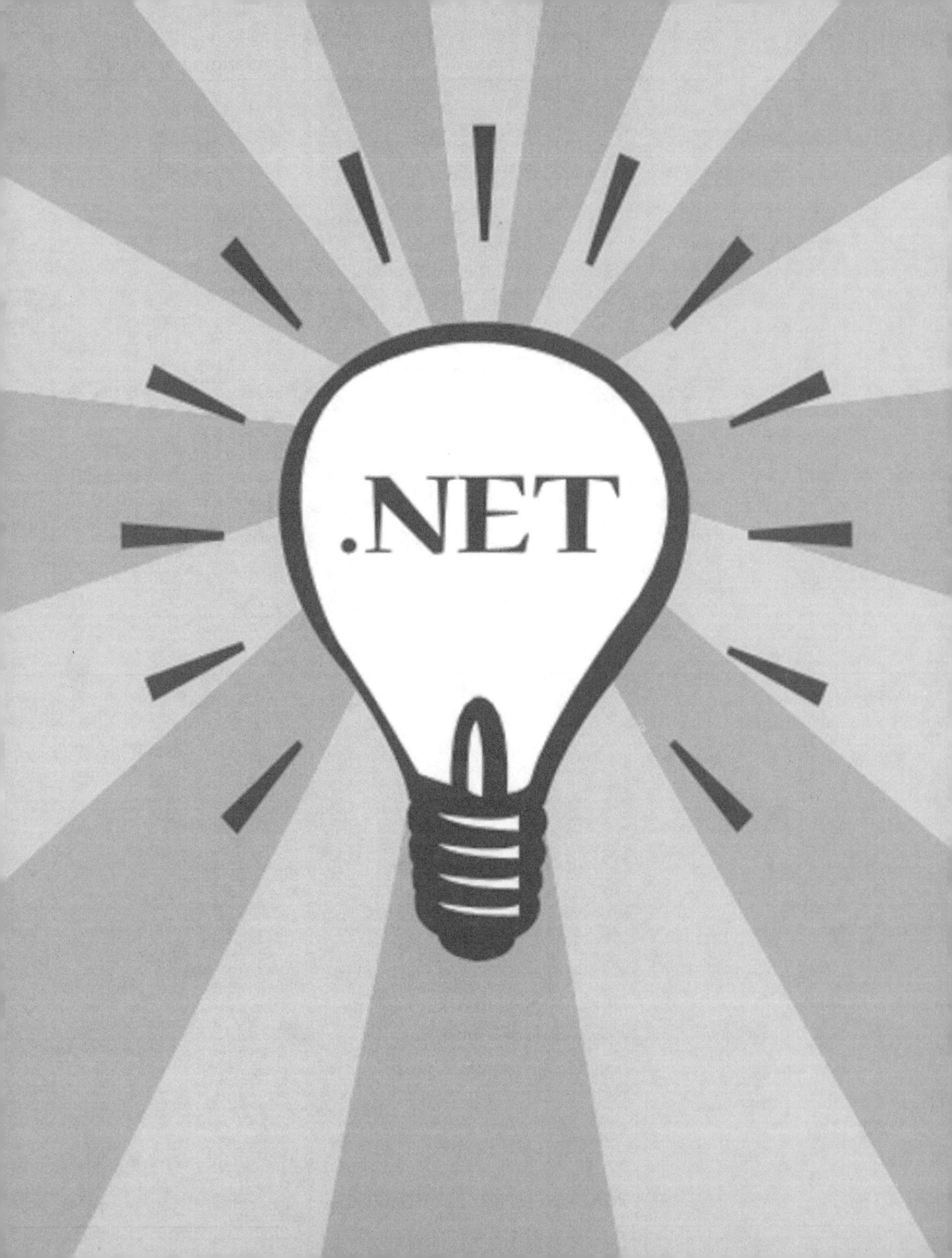
.NET

3

Web Development

We have probably all heard the phrase "there's nothing as constant as change" applied to Web application development one too many times. But there is a definite grain of truth to that. Not even a decade ago – just as the Hypertext Mark-up Language (HTML) 2.0 became the state of the art – developers were already looking for ways to make it both dynamic and interactive. Today, we have truly exciting technologies in our portfolios like Flash, XML and phone-top browsers. Futurists tout how our "smart devices" will communicate wirelessly with remote "Web Services", thus seamlessly weaving the Internet into our autonomic lives. Along the way, companies have introduced and will continue to introduce products they dub as "revolutionary" and "evolutionary." However, very few other products will likely have the impact that .NET will on the web development community both today and in the future.

So exactly why do we say that .NET will have such an impact? There are five answers to that question:

❑   .NET was designed and built from the very first byte to be completely Internet-technology based. With .NET, Microsoft has shed many of the limitations on its technology that made implementing modern Web applications both challenging and time-consuming.

❑   Changes to the ASP processing model make it possible for ASP.NET to have higher performance and better fault tolerance ensuring higher application reliability.

❑   The .NET Framework makes developing XML Web Services as simple as possible with a minimum loss of fine control over the request and response.

❑   Visual Studio.NET makes developing complex Web Applications and Web Services just as easy as developing Desktop Applications through the use of Drag-and-Drop control placement.

❑   The new Mobile Internet Toolkit finally makes it possible to develop cell phone-based applications using the same Integrated Development Environment (IDE) we use to develop other Internet-based applications.

Our goal in this chapter is to help you understand what .NET means to you as a Web Developer today and into the likely future. We want to give a snapshot of what the state of Web Development is today and how it got here. We will compare this to how Web Development works in the .NET environment and how all of this shapes the future. One thing to keep in mind is that .NET will keep changing; as new technologies emerge Microsoft will expand the Framework to include them. The Framework will continue to evolve for many years to come.

In this chapter, we will review:

- ❑ How Web Development is transitioning from an artisan skill to a methodical discipline. This section will review how the speed of development is changing, how performance is improving and how new fault-tolerance features will help applications meet the demands placed on them.

- ❑ How Active Server Page (ASP) development changes in .NET compared to the "classic" ASP environment. We will compare and contrast ASP development to ASP.NET development in terms of code mixing, execution, and data typing.

- ❑ The design surfaces for ASP.NET pages – Web Forms. As Web Form pages are built up from a series of controls, we will spend time looking at HTML Controls, Server Controls, and Mobile Controls explaining the advantages and disadvantages of each.

Web Development in Transition

Finding anything that has undergone as much change as quickly as web application development has in the last few years is certainly a challenge. We have gone from very basic static HTML web sites to customizable dynamic web sites. The demand for dynamic content, along with advances in technology, has shaped the Web we have today, along with the toolsets available. It is important to understand these changes and why they have occurred. Doing so will help us understand why the new features in .NET are important. The three major areas of change, we will look at include the speed of development, application performance changes and fault tolerance. One thing to consider when picking a tool or a technology is the maintainability of code produced. After the initial development, more often than not, changes will be required. How difficult will the code be to maintain? With Visual Studio and the .NET Framework, you can rest assured that if an application is coded properly initially, further maintenance will be very easy.

Speed of Development

Speed of development typically measures how much (or little) time passes from the inception of the development project to when the application finally goes into production. The dominant factors in that tend to be the number of features the users demand, the complexity of the features sought and the number of developers participating in the project. Ideally, the features that the users want will be expressed as well stated requirements. Since different approaches to web application development have different advantages and disadvantages, picking the right tool for the job helps accelerate the speed of development.

> **Nothing seems to stymie a project like users...**
>
> Or least users who keep changing requirements during development. You've probably been there yourself. After seeing a prototype or a test build of an application, the users will come back with either a laundry list of changes including bugs, "missed" features and new things they want added, or they will be anxious to put it into production (not realizing it still needs to be completed behind the scenes). After getting a grip on these changes, we frequently find that the development effort will take longer, more developers, or both.
>
> Very few off-the-shelf tools will help combat this, although some development techniques react better to changes than others. The most effective way to deal with changes like this is typically though the development methodologies. A methodology that deals particularly well with "dynamic requirements" is known as "Extreme Programming". For a gentle introduction to Extreme Programming, see http://www.extremeprogramming.org/.

Common Gateway Interface (CGI)

The Common Gateway Interface (or simply CGI) was the one of the first ways developers had to interact with the request-response cycle for a web page. Technically CGI is a way for the web server process to share information in the request to an application and to stream the response generated back. In most CGI-based applications, the information contained in the request is passed to the application in a string format. Parsing that information and acting on it is left to the program. It is a fairly bare-bones approach too: the CGI process does little internal processing of the request before the application sees it, and it rarely does any processing against the response.

In its heyday, the major advantage for CGI was that it was about the only standardized way that developers could get at the information in the request to generate a programmatic response. Since just about anything from a basic shell script to a C++ executable could be called, it offered a great deal of developer flexibility. At the same time, CGI is not suitable for building complex web applications due to the fact that the programs or scripts would become very complex to write and maintain.

Another major downside to CGI is that it spawns the destination process execution. Frequently the destination for a CGI request would be a script file. When this script file was called, it had to be fetched from disk and passed to an interpreter that also had to be loaded and executed. The net result of all of these comparatively slow efforts was to make CGI responses seem terribly slow overall.

A simple Perl script – called through CGI – for showing the current date and time in effect for the web server would look something like this:

```
print "HTTP/1.0 200 OK\n";
print "Content-type: text/html\n\n";

($sec,$min,$hour,$day,$month,$year,$wd,$yd,$isdst) = localtime(time());
$now = sprintf("%04d-%02d-%02d
%02d:%02d:%02d",$year+1900,++$month,$day,$hour,$min,$sec);
print "<html>\n<head>\n<title>Server Time</title>\n</head>\n";
print "<body>\n<h1>Server Time</h1>\n";
print "<p>The local server time is $now</p>\n";
print "</body>\n</html>\n";
```

In CGI scripts, literally all of the response must be written out by the script or destination program.

Did the so-called "Script Kiddies" make web application development a possibility?

Scripting languages like Perl were developed to help automate operating system tasks. However, some professional programmers have chosen to treat applications developed in scripting languages with a certain measure of distain. Worse, these same developers will sometimes deem those whom chose to use these languages as "Script Kiddies". They reason that a scripting language by its very nature can never be used to develop complex, powerful, and professional level applications. Sadly, the users who are using scripting languages to develop solutions are also cast in the same light. What these developers fail to realize is that without this artisan effort, web application development would have taken much longer and have a much less important role that it has today. It was largely due to the fact that tools like Perl and CGI came about that the Web became meaningfully programmable by the average developer.

We will take a more enlightened view of the "Script Kiddie". For the rest of this book, consider the "Script Kiddie" approach to be more ad-hoc than planned, more concerned with meeting immediate needs than long-term goals, and with "getting the job done quickly" than "getting the job done fancy".

Server-Scripting

The performance issues of CGI made it clear that so long as the processing of script remained outside of the web server process (that is, a process must be spawned) something better was needed. The first generation of such improvements included the original ISAPI filters/extensions, Active Server Pages (ASP), Allaire's ColdFusion, and PHP. Here, the programming logic is mixed directly in with the HTML page that the web server is supposed to send as its response. When a request is made for such a page, the web server process fetches that page and passes it off to some in-memory process for action. That in-memory process is typically a scripting language interpreter. This process parses the read file looking for special tags. When one of these special tags is encountered, the process then resolves the code and replaces the result back into the HTML document. Interpreted pages are usually processed on a read-and-single-pass respond process. Once the response has been generated, any information that was made with the request (POST/GET) or computed during the generation of the page is discarded once the page is returned to the client and the script completes.

The second generation of server-side scripting is exemplified by Java Server Pages (or JSP). In JSP each Web Page is associated with a "Servlet." These servlets are similarly asked to parse the page in question and update the response before it is dispatched to the client. The big difference is that JSP Servlets are compiled classes that can maintain a certain amount of state.

In either case, the advantages are:

❑   Faster processing because no external processes have to be spawned to generate the response

❑   Less coding because the Web Server or the page interpreter process frequently takes care of parsing inbound requests and adding appropriate response headers automatically

However, both approaches have a couple of disadvantages to keep in mind:

❑ The mixing of HTML and application code can make it easy to write fairly sloppy, inefficient code and can make maintaining such pages more difficult

❑ In first generation server-side scripts, the reuse of code is commonly reduced to "copy and paste" or including files of shared code into the page rather than more efficient methods

An ASP that displays the local time of the server where it's being run looks like this:

```
<html>
<head>
<title>Server Time</title>
</head>
<body>
<h1>Server Time</h1>
The local server time is <%= now %>
<body>
</html>
```

As you can see the dynamic portion of the page (<%= now %>) is embedded right in with the HTML, making it difficult to maintain and reuse.

> **It is at least partially this mixing of code and presentation mark-up that has earned the server-side scripter a bit of a reputation as being a "Script Kiddie". The fantastic ease of writing such scripts has made it just as easy to write "bad" programs in the long-term. It is fairly easy, in an adhoc way, to generate complete Web-based applications. Because there is very little distribution overhead, such applications are frequently made to solve immediate needs rather than long-term problems or for reusability or sustainability.**

Component Programming

Component Programming involves the development of rich sets of programming logic bundled up into binary-format libraries. The components are then called by server-side scripts or CGI programs. For example, in the Windows environment, it would be common to have functions for working with the database or validating user inputs against business rules encoded into a Dynamic Link Library (DLL). In many cases the developer or an administrator would then use some system process – such as Microsoft Transaction Server or Component Services on the Windows platforms – to host these libraries. Server-side scripts would then be written to make use of these libraries.

In practice, the process works like this. The developer (or developer team) sets out to identify what entities and interactions exist in the problem domain. They will then identify what attributes of the entities must be known to solve the business problem and how the interactions between the entities must work to achieve the same goal. A class will then be designed for each entity. This class acts like a template for creating instances of the class known as objects. The class will normally hold and expose all of the germane attributes for the entity as well as offering methods as ways of interacting with it. Code will then be written for each class that affects these attributes and methods. Each class may then be individually compiled into a library or all of the classes needed by a solution may be compiled into a single solution.

An example may make the preceding easier to understand. Suppose you are working on a simple customer tracking application for your local bookstore. Chances are you will have at least three entities in that system: Customers who buy books, Books offered for sale and Transactions that record a given customer purchasing a given book. For customers, we might know their name, address and home phone number. For titles, we should know the title of the book, our price for it, and the name of the publisher who published it. When a customer buys that book, the transaction will record who the customer is, what the book purchased was, and what price we charged for the title. The names, addresses, phone numbers, titles, and prices are all attributes of our Customer, Book, and Transaction classes. Each time a book is sold, we need to record that. Customers move, so we will likely need ways of updating the addresses we have for them. Publishers love to publish, so will likely be adding and removing titles from inventory frequently. The programmatic means we offer to update customers, record transactions, and manage the inventory of books become the methods of these classes.

Focusing on the customer class, a developer would codify a class for holding the attributes like name, address, and phone number. They might write the logic needed to load and save that information to a persistent data source, like a database, into that class, or it might be in a different class that will be shared by the transactions and titles classes. However, the developer will make sure that a method for updating the customer's address is available. Once this class has been completed, the developer will compile it – along with any others – into a library. If the developer used Visual Basic 6.0, for example, to codify this class, they might then produce or one more DLLs with all of the functionality for all of the classes. These DLLs could then be called by ASP. To get a higher level of performance by distributing the work of the DLLs over more processes or more than one computer, the DLLs may be installed into Component Services. Component Services "spins up" an in-memory version of a DLL so that other processes can quickly create instances of it for use. The instance can be on the same computer as the ASP requesting the object or on a different computer. Component Services normally takes care of the details involved in communicating with the instance automatically.

The major advantages of Component Programming include:

❑ **Ease of use**: Properly written components will tend to abstract the internal workings of a class into a simple programmatic interface. Consider the case of needing to update a customer's address. Rather than having to know all of the details of what database to update and how, the developer will probably just need to call one simple looking method on the object representing the customer. By cutting the interface down to a single method call, the object becomes easier for ASP developers to use than having to write all of the code themselves.

❑ **Ease of reuse**: A well written component will more readily lend itself to being used by more than one application. In our example, the customer class was used to provide a shipping address for an order. However, that same information could just as easily be used to provide a mailing programming with the customer's address, so we can send them announcements about sales and in-store events.

❑ **Enhanced performance**: Because the component is distributed as a compiled binary, it will execute much faster than the same code left to a script interpreter would. If it is placed into a hosting environment that takes care of bringing the object up to operational speed beforehand, that will also improve the overall performance of the application.

❑ **Better ability to scale up and scale out**: The pre-compiled nature of components allows them to consume fewer system resources during their lifecycle than having all of the code in an interpreted script would do. It also means that, through use of technologies like Distributed COM, components can be hosted on a remote computer. Lower usage of local resources means that more of them can be created on the local machine, thus "scaling up" the application more readily. Being able to run parts of the application on a remote computer means the application can "scale out" over multiple hosts.

The disadvantages of Component Programming include:

❑ **Complexity**: Having an application "layered" into components is inherently more complex than having an "all-in-one-solution" in the minds of many developers. It definitely requires better documentation of what parts of the application are where and what the dependencies are between the parts.

❑ **Requires disciplined programming**: In order to enjoy the fruits of Component Programming, the developer must be more disciplined than they might otherwise be. This is particularly true if the component being developed is expected to be used by more than one application at a time. More time must be spent up front making sure that all of the attributes and methods needed are actually exposed. Failing to do this, then redeveloping the component, can start a catastrophic cascade of changes throughout complete systems.

❑ **Harder to develop incrementally**: Developers whom have come through the ranks of web Application development from the early "Script Kiddie" days will often write their applications function by function, testing each function as part of the overall script until the script is complete. Due to the requirement imposed by IIS on components (we briefly mentioned "DLL Hell" in Chapter 1), this approach does work nearly as for Component Programming.

❑ **Harder to debug**: When a bug does manifest itself in a component-based application, the first step in fixing it is to figure out where and why the problem is occurring. However, using components makes this harder because you will not always know where in the component an error is occurring or why. It's also harder to debug the total application using a visual tool because the interaction between the web server and the component gets in the way. Lastly component development comes in many flavors – Visual C++, ATL, and Visual Basic to name a few. Each of these requires different languages, skill sets, and toolsets to debug and find the problem.

❑ **Deployment**: Depending on the technology used this could mean downtime for the web site. For instance, in order to move a new version of a COM component in you may need to have some downtime. In order to avoid this, a complex web farm may need to be implemented.

> **Component Programming with ASP is bound to be late!**
>
> No, we're not saying that you will automatically deliver your application past its due date if you choose to use component programming. In "classic ASP" – the ASP we had before we had .NET – all objects were "late bound". This means that the interpreter did not expect to know anything about the class until it created an instance of it. In most cases this allowed a program to load faster, but run slightly slower, as it worked through creating instances of classes. At the other end, "early bound" code knows all about the classes it uses and prepares to use them as the program initializes. This causes the program to start up a bit slower, but run a bit faster overall. The problem with early-bound code is that it can inefficiently lock up resources for the life of the application if not disposed of properly, which becomes a performance buster for web applications. The key point is that both early and late binding have pros and cons that need to be weighed for each situation.

Returning to our "Server Local Time" example, a Visual Basic 6.0 class for getting the current time might look like this:

```
Option Explicit

Public Property Get CurrentLocalTime() As String
    CurrentLocalTime = CStr(Now())
End Property
```

This class, `clsTimeOfDay`, was defined in a project named `Chp4Com`. It is compiled into a DLL that is then hosted via COM+. The server-side script that calls the class looks like this:

```
<HTML>
<HEAD>
<TITLE>Server Time</TITLE>
</HEAD>
<BODY>
<h1>Server Time</h1>
<%
Dim TimeOfDay
set TimeOfDay = Server.CreateObject("Chp4Com.clsTimeOfDay")
Response.Write "The current server time is: " & TimeOfDay.CurrentLocalTime
        & VbCrLf
Set TimeOfDay = nothing
%>
</BODY>
</HTML>
```

> **"Real Programmers"** seem to think the Component Programming approach to designing and building web applications is more mature than what "Script Kiddies" are frequently noted for doing. Developing one or more components then using them in a single application does tend to force more separation between the mark-up and programmatic code. If the component developer designs their component generically enough and it works with data that many applications may need to use, then the chances of reuse are also improved.

.NET Changes

Much of what we have come to know and appreciate about web development only gets faster, easier, or more "professional" with the introduction of .NET. This is particularly true for the ASP-centric developer. Although we can finally bid farewell to tools like Visual InterDev and FrontPage, much of what we learned in these environments still applies. If you've done any development in Microsoft's other Visual development tools, much of what you have learned there applies in the .NET environment.

One of the most striking changes is in how ASP.NET pages are processed compared to previous versions of the technology. We had previously said that ASP was a server-scripting approach to web development. That means that when a page was requested, the ASP processor (ASP.DLL in most cases) would receive the text of the page from IIS and would parse out certain tags. These tags were further processed against a script interpreter. The results of these calculations were inserted back into the document. When processing was completed, the results were passed back to IIS for dispatch to the client. The actual process is a bit more complicated than this, of course, but this description should give you the idea – ASP pages are parsed as semi-structured entities in a linear fashion.

That model changes a bit in ASP.NET. ASP.NET pages are more commonly called Web Forms. Web Forms are considered to be well-formed files consisting of HTML Controls and the source code for the page. The HTML in a Web Form serves the same purpose that it did in classic ASP – to define, position, and style visual elements. Controls, on the other hand, do not have an equivalent in classic ASP. In ASP.NET, controls are typically components that are executed as ASP.NET parses the Web Form. The results of executing a control are inserted in situ into the response. In some sense then, controls fill the role that blocks of server-side executed code did in classic ASP. However, since they are components, they save you the development effort of writing that code. They also tend to execute faster and are more resource efficient than interpreted code. One thing to note about the components is that they are regarded as one of the pieces that ASP.NET pulls together during compilation (HTML, controls, and code behind) and then builds the final program, outputting the HTML back to the client.

There are three basic ASP.NET control types:

❑ **HTML Controls:** HTML Controls more or less mimic the HTML 4.01 tags with programmatic elements. HTML Controls exist for a very pragmatic reason – to abstract the desired HTML tag so that ASP.NET can freely use a different tag if needed. Consider what happens if you decide to use a tag that only Internet Explorer implements, yet a user running Netscape Navigator asks for the page. If you had instead used an HTML Control, ASP.NET can detect what "user agent" (browser) requested the page and can, therefore, generate an HTML tag appropriate for that browser instead. There are two sub-types of HTML controls: Input Controls and Container Controls. Input Controls represent those HTML tags you might commonly use to gather information from a user such INPUT and BUTTON. Container Controls represent tags like DIV and SPAN.

Another key point to keep in mind about HTML Controls is that literal HTML tags cannot be accessed programmatically, but Web Form Controls can be. By using HTML Controls, you can change the content of a tag as the Web Form is processed.

❑ **Web Server Controls:** Web Server controls are the pre-compiled bits of functionality that generate HTML. .NET ships with quite a healthy stack of such controls from `AdRotator` (which generates in line banner ads) to XML (which easily applies a transform or style sheet to an XML Document.)

Web Server Controls are explicitly accessible to any programming logic that runs as the Web Form is processed. This happens so that you can adjust the properties of the control at run-time to generate exactly the output desired.

❑ **Custom Controls:** Realizing that not every function possibly needed in an application could be made available as an HTML or Web Server Control, Microsoft has made it possible for us to write our own controls. These are called **User Controls** or Custom Controls. Writing application logic into Custom Controls allows us to use – and reuse – that block of code on any appropriate web page.

Custom Controls are also available for programmatic access and control.

Another major difference between ASP and ASP.NET is that ASP.NET is able to use any .NET classes and .NET language seamlessly. Contrast this with ASP, where using a Win32 Application Programming Interface (API) calls involved a fair amount of workarounds. This means ASP.NET applications can easily use the full range of richness of the .NET framework.

One important thing to note about the ASP.NET pages is that they are actually classes compiled in two phases, as opposed to classic ASP, which is interpreted at each run. In ASP.NET the first phase occurs when the code-behind class files (inherited from the `System.Web.UI.Page` base class) are compiled into a dynamic link library (`.dll`) by Visual Studio during development. In the second phase, a user requests the web page (`.aspx` file) and ASP.NET will create a .NET class that is inherited from the class created in the first step (code-behind files compiled into a `.dll`). The `Inherits` attribute of the `@Page` directive is used to link the `.aspx` class to the web page. The point here is .NET's extensive use of classes to represent the various components of the page.

When using the various object-oriented languages built for .NET, ASP.NET applications gain full access to all the features that object-orientation brings to the table. That means that our ASP.NET pages can inherit functionality from other Web Forms or be used to provide functionality to other pages. Our web pages can also be used as sources of functionality from other Web Forms.

All .NET inheritance is limited to single inheritance.

Thinking about all of the ways you could inherit one Web Form from many others? Stop – .NET only supports one class inheriting from zero or one other class. While inheriting from more than one class is useful in some situations, the .NET Framework simply does not support it at this point. So if you need to build a Web Form class from more one other Web Form classes, you need to nest these pages in series. For example, if Web Form Z needs to inherit from classes A, B and C, B would need to inherit from A, C would need to inherit from B, and Z would need to inherit from C. In most cases, it might be wiser to use Custom Controls to retain the most flexibility instead of using this much inheritance. Often the use of interfaces can also take the place of multiple inheritance.

One of the most frustrating things to make work with ASP was visual debugging, particularly if you had added Visual Basic components into your page. One of the best features in Visual Studio.NET is that you can easily debug ASP.NET – complete with variable watches and break points – on local and remote servers and through class and process boundaries. Also, because ASP.NET has full and unfettered access to the .NET Framework, it can make use of the System.Diagnostics classes, including:

- ❑ Debug: This class allows you write messages to a log and test assertions about conditions. Code from this class is automatically removed from "release" builds of the solution.

- ❑ EventLog: This class allows you read and write from Windows-style event log files.

- ❑ PerformanceCounter: This class allows you to create and control performance counters within your application.

- ❑ Trace: Like Debug, trace allows you write messages to a log. Trace is intended for in-production applications, catching exceptions and errors as they occur. Unlike Debug, instances of the Trace class are not discarded in release builds.

Improve Performance

We have mentioned that web development in the .NET environment will enjoy enhanced performance, but exactly what do we mean by that? This section sets out to compare four facets of performance between previous web development techniques and .NET: load time, execution speed, database connectivity, and caching.

Binary Executables

When we discussed the CGI approach to Web Development, we noted that one of its shortcomings was that it was very slow to fetch the target application code from disk into memory before it could be executed. Almost any time that data or an application has to be fetched from disk, it will be two, three or more orders of magnitude slower than having the application already loaded in memory.

However, if the code to be loaded is already a compiled program – a binary executable – the time saved interpreting and converting the in-line script into executable code may offset the time required to load the program into memory. This is particularly true as the complexity of the compiled code increases.

Script Interpretation

The script-interpretation approach to web development keeps the programming logic in a non-compiled form. When the page containing the script is requested, that script is loaded, parsed, and executed. Because the script interpreter is commonly integrated with the processing engine, this approach tends to load the script faster, but executes more slowly than a binary executable.

An ideal web development solution would store programs in compiled form and keep them resident in memory so as to avoid the overhead of loading them from disk. The first way .NET achieves better performance is by doing just that.

Virtual Compile

As we know from previous chapters, .NET program files are not actually immediately executable. Instead, they are normally in the form of intermediate format or "P-code" format. When the program is actually executed, it is loaded into memory and "just-in-time" compiled into actual executable instructions. This process is actually very efficient, as the code produced by the first compilation process can normally be very quickly converted to actual instructions and readily stored in memory. While the JIT-compiled code runs very efficiently, it is still slower then a native pure executable. As future versions of .NET are released, I think it is safe to assume we will keep seeing optimizations made to narrow the gap further.

By virtually compiling ASP.NET Web Forms into cached applications, a great deal of the processing overhead of web applications is neatly bypassed.

Standard Database Network Connection Libraries

Active Data Objects (ADO), Open Database Connective (ODBC), and Object Linking and Embedding for Databases (OLE DB) are common technologies that are heavily used by most Web Developers who regularly use classic ASP. Each of these technologies plays a role in allowing ASP-based applications to select, insert, update, and delete data on Relational Database Management Systems (RDBMS). This trio has earned much popularity with developers because, when combined, they offer a uniform way for our applications to interact with virtually any RDBMS. Having a single standard means that developers could concentrate on learning just one way of working with data, freeing them to spend more time productively working on their applications.

However, this approach to database access has a couple of drawbacks. First, because these technologies strive to provide a standard way of working with any RDBMS, any of the functionality that the RDBMS may offer over and beyond the standard will not normally be available to the developer when using ADO, OLE DB, or ODBC. The other problem is that both OLE DB and ODBC impose a standard design on the communications between the RDBMS and ADO. Adhering to these standards typically causes the total performance of applications that use these technologies to be lower than it otherwise would.

Custom Database Network Connection Libraries

Microsoft understands that while one programming model for database access is ideal for developers, it is less desirable from a performance standpoint. In the .NET model, Microsoft has addressed this by having a uniform programming model (ADO.NET) and distinct .NET Data Provider classes. These .NET Data Providers are written to a general data access model, like the OleDb Data Provider, which can be used with any OLE DB driver, or they can be written for a specific database – like the SqlClient class that is designed specifically for use with Microsoft SQL Server 7.0 and newer. Since such .NET Data Providers are specifically designed to a given RDBMS, they can take full advantage of all of the speed and features of the underlying RDBMS. These providers implement the same basic interface, so that they all perform the same basic operations that we would expect, and is very easy to switch between them.

We will talk more about the data access between classic ASP and ASP.NET in the next chapter.

Caching

One of the ways developers enhance total application performance is through caching. This caching can be of script responses on the server or client, or of data on the serverside by the application.

Classic ASP could be configured such that for each request, the response generated could be cached in memory. If the same request were made again, ASP would fetch and return the cached response rather than processing the script again. Although this certainly could improve overall application performance, setting it up required administrator participation in configuring IIS to properly cache the pages.

ASP.NET offers caching in several flavors to enhance performance of your web application:

❑ **Page caching** (output caching) – This allows an entire page to be cached by browsers, proxy servers, and the originating web server based on a specified time. Another way that caching can be used to improve performance is to allow the client to cache response pages itself. In this way, the browser could check to see if it held a current response for the given parameters, and it if did, no request would be generated to the Web Server. However, this approach has a few catches that have caused some developers to avoid it altogether. First, the browser must support caching. Most current desktop browsers do, but few compact form-factor browsers don't (Web-enabled cell phones for example). Programming for effective client-side browsing also requires the developer to pay meticulous attention to writing the proper headers as part of the response, or the administrator to apply generic settings at the server level.

❑ **Partial page caching** – This allows you to identify parts of the page that are most resource intensive or rarely change and cache the results on the server for future requests. Typically this is done by creating them in Web Forms user controls and then setting the expiration on the control itself.

❑ **Caching Application Data** – The .NET Framework also provides a very flexible class called "Cache" that simply stores references to data. The Cache class also provides for the expiration of the data and prioritizing the data amongst itself. The cache is tied to a single application and its lifetime is therefore tied to that of the application, if the application is restarted the cache is emptied.

For "rich browsers" – those that support client-side scripting – a better solution was to embed the certain parts of the page data in "data islands." The browser could then work directly with these data islands to update the page without generating another request to the server.

.NET Changes

ASP.NET makes several performance-related improvements compared to what came before. When an ASP.NET page is requested, the class on which that page is based is two-phase compiled like any other .NET program. The results of the second compile are placed in the memory of the web server. The next time that particular page is called, the class executes with all of the speed of a binary executable stored in memory. The increase in performance that this approach offers can be quite dramatic, particularly for complex or otherwise slow running scripts. However, the first request for a page is a bit slower because the ASP.NET processor must fetch the files from disk and compile them.

We have already discussed how data-centric ASP.NET applications can use an RDBMS-specific class to work with a data source. But how big of a difference can that really make? According to some of the results published by Microsoft in its their testing, the combination of using compiled classes and the SQL Server .NET Data Provider allows hundreds of times more responses to requests in the same interval as classic ASP. Although achieving results like this requires some fairly specific programming (making the best use of caching and tightly written code for example), it is not uncommon for data-centric ASP.NET applications to be able to handle ten times as many requests in the same time period as classic ASP without such programming efforts.

Fault Tolerance

We can have most tightly optimized code, the best partial page caching the and excellent throughput to our RDBMS and still have poorly performing applications. This can be result of blocking processes, competing processes, or errors that we simply overlooked in the code. From the ASP.NET prospective, a number of new features have been added to make our applications more fault tolerant.

.NET Changes

ASP.NET now offers several different mechanisms for saving user state that support a web farm environment. With these a server crash will not cause all users to lose their session data and be forced to start over, as in the past when using default session management. It also allows for more dynamic balancing techniques to be used.

ASP.NET offers four ways to detect if an application has failed. Each ASP.NET application uses a pool of Worker Process Threads (WPT). WPT are threads of execution managed by the Operating System and the CPU. When ASP.NET detects that an application has failed, it will attempt to gracefully start a new instance of WPT for the application. When the new instance starts, new requests for the application are automatically directed to the new WPT instance.

❑ When the ASP.NET processor starts a WTP for an application, it may optionally check to see if that application is running by checking its "heartbeat". In this approach, the ASP.NET processor sends periodic messages to the application. If the application fails to respond to enough of these messages, the application is considered to have failed.

❑ It is possible that an ASP.NET application may exhaust its pool of WPT if it has been assigned a fixed number of them. The ASP.NET processor can check to see if this is the case. When this occurs, ASP.NET can restart the application with a new pool of threads.

❑ ASP.NET applications can become swamped with requests for pages. ASP.NET offers two ways of dealing with these overload situations, both of which result in a second instance of the application being generated to handle the extra workload. First, if too many requests are coming in, ASP.NET can create a new instance to handle these requests automatically. Second, if too many "Server Too Busy" (HTTP response code 503 messages) have been generated, a new instance of the application will be started.

❑ One last way that ASP.NET can detect faults is if a process has requests pending, but that process has not provided a response for some time. This processes can be considered as having failed and thus restarted.

Each of these methods is based on the `<processingModel>` directive element found in the `Web.Config` file for each ASP.NET application. The heartbeat method is controlled by the `<pingFrequency>` and `<pingTimeout>` elements. The number of WPT available to an application is controlled in by the `<maxWorkerThreads>` elements. A new pool of WPT is started when the number of WPT specified is exceeded. The threshold for too many requests is controlled by the `<requestLimit>` element. The threshold for too many 503 error messages is controlled by `<requestQueueLimit>` element. Finally, the `<responseDeadlockInterval>` controls how "locked up" processes are detected, whereas `<responseRestartDeadlockInterval>` controls how such processes are dealt with when detected. For more information on `Web.Config` see *Professional ASP.NET 1.0, Special Edition* from Wrox Press (ISBN 1-861007-03-5).

How ASP Development Changes

We have already seen some of the key ways that .NET impacts on web development for the ASP developer. In this section, we will dig a bit deeper into some of the key changes.

Web Form Front End

One of the most significant changes is that, from a design prospective, ASP.NET pages are not conceptually treated so much as simple linear pages, but more as Forms.

In the past, the processing model of ASP was:

- ❑ Parse the request for any parameters and load those into the matching object model receptacles for these items
- ❑ Check the cache for matching responses; immediately return them if appropriate.
- ❑ Load the requested page from disk
- ❑ Parse the page element by element for server-side scripts
- ❑ Execute the scripts as they are found, inserting the results into the response stream
- ❑ Dispatch the response back to the client

The ASP.NET processing model follows this model:

- ❑ Parse the request for any parameters and load those into the matching object model receptacles for these items.
- ❑ Check the cache for matching responses, immediately return that if appropriate.
- ❑ Check the application cache for compiled versions of the requested class. If present, load that class for execution. If not, load the request page from disk, compile, and cache.
- ❑ Parse the page element by element for controls. Add each of the controls to a collection of controls. Controls may register themselves as event handlers in this phase. The events are generated by actions from the client, such as clicking a button.

❑   Examine the request to see if it represents any event. If so, dispatch the event to any control registered as the handler for that event.

❑   Execute each control, inserting its output in the response where the control occurred in the Web Form.

❑   Dispatch the response back to the client.

❑   The major difference is that ASP.NET Web Forms are classes that can be compiled, and Web Forms are built up from controls. Controls are used to react to events.

Code-behind Class

We just said that Web Forms are based on classes, but what exactly do we mean by that?

Regardless of how an ASP.NET page is written, the ASP.NET processor will convert each Web Form into a .NET class so that it can identify any controls within the page. In turn these controls can be used to react to events. This is an important change to the web developer because it brings ASP.NET much closer to the visual programming model used by Microsoft's other development tools – namely Visual Basic. It means that the differentiation between web development and Windows development is blurred considerably and that developer skills will apply equally to each type of development.

ASP.NET pages may be written such that 100% of programmatic code is in the same file as the HTML mark-up. We know that the ASP.NET processor will treat all pages (Web Forms) as classes. We also know that classes can inherit from other classes. This gives rise to the idea of **Code-behind Classes**. Code-behind Classes are simply classes that contain the logic needed for reacting to standard and control-raised events. These classes are inherited by the actual Web Form.

The Code-behind Class is an important advance for web development because it allows the more or less clean separation of programmatic code from the HTML mark-up. Such separation allows designers and other "look and feel specialists" to change the page mark-up as much as they desire, while allowing the developers to do the same with the Code-behind Class. Such flexibility helps decrease the total time it takes to develop an application.

Most ASP.NET developers, particularly those who use Visual Studio.NET, will prefer to use the Code-behind Class concept to separate their code from the mark-up content. However, this isn't a requirement – you can still put all of the programmatic code in the mark-up file. ASP.NET will still treat the page as a Web Form in either case.

Early or Late Bound

The .NET compilers perform a task known as binding when an object is assigned to a variable. Two types of binding exist. Early binding occurs when an object is assigned to a variable declared to be of a specific object type. The early binding of objects allows the compiler to pre-allocate memory before the application executes. Being early bound, Visual Studio will know what methods and properties are available and therefore can provide IntelliSense in the development environment. When an object is late bound, it is declared to be of type Object. Objects can reference any type of object. Late bound objects are populated when assigned to instances of new classes. Late binding allows for some programming flexibility. Classic ASP only supports late binding.

The code you write in for an ASP.NET class may use either late or early binding or a mix of both. Early binding is generally preferred because it allows the complier to generate the most optimized code, and it also allows the compiler to verify the method calls during compilation.

Understanding Web Forms

It is pretty easy to understand then that Web Forms and controls depend on each other – but what exactly does a Web Form containing controls look like? In the designer view, a simple page that allows for scheduling one of three conference rooms might look like this:

HTML Mark-up

We know that an HTML-based document underlies this Web Form. The following code shows that page – this could also have been built using the graphical environment in Visual Studio.NET with simple drag and drop.

The first line – the Page directive – controls how the ASP.NET processes this page – on the server in or client–side script. The language attribute defines that this page will be written in Visual Basic .NET. The AutoEventWireup attribute means that as users click on or change the values of controls an event is fired back to ASP.NET for processing.

The Inherits attribute identifies the class that the Web Form will inherit from – essentially our code-behind class. The Codebehind attribute gives the the name of the file where that class's source code is located:

```
<%@ Page Language="vb" AutoEventWireup="true"
                Codebehind="schedule.aspx.vb" Inherits="WebForm1"%>
```

The Codebehind attribute is used by Visual Studio .NET and for debugging purposes. But when we build the application in VS.NET, the code-behind class is compiled and included in a file called Web.dll. If we want ASP.NET to compile the code-behind automatically as required, we use Src instead of CodeBehind:

```
<%@ Page Language="vb" AutoEventWireup="true"
                        Src="schedule.aspx.vb" Inherits="WebForm1"%>
```

The next block of code is simply common HTML page elements:

```
<!DOCTYPE HTML PUBLIC "-//W3C//DTD HTML 4.0 Transitional//EN">
<HTML>
 <HEAD>
  <title>Schedule A Conference Room</title>
 </HEAD>
```

As we might expect, the <Body> of the HTML document contains the normal HTML tags, the HTML Server Controls, and the Web Server Controls.

How does ASP.NET respond to my input?

If you are already familiar with web development, you probably know that certain HTML tags will provide information back from an HTML page to the web server. These tags are informally known as input controls. Each of the needed input controls must be nested inside of a Form tag.

ASP.NET follows this same rule regardless of the type of control used. Since all controls are eventually expressed as HTML tags and literal data, so long as a given control is rendered into a Form tag set, the value a user sets for it is returned to ASP.NET. In other words, no special processing is needed to extract the user's input from any type of ASP.NET controls.

```
<body>
 <form id="Form1" method="post" runat="server">
```

The attribute runat="server" tells the .NET Framework that the control should be processed during server-side processing. Following the Form tag, we have a small amount of HTML mark-up for putting a header on the page and defining a table to hold our controls and their captions.

```
   <H1>Schedule A Conference Room</H1>
   <P>
    <TABLE id="Table1" cellSpacing="1" cellPadding="1" width="100%"
                                                         border="0">
     <TR>
      <TD>Conference Room:</TD>
       <TD>
```

Here is our first example of a Web Server Control. This particular control – `DropDownList` – simply generates an HTML `<select>`...`<option>` set of HTML tags in the output. Our program will know this particular control by the value of its ID attribute: `DropDownList1`. We have another control immediately following the first. The second control is a `RequiredFieldValidator` (or RFV). An RFV Control simply checks that the control it is associated with (via the RFV's `ControlToValidate` attribute) has a value specified.

```
<asp:DropDownList id="DropDownList1" runat="server">
</asp:DropDownList><BR>
<asp:RequiredFieldValidator id="RequiredFieldValidator1"
      runat="server" ErrorMessage="You must select a conference room."
      ControlToValidate="DropDownList1">
</asp:RequiredFieldValidator>
</TD>
```

> **Wait – aren't you missing something? Like the options for the `Select` tag? And how does RFV actually validate that something was selected?**
>
> **No, not really. We will add the list of available conference rooms programmatically when we look at the code behind this file. As to how the RFV works – that depends. If ASP.NET detects that the client receiving this page can use JavaScript, it will insert a client-side function into the HTML page to do the validation before the value is sent back to the web server. If the browser does not support client-side scripting, ASP.NET will build the validation logic back into our server-side program that processes the page. As Microsoft likes to say about .NET – "it just works!"**

The Web Form continues defining the literal HTML and controls used. It has another required input that demands that the requestor explain why they want to use a specific conference room. This is followed by a **Calendar Control** named `Calendar1`. And yes, that's really all of the code you need to write to put a fully functional date-selecting calendar on a Web Form!

```
</TR>
 <TR>
  <TD>Scheduling Notes:</TD>
  <TD>
   <asp:TextBox id="TextBox1" Runat="server" Rows="3"
                              Columns="35" Height="75px" />
   <asp:RequiredFieldValidator id="RequiredFieldValidator2" runat="server"
   ErrorMessage="Please explain why you want to use this conference room."
   ControlToValidate="TextBox1"></asp:RequiredFieldValidator></TD>
 </TR>
 <TR>
  <TD>Date to Schedule:</TD>
  <TD>
   <P>
    <asp:Calendar id="Calendar1" runat="server"></asp:Calendar></P>
  </TD>
 </TR>
 <TR>
```

```
<TD></TD>
<TD>
```

We then have a control that triggers the processing of the form on the server. When the user clicks on this button, the text values held by the controls on the Web Form are packaged and sent to the web server. The way that the various controls (button and image button) within a form post events is through the use of a client-side JavaScript function __doPostBack. This function is called by the controls that submit a form with the view state information as well as any arguments needed.

In reality, ASP.NET will generate an INPUT HTML tag, with its type set to Submit, for this Web Server Control.

```
        <asp:Button id="Button1" runat="server" Text="Submit">
        </asp:Button></TD>
    </TR>
    <TR>
     <TD></TD>
```

Finally, we have an HTML Control that we will programmatically update with confirmation of the conference room registration. Note that unless the runat server attribute is specified, this control will not be available to us as we process the response.

```
        <TD><p runat="server" id="p1"></p>
        </TD>
        </TR>
       </TABLE>
     </P>
    </form>
   </body>
  </HTML>
```

When the user views the final version of this page in a browser, they see roughly the same page as previously shown:

So how exactly did the line confirming the conference room date and reason work its way into the response? We already know that the DropDownList, the TextBox, and the Calendar Controls are within a set of <Form> tags. So far, that is not much different than traditional ASP development; but what happens next is.

Code-behind Class

The Code-behind Class for this page follows. As we might expect, that class consists mostly of functions that handle events generated by the Web Form when the user interacts with it in the browser. To be used as a Code-behind Class, this class must inherit the System.Web.UI.Page class.

```
Imports System.Web.UI.WebControls, System.Web.UI.HtmlControls

Public Class WebForm1
  Inherits System.Web.UI.Page
```

Next, each of the controls on the Web Form is represented (declared) in this class by an object. Each of these objects is referenced by a variable shared throughout the class. So they can be used as sources of events, they are declared with the WithEvents attribute as well.

```
Protected WithEvents Calendar1 As Calendar
Protected WithEvents Button1 As Button
Protected WithEvents DropDownList1 As DropDownList
Protected WithEvents RequiredFieldValidator1 As RequiredFieldValidator
Protected WithEvents p1 As HtmlGenericControl
Protected WithEvents TextBox1 As TextBox
Protected WithEvents RequiredFieldValidator2 As RequiredFieldValidator
```

> The classes codifying the Web Server Controls are defined in the **System.Web.UI.WebControls** namespace, whereas HTML Control classes are defined in the **System.Web.UI.HtmlControls** namespace.
>
> Custom Controls normally inherit from the **System.Web.UI.Control** class. If the Custom Control would actually provide HTML mark-up in the response, you should inherit from the **System.Web.UI.WebControls.WebControl** instead.

The next bit of code is automatically generated by Visual Studio.NET when you create a Web Form. If you change any of the properties of the Web Form, the code will automatically be adjusted to reflect the changes made. If you are not using Visual Studio.NET to create your applications, you will only need to include the Page_Init subroutine calling the InitializeComponent method and the line of code before it that declares InitalizeComponent().

```
#Region " Web Form Designer Generated Code "

  'This call is required by the Web Form Designer.
  <System.Diagnostics.DebuggerStepThrough()> Private Sub InitializeComponent()

  End Sub
```

```
Private Sub Page_Init(ByVal sender As System.Object, _
                           ByVal e As System.EventArgs) Handles MyBase.Init
  'CODEGEN: This method call is required by the Web Form Designer
  'Do not modify it using the code editor.
  InitializeComponent()
End Sub


#End Region
```

> **Other than the methods you will write to handle events on the controls, Web Forms
> will typically have two other methods: `Page_Init` and `Page_Load`. The code for
> `Page_Init` is executed the first time the page is processed (new or changed) by
> ASP.NET. `Page_Load` is executed each time the page is requested. A variable,
> `IsPostBack`, indicates if the current request is the first request made by the browser
> for the page in question. If it is not, `IsPostBack` will be true. Testing this value
> allows you write code that will be executed only the first time a request for page
> is processed.**

In the real world the information about our conference rooms might come from a database or XML file.
We will look at how ASP.NET uses these types of data in the next chapter. This application has a simple
function that populates the conference room list. The `DropDownList` Web Control has a property
called `Items`. These will be translated to `<option>` items in the select HTML `<select>` tag. The `New`
operator creates instances of the `ListItem` class that represents each `<option>` tag.

```
Private Sub PopulateConferenceRooms()

 DropDownList1.Items.Clear()

 DropDownList1.Items.Add(New ListItem("Blue"))
 DropDownList1.Items.Add(New ListItem("Green"))
 DropDownList1.Items.Add(New ListItem("Red"))
End Sub
```

After the `PopulateConferenceRooms()` subroutine we have the `Page_Load` subroutine that tests the
`IsPostBack` variable to see if the current request is the first request made for the page. If it is, the
`PopulateConferenceRooms` subroutine we just looked at is called. The Calendar Web Control –
`Calendar1` by variable name – is also set to the current date.

```
Private Sub Page_Load(ByVal sender As System.Object, ByVal e As System.EventArgs)
Handles MyBase.Load
  'Put user code to initialize the page here
  If Not IsPostBack Then
   PopulateConferenceRooms()
   Calendar1.SelectedDate = System.DateTime.Now
  End If
End Sub
```

If it is not the first time it is requested the automatic state saving will contain the conference room information and will repopulate it to the web page. The last bit of code in the last class handles the event created when the user clicks on the form's Submit button. We know that the subroutine does handle these events by reading the `Button1_Click` text following the formal parameter list. When the event is processed by ASP.NET, this function updates the HTML Control named `p1` so as to display a confirmation of the conference room request.

```
Private Sub Button1_Click(ByVal sender As System.Object, _
                    ByVal e As System.EventArgs) Handles Button1.Click
  p1.InnerText = "You have requested the " & _
  DropDownList1.SelectedItem.ToString() & _
  " Conference Room on " & Calendar1.SelectedDate & " " & _
  "for " & TextBox1.Text
End Sub
End Class
```

The user, of course, sees the response rendered as a web page that looks like the following:

Mobile Controls

There is one more set of controls worth knowing about: The Mobile Web Controls from the Mobile Internet Toolkit. These controls are specifically designed to work with Mobile Web devices like cell phones and PDAs. These controls are supplied with the Mobile Internet Toolkit. You need to download and install the Mobile Internet Toolkit in order to use them. Another download, the Microsoft Mobile Explorer 3.0 Emulator, makes it easy to test your Mobile Control-based applications from within the Visual Studio.NET environment.

> You can download the Mobile Internet Toolkit from
> http://www.microsoft.com/downloads/release.asp?ReleaseID=35406 and the
> Microsoft Mobile Explorer 3.0 Emulator from
> http://www.microsoft.com/downloads/release.asp?releaseid=30578.

Like HTML Controls, the Mobile Controls automatically generate the correct form of HTML, XHTML, or WML that the target devices uses, based on what the ASP.NET processor detects about the user agent requesting the Mobile Web Form. Many of the key Web Form controls, like the Select List and Calendar Controls are made available as Mobile Controls as well. The best thing about using the Mobile Controls is that since they are based on the ASP.NET Web Form architecture, they are just as easy to program against. It is also easy to write your own User Agent detection that redirects "rich agent" requests to Web Forms based on the standard Web Controls and requests from "mobile agents" to Mobile Web Form applications.

Summary

While there is probably nothing as constant as change, Visual Studio.NET is one tool that will help the web developer cope efficiently and effectively with change. Just as tools like FrontPage and Visual Studio made it easier to generate web applications based on HTML and ASP, Visual Studio.NET will make it easier to generate both Web Services and Web Forms. The use of controls to generate interactive objects will make it easier to adapt to client platform changes as well. Microsoft is betting its future on .NET and Visual Studio.NET is the best way write .NET-based applications for the following reasons:

❑   .NET was designed and built from the very first byte to be completely Internet/network-technology based. With .NET, Microsoft has shed many of the limitations on its technology that made implementing modern web applications both challenging and time-consuming.

❑   Changes to the ASP.NET processing model make it possible to have higher performance and better fault tolerance, ensuring higher application reliability.

❑   The .NET Framework makes developing XML Web Services as simple as possible with a minimum loss of fine control over the request and response. Visual Studio.NET makes developing complex Web Applications and Web Services just as easy as developing desktop applications through the use of drag-and-drop control placement. Web Services will be covered in detail in Chapter 7.

❑   The new Mobile Internet Toolkit finally makes it possible to develop cell phone-based applications using the same Integrated Development Environment (IDE) we use to develop other Internet-based applications.

In this chapter, we reviewed:

❑   How web development is transitioning from an artisan skill to a methodical discipline. We saw how the speed of development is changing, how performance is improving, and how new fault-tolerance features will help applications meet the demands placed on them.

❑   How Active Server Page (ASP) development changes in .NET compared to the "classic" ASP environment. We compared and contrasted ASP development to ASP.NET development in terms of code mixing, execution, and data typing.

❏   The design surfaces for ASP.NET pages – Web Forms. As Web Form pages are built up from series of controls, we spent time looking at HTML Controls, Server Controls, and Mobile Controls, explaining the advantages and disadvantages of each.

In the next chapter we will see ASP.NET and .NET new data technologies will work together to form a great overall Web Development solution.

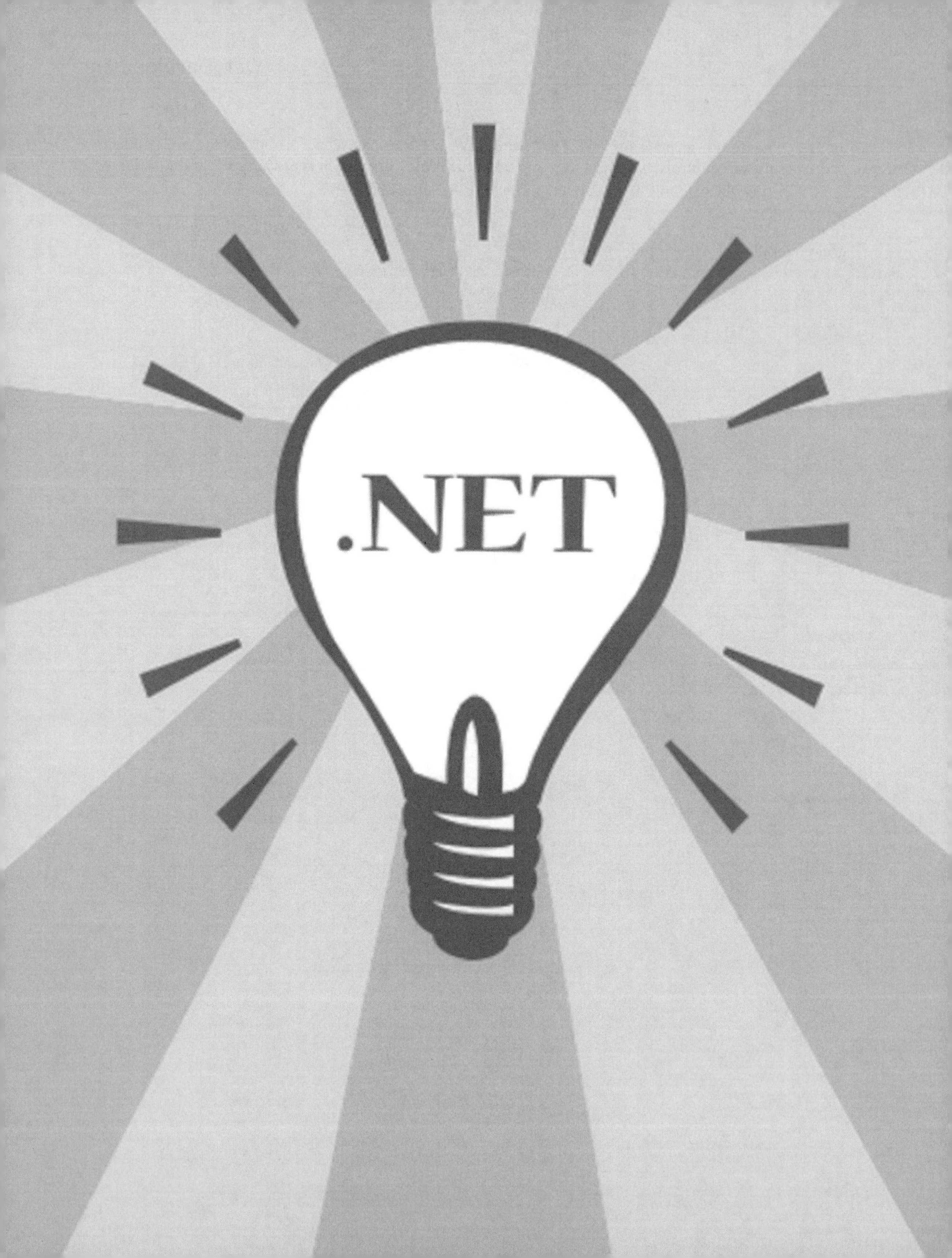
.NET

4

Windows Client Development

Whatever you may hear, rich-client development has not passed on. It has not ceased to be. It is not pushing up the daisies, and it does not rest in peace. It has not shuffled off its mortal coil. It is not an ex-software architecture.

Recently trendy developers have used a web browser on the client, and put all the power into the server. But the .NET Framework wakes up rich clients, bringing them back with a vengeance.

If a particular application requires a demanding user interface and high performance then ignoring the capabilities of a rich client in favor of the browser-based trend is stupid. HTML rendered in a browser just isn't going to cut it for many applications. For example, can you imagine trying to develop a decent CAD or digital video editing application with an interface that is limited to the capabilities of HTML input and output standards? Games are another category that always push the limits of a platform. While checkers or chess in the browser may be fine, I don't think we're going to be seeing the next MechWarrior, Quake, or Unreal Tournament playable from within Opera, Netscape, or IE. Even multi-player Internet games consist of super-rich, high-performance local clients that connect to a web server backend.

Picture the long line of Christmas customers waiting at a busy checkout. Poor responsiveness is not an option for your point-of-sale application. When a thin client system stops working because the server goes down or because of a lost connection, we wish that the client wasn't so thin. If the system was more than a dumb terminal, it could cache larger amounts of data, perform complex operations on the cached data, and merge with the master database when connection is resumed. Have fun trying this with cookies and a browser on your store's intranet!

In the past, however, developing and deploying Windows applications has been no picnic. Choose C++ and be burdened with cumbersome tools like MFC/ATL while trying to avoid reinventing common graphical controls and message processing behavior. Or choose Visual Basic as your tool so you can concentrate on business logic instead of low-level interface details ... only to find out that occasionally you need access to some advanced Windows functionality that has been abstracted away by the tool.

With .NET we are no longer forced to make language choices with such unfortunate ramifications. The .NET Framework's Windows client programming model blends the flexibility of C++ with the pre-packaged functionality of Visual Basic. We are not bound to VB.NET for rapid GUI development, or to C#/C++ for advanced Windows features.

The .NET Framework provides namespaces for Windows forms development, accessible to any language that targets the CLR. Windows Forms is fully integrated into the .NET Framework, giving Windows applications support for advanced graphics functions (using GDI+), ADO.NET, XML, remoting, and Web Services. Web Services and Windows applications provide a formidable partnership, combining many of the benefits of web-based applications with the power and stability of rich clients. As these benefits are realized, we will see more Internet applications with rich, Windows front ends.

In this chapter, we will explore:

- ❏ Simple Windows Forms applications using the standard components and controls provided with Visual Studio .NET. We will not explore all of the available components, but will see a few examples to demonstrate the concepts.

- ❏ Methods and strategies for developing our own custom components and controls for Windows development.

- ❏ An example demonstrating the power of visual inheritance.

- ❏ Changes in form menu development, Windows messaging, MDI applications, data binding, consuming Web Services from within a Windows application, and console applications.

- ❏ The .NET Compact Framework, briefly.

Windows Forms: The Big Picture

Before we start working with Windows forms, let's take a look at some of the big questions that first contact with this new technology tends to raise:

- ❏ **Q: Can I graphically design my forms in Visual Studio .NET like I can in Visual Basic?**

    A: Yes. The Visual Studio .NET Windows Forms Designer is just as easy to use as the Visual Basic forms design package. You'll also find new form properties such as docking and anchoring at your disposal to make designing for resizing easy instead of painful. Get ready to be impressed with the new menu designer too, along with lots of other labor-saving features.

❑ **Q: What about my existing third-party and in-house custom controls? Will I be able to use my existing library of DLLs and OCXs?**

A: New solutions developed exclusively within the .NET Framework do not involve COM or ActiveX since the architecture is quite different. If this statement gives you flashbacks of the nightmarish 16 to 32-bit Visual Basic shift, where custom and third-party VBX components died overnight, don't worry. History is not due to repeat itself just because you can't suddenly rebuild everything right away using .NET.

When you drop an ActiveX control on a Windows form in Visual Studio .NET, VS.NET will create a runtime-callable wrapper class for you. This wrapper is a .NET façade for the ActiveX control, allowing managed code within the Framework to access the control as if it were a native .NET component. While this works flawlessly most of the time, you may have some controls with special requirements. We will look more closely at integrating existing components with .NET in Chapter 6.

❑ **Q: I heard I could develop .NET components than can be used in my VB or VC++ applications, is this true?**

A: Yes. This will help migration as it allows you to begin developing new .NET components that plug in to your legacy systems, or to slowly start replacing components from these production systems. Like the runtime-callable wrapper created by .NET when you host an ActiveX or COM component, you can have .NET create a COM-callable wrapper for you. This puts a COM façade on the .NET-managed component. You can register this wrapper and consume it like any COM object, although the .NET runtime must be installed on any machine that uses .NET components – even if they are wrapped in COM.

❑ **Q: Since the .NET Framework is object-oriented, does this mean that I can develop a standard Windows form for an application and inherit it to establish a consistent look and feel? Is 'cut-and-paste' GUI inheritance finally dead?**

A: Yes! Visual inheritance works because a form is just a class. Like all inheritance, the potential for misuse through overuse exists. But this is still a wonderful opportunity for consistency in applications with many similar forms.

Now let's look at some Windows Forms code. For a well-behaved Windows Forms application, it doesn't get too much simpler than the following C# code. These few lines don't look as if they could possibly achieve much, but behind them the .NET Framework is doing a lot of work:

```
public class EasyForm
{
  public static void Main()
  {
    System.Windows.Forms.Application.Run(new System.Windows.Forms.Form());
  }
}
```

The public static method named `Main()` is required to serve as the program's entry point. The `Application` class provides the static `Run` method to start Windows applications. Here we pass the `Run` method a new instance of the `Form` class. A regular application message loop thread starts and the form executes as a GUI application.

What does that mean? It means that a blank form appears and waits for system messages (mouse events, keyboard events, and so on). We can terminate the program by clicking on the form's close button, which stops the message loop thread, and the Run() method returns. Since there is no more code in the Main() method after the call to Application.Run, the application terminates.

If you come from a Visual Basic background, you already expect your development tool to serve up a form on a silver platter – you expect a blank form application working as described earlier with absolutely no visible code. But if you're experienced with MFC/ATL then you have a good idea just how much background plumbing is involved.

> **VB 6 programmers may think of the .NET static `Main()` method as VB's `Sub Main()`, but in .NET we are required to use it in every application as an entry point. The `Sub Main()` approach in VB 6 gave us more flexibility, and we could display a form by loading it in our `Sub Main()`. We're doing something similar here: a new instance of the `Form` class is created and displayed.**

In our first simple example, we can see that the Application and Form classes hail from the System.Windows.Forms namespace. Usually we would create a class that inherits from the Form class to include all the controls and other stuff that we want. The following illustration gives us more insight into the Form class's place in the .NET Framework hierarchy:

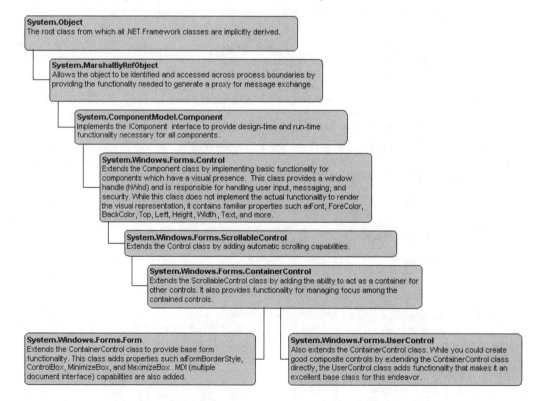

`Object` is the ultimate base class in .NET. Each class along the way inherits the features of its base class and then adds new features of its own or modifies features it inherited. We can see from the ancestry of the `System.Windows.Forms.Form` class that it is the culmination of many classes and is quite robust because of its inheritance.

Now we can clearly see how the few lines of code in the simple example implemented so much. When we instantiate a new object of type `Form` and pass it to the `Application.Run()` method, by default the form object contains an amazing amount of functionality derived from other classes in the Framework. The form already contains methods to display itself and process basic system events. The `Application.Run()` method actually takes care of calling the form's display method for us (named `Show()` and inherited by the form from the `System.Windows.Forms.Control class`).

Unlike Visual Basic 6, .NET is completely object-oriented. This translates into the developer being able to choose the level of abstraction. Like things canned for you? Then use the feature-rich base classes provided by the Framework and start from there. Don't like a few things about a provided class? Then inherit it and extend it by overriding or hiding/replacing its members.

Windows Forms in Visual Studio .NET

The first tiny code example in this chapter was something we could have created with a text editor and a working knowledge of the appropriate C# compiler command and switches. In fact, it is possible to create any .NET application with a text editor. However, the graphic form-design features in Visual Studio .NET are great, and in this chapter we will choose them over coding in a text editor. We'll also examine the code that VS.NET generates, which will provide an idea of the sort of code it would take to produce Windows Forms applications without a form designer.

Visual Studio .NET marries the wonderful Rapid Application Development capabilities that have been available to Visual Basic developers with the power that has been available to C++ developers. To begin a new Windows application in Visual Studio .NET, select File | New | Project and choose the Windows Application template (the examples in this chapter will use the C# language, although the techniques would be similar in VB.NET):

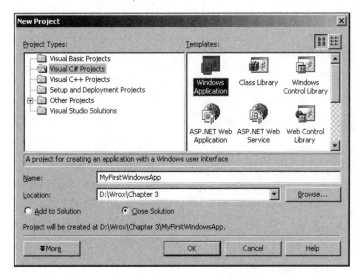

Visual Studio .NET automatically generates several new files for the project, but we want to examine the following code in the file named Form1.cs:

```csharp
using System;
using System.Drawing;
using System.Collections;
using System.ComponentModel;
using System.Windows.Forms;
using System.Data;

namespace MyFirstWindowsApp
{
  /// <summary>
  /// Summary description for Form1.
  /// </summary>
  public class Form1 : System.Windows.Forms.Form
  {
    /// <summary>
    /// Required designer variable.
    /// </summary>
    private System.ComponentModel.Container components = null;

    public Form1()
    {
      //
      // Required for Windows Form Designer support
      //
      InitializeComponent();

      //
      // TODO: Add any constructor code after InitializeComponent call
      //
    }

    /// <summary>
    /// Clean up any resources being used.
    /// </summary>
    protected override void Dispose( bool disposing )
    {
      if( disposing )
      {
        if (components != null)
        {
          components.Dispose();
        }
      }
      base.Dispose( disposing );
    }

    #region Windows Form Designer generated code
    /// <summary>
    /// Required method for Designer support - do not modify
    /// the contents of this method with the code editor.
    /// </summary>
```

```
    private void InitializeComponent()
    {
      this.components = new System.ComponentModel.Container();
      this.Size = new System.Drawing.Size(300,300);
      this.Text = "Form1";
    }
    #endregion

    /// <summary>
    /// The main entry point for the application.
    /// </summary>
    [STAThread]
    static void Main()
    {
      Application.Run(new Form1());
    }
  }
}
```

We see that the designer by default creates a new class named `Form1`. This new class is derived from `System.Windows.Forms.Form`:

```
public class Form1 : System.Windows.Forms.Form
```

As we saw earlier, if we made no further changes to the `Form1` class, it would already include a ton of functionality. Any modifications we make to the form in Visual Studio .NET's Forms Designer will generate code that customizes the `Form1` class. Visual Studio .NET places the code in the `InitializeComponent()` method found between the #region and #endregion directives.

The Forms Designer uses the container-called components to help instantiate, organize, and dispose of any components we add to the `Form1` class in visual design.

The `[STAThread]` attribute marks the application as single-threaded apartment (STA) mode, which as the name implies allows only one thread. While the .NET Framework does not use apartments (logical containers) for threading, apartments are vital to COM classes. This attribute is only meaningful to a .NET application if it utilizes COM interop functionality. For more information about COM interop, see Chapter 6 – Enterprise Development.

As we mentioned in our earlier example, the static `Main()` method is a required entry point for all C# applications. In our first example, this method simply instantiated a new `Systems.Windows.Forms.Form` object and passed it to the `Application.Run()` method.

All C# code must be contained within some class, so don't get confused in our latest example just because the `Main()` method actually exists inside the `Form1` class definition itself. The special static entry point must exist in some class of our application, even if it is inside of a class that is used *within* the `Main()` method:

```
static void Main()
{
  Application.Run(new Form1());
}
```

This is standard procedure when a form class is to be your startup object in an application.

Consuming Controls

To add controls in Visual Studio .NET's form designer, click on one of the controls in the Toolbox window, drag it over the form design surface, and then drop it where you want it. The Properties window configures forms and controls. Let's see how to add some standard controls to a form.

Drag, Drop, Generate Code; Repeat as Required

Our previous example demonstrated that creating a project using Visual Studio .NET's Windows Application template will create a new form class with a default name of Form1. The designer follows the same naming pattern when it generates code to add controls to the form (Button1, Button2, and so on).

The following image shows a button being added to a form via the designer. We could use the Properties window to change the form class's name from Form1 to frmMain and the button's name from Button1 to btnDesignTime. Setting the form's Text property to Adding Controls changes the form's title bar. We also specify Design Time as the text to display on the button face by setting its Text property:

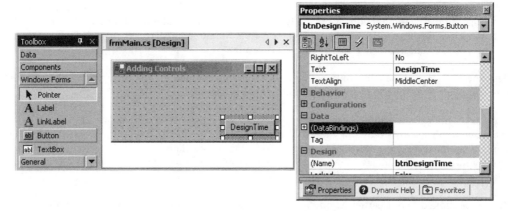

To see the code the form designer automatically generates for our design-time changes, look for the file named frmMain.cs in the AddControls chapter example and search the for the string btnDesignTime. First you should notice that the designer adds code to the declaration section of class frmMain. A new object of type System.Windows.Forms.Button is declared:

```
// Form Designer Added this Declaration
private System.Windows.Forms.Button btnDesignTime;
```

As we mentioned earlier, the designer saves our Properties window changes in the InitializeComponent() method, which is executed in the form's constructor. Older versions of Visual Basic stored your design settings in a part of the FRM file hidden from the Visual Basic editor.

The designer inserts code to instantiate the button object, which is declared earlier in the source file, and sets any properties we had specified at design time (location, name, text to display). Finally the Button is added to the Controls collection (note that the keyword this refers to the form itself).

This control instantiation was something else hidden from us in classic Visual Basic. Visual Studio .NET, however, incorporates the property setting and control instantiation details in code. This allows us to see what is really going on, and reminds us that we could do all of this with a text editor:

```
private void InitializeComponent()
{
    this.btnDesignTime = new System.Windows.Forms.Button();
    this.SuspendLayout();
    //
    // btnDesignTime
    //
    this.btnDesignTime.Location = new System.Drawing.Point(168, 64);
    this.btnDesignTime.Name = "btnDesignTime";
    this.btnDesignTime.TabIndex = 0;
    this.btnDesignTime.Text = "DesignTime";
    //
    // frmMain
    //
    this.AutoScaleBaseSize = new System.Drawing.Size(5, 13);
    this.ClientSize = new System.Drawing.Size(248, 93);
    this.Controls.AddRange(new System.Windows.Forms.Control[]
                        {this.btnDesignTime});
    this.Name = "frmMain";
    this.Text = "Adding Controls";
    this.ResumeLayout(false);
}
```

The designer uses the Controls.AddRange() method, to enable numerous controls on the form. Each control object is be created and configured, and then all are added to the Controls collection with one method call. The syntax used may look a little strange at first glance:

```
new System.Windows.Forms.Control[] {this.btnDesignTime}
```

This simply creates a new array object of type System.Windows.Forms.Control. The items between the brackets are immediately assigned to this array object. Suppose we add four buttons to a form. The designer might create code that passes the following array to the AddRange() method:

```
new System.Windows.Forms.Control[]
    {this.Button1, this.Button2, this.Button3, this.Button4}
```

The System.Windows.Forms.Button class is derived from the System.Windows.Forms.ButtonBase class, which in turn is derived from the System.Windows.Forms.Control class. This demonstrates another benefit of the object-oriented nature of Windows Forms: because controls in the toolbox inherit the Control class, they can be treated as objects of type Control (as we see here when Button objects are added to the array). This type-inheritance is an extremely useful form of **polymorphism** that we can fully exploit in Windows Forms.

This visual designer coupled with automatic code generation is wonderful for design-time, but what about adding controls dynamically at run time? We could enter the following code in the constructor of the `AddControls` example to add a second button without designer help. Here we're doing it in the form's constructor for demonstration purposes, but we could do it in any method we wished to dynamically create controls in response to events:

```
public frmMain()
{
  //Required for Windows Form Designer support
  InitializeComponent();

  // Adding a new Button at Run Time
  System.Windows.Forms.Button btnRunTime =
                   new System.Windows.Forms.Button();
  btnRunTime.Location = new System.Drawing.Point(75, 64);
  btnRunTime.Name = "btnRunTime";
  btnRunTime.TabIndex = 1;
  btnRunTime.Text = "RunTime";
  this.Controls.Add(btnRunTime);

  // Assign handlers to button events
  btnDesignTime.Click += new System.EventHandler(ButtonClick);
  btnRunTime.Click += new System.EventHandler(ButtonClick);
}
```

First, a new instance of a `Button` is created. Next, the desired properties of the button are set, and finally it is added to the form's `Controls` collection. We'll talk about the code using `System.EventHandler()` in the next section when we talk about events. For now, if you build and run the `AddControls` sample project, you will see the following results:

Events

Like properties and methods, events are members in .NET Framework classes. The `Control` class contains numerous event members including `Click`, `GotFocus`, and `MouseHover`. An event is a message sent to signify that a certain action has occurred. The `Click` event, for example, is triggered when the user clicks on the graphical surface of a control. Just exactly where is an event message sent, though? It needs to be sent to a method that is expecting the event and can process (handle) it.

In .NET we must specifically assign handler methods to events, otherwise nothing will be 'listening' for the events. This was also the case in Visual Basic 6, but it just wasn't so obvious. When you double-clicked on a control for the first time in design mode, Visual Basic would add an empty event handler method for the control's default event. Visual Studio .NET can do the same thing for us, but we'll see that we also have much greater flexibility regarding events in .NET. Visual Basic 6 had a strict event handler procedure naming convention (`ControlName_EventName`), but .NET allows you to name your handler methods as you desire.

> **Double-clicking a control in Visual Studio .NET will also automatically create an empty event-handler method for the control's default event, and assign it to the event. It will then open the code window, ready for us to write the event-handler code. The effect of this is very similar to Visual Basic. However, we will manually create most of our event handler methods in this chapter and assign them ourselves, because it makes the concepts involved clearer and gives us more flexibility.**

In .NET, the event member of a control is actually a specific kind of delegate object (System.EventHandler) encapsulated in the control. If you are familiar with function pointers in C++, then you already have an idea of what a delegate is. You can think of a delegate as a sort of type-safe function pointer. By assigning a method to an event, the delegate then knows which method to invoke, or you might say it knows where to pass its message.

If the delegate is type-safe, then this must mean there are rules about the methods that can be assigned. The signatures of the assigned methods must match the delegate's definition. The Click event of the Button class, for example, is defined to require a signature with two arguments as follows:

```
void HandlerMethodName(object sender, System.EventArgs e)
```

While it is type safe, it's unbelievably flexible. The sender argument is of type object. Remember that every class in the .NET Framework is derived from the object class, so sender could be anything. The sender argument is a reference to the object that is firing the event – in this case the button that was clicked.

The e argument is of type System.EventArgs. This argument will contain any important additional information about the event. The class System.EventArgs doesn't contain any place for additional information and is used directly in event definition by simple events such as the click of a button. For more complex events, the System.EventArgs serves as a base class for more complicated event argument classes that do contain important information. We'll talk a little more about other event argument types later, but for now let's finally look at a method that could be assigned to a Button control's Click event:

```
private void ButtonClick(object sender, System.EventArgs e)
{
  MessageBox.Show("Button Event Handler",
                ((Button)sender).Name + " Clicked");
}
```

In this event-handling method, the sender object is cast into a Button so its Name property can be accessed to display which button triggered the event. In the real world, it might be appropriate to do some type checking on the sender object via its GetType() method to make sure it is the expected type. For this simple example, however, the ButtonClick event handler method will only be assigned to the Click events of actual Button objects.

We now have an event handler method, but we need to assign it to the Click event of the button. Earlier, we looked at the constructor code of the frmMain class in the AddControls project. We didn't explore the meaning of these lines:

```
// Assign handlers to button events
btnDesignTime.Click += new System.EventHandler(ButtonClick);
btnRunTime.Click += new System.EventHandler(ButtonClick);
```

The += is an additive assignment operator. In this case, we create and add the event handler delegate to the event. This new delegate instance takes the name of a handler method as the argument in its constructor. Now when the user clicks on btnDesignTime or btnRunTime, its Click event is fired and the delegate knows to invoke the ButtonClick() method.

In Visual Basic 6, in order to have multiple controls invoke a single handler, we were forced to put the code in a separate subroutine and then have each control's event handler call this subroutine. As you can see in our example, with .NET it is easy to assign multiple events directly to the same handler method.

The 'additive' part of the += assignment operator we discussed earlier is very important because it enables us to attach multiple delegates to the same event. This means we can have multiple handler methods execute in response to a single event. In the following code, MyMethod2 does not replace MyMethod1 as the assigned handler for the click event. In this case, both methods would be invoked when the button is clicked.

```
btnMyButton.Click += new System.EventHandler(MyMethod1);
btnMyButton.Click += new System.EventHandler(MyMethod2);
```

Handler delegates can also be easily disconnected using the -= operator. As is often the case, you may have critical code in a handler method that must complete before the handler is invoked again (ever seen an impatient user clicking a button over and over and over rapidly?). The code below disconnects the handler method from the event, processes critical code, and then reconnects the handler method so that button clicks can again be processed:

```
private void LongProcess(object sender, System.EventArgs e)
{
    ((Button)sender).Click -= new System.EventHandler(LongProcess);
    // Critical Code Here
    ((Button)sender).Click += new System.EventHandler(LongProcess);
}
```

Earlier we mentioned special types of event arguments in the method signatures for handler methods. The Control class's Paint event is a good example of this. The Paint event is a notification that the control needs to be drawn or redrawn. For example, when a messagebox overlays part of a window and then the user clicks OK to dismiss the messagebox, the window must be redrawn to return it to its former appearance. The following signature is specified by the System.Windows.Forms.PaintEventHandler delegate:

```
void HandlerMethodName(object sender, PaintEventArgs e)
```

The System.Windows.Forms.PaintEventArgs class is derived from the basic System.EventArgs class we used earlier. It extends the base EventArgs class by adding the Graphics and ClipRectangle properties, among other things. The Graphics property is a GDI+ drawing surface belonging to the sender control. The ClipRectangle property is a System.Drawing.Rectangle object defining the rectangular region of the sender control. We can see from this that it is imperative that you investigate event delegate definitions and implement the proper arguments when creating event handler methods.

Getting in the (Message) Loop

Controls expose and fire events, but how do the controls actually know when they've been clicked on? Because Windows sends them a message. In .NET, Windows sends messages to the control's WndProc() method, which can fire the appropriate event based on the message received.

Controls that inherit from the System.Windows.Forms.Control class have access to this method. We can override this method and respond to Windows messages any way that we like. For example, adding the following method to a form would allow us to directly respond to the right mouse button being pressed on the form:

```
protected override void WndProc(ref Message m)
{
   int WM_RBUTTONDOWN = 0x0204;

   MessageBox.Show("Responding To The Right Mouse Button Press",
                   "Intercepting Message");
   base.WndProc(ref m);
}
```

The source for this form in the Form1.cs file of the WndProcTest project in the code download.

We respond to the message and then pass the message to the base class so that other actions, including firing the exposed MouseDown event, can be processed. This is a *very* important step that must not be forgotten.

The integer values for the messages such as right mouse button down can be easily found in the WinUser.h include file in the Microsoft Visual Studio .NET Visual C++ 7 PlatformSDK directory.

So ends our introduction to using the System.Windows.Forms.Form class. Now let's look at rolling our own controls.

Rolling Your Own Controls

So far, we've only been using forms that contain standard controls from Visual Studio .NET's default toolbox. Now we're going to look into authoring our own components and controls. The terms 'component' and 'control' are often used interchangeably – as we go through, we'll see the subtle difference in their meaning.

Understanding Components

Calling something a **component** in .NET implies that it implements the System.ComponentModel.IComponent interface. The IComponent interface specifies design-time and run-time behavior for components. The IComponent interface is derived from the IDisposable interface, which specifies a Dispose() method for the explicit release of any unmanaged resources (possibly disk files or database connections). For a class to expose members to the forms designer and exhibit design-time functionality it must implement IComponent.

Controls are components that also implement the `IWin32Window` and `ISynchronizeInvoke` interfaces, which enable the control to respond to Windows messages correctly. For this reason, writing a component is similar to writing a control – only easier. We will look at developing a control later. For now we will examine the standard `Timer` control, to see how it works, and how this impacts on developing our own components.

The `Timer` (`System.Windows.Forms.Timer`) component inherits the `System.ComponentModel.Component` class. It is easier to inherit from the `Component` class than to directly implement the `IComponent` and `IDisposable` interfaces – the `Component` class already implements both interfaces and adds some additional features such as the `Container`, `Site`, `Events`, and `DesignMode` properties.

Let's examine the design-time behavior of the `Timer` component in Visual Studio .NET. Dragging the `Timer` component over to the form designer will not site a graphical control on the actual form design surface. Instead, a design icon for the `Timer` is displayed in a component tray below the form:

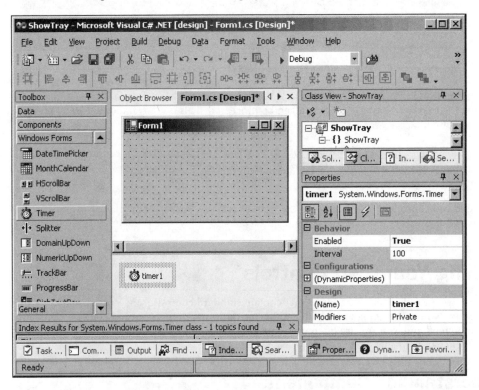

This is because the `Timer` is a component, not a control. Selecting this icon, will give us access through the **Properties** window to the design-time properties of the component (see screenshot above). If we want the timer to automatically start when the form is initialized, we can set the `Enabled` property to `True`. The **Properties** window shows that the value has been changed from its default by displaying the **True** value in bold.

Adding the `Timer` to the form causes the designer to produce the following declaration in the form's constructor:

```
    private System.Windows.Forms.Timer timer1;
```

and the following in the form's `InitializeComponent()` method:

```
private void InitializeComponent()
{
  this.components = new System.ComponentModel.Container();
  this.timer1 = new System.Windows.Forms.Timer(this.components);
  //
  // Form1
  //
  this.AutoScaleBaseSize = new System.Drawing.Size(5, 13);
  this.ClientSize = new System.Drawing.Size(208, 117);
  this.Name = "Form1";
  this.Text = "Form1";
}
```

`timer1` is also added to the form's `components` container so it can participate in the form's standard cleanup logic:

```
protected override void Dispose( bool disposing )
{
  if( disposing )
  {
    if (components != null)
    {
      components.Dispose();
    }
  }
  base.Dispose( disposing );
}
```

Changing the `Enabled` property to `True` will cause the following change to `InitializeComponent()`:

```
private void InitializeComponent()
{
  this.components = new System.ComponentModel.Container();
  this.timer1 = new System.Windows.Forms.Timer(this.components);
  //
  // timer1
  //
  this.timer1.Enabled = true;
  //
  // Form1
  //
  this.AutoScaleBaseSize = new System.Drawing.Size(5, 13);
  this.ClientSize = new System.Drawing.Size(208, 117);
  this.Name = "Form1";
  this.Text = "Form1";
}
```

Let's see what this tells us about authoring our own components. Suppose that we built a class to implement FTP (File Transfer Protocol) functions. Should we create a component by deriving our class from the System.ComponentModel.Component class, or should we simply implement the IDisposable interface in our class?

While an FTP object would definitely need some resource management via the IDisposable interface, it may not need design-time functionality. If we don't need the control to appear on the ToolBox and support a Properties window in Visual Studio .NET, then we can just implement the IDisposable interface – it will be more efficient. If we want design-time cooperation with Visual Studio .NET we will definitely want to take advantage of what the Component class has to offer.

Controlling Your Controls

We know from earlier discussion that a Windows Form is itself a complex control. A button is a simpler control, but it still has a visual representation at both design time and run time. It has more design-time behavior than a component because it is actually rendered on the form surface in the designer.

The Timer we discussed earlier is a .NET component, not a control, since it derives from the System.ComponentModel.Component class rather than from the System.Windows.Forms.Control class. The Control class inherits the Component class but also implements the IWin32Window and ISynchronizeInvoke interfaces for exposing window handles and executing delegates.

The Control class provides a lot of the features we expect for Windows GUI programming: basic appearance and position of the visual elements, handling user interaction such as keyboard and mouse events, providing a Windows handle (hWnd), and dealing with messaging.

We're going to explore examples of developing our own controls in three ways:

❑ **Extended Controls** – Controls based on existing controls

❑ **Composite Controls** – Controls composed of several other controls

❑ **Custom Controls** – Controls that implement a customized graphical appearance

Extended Controls

In this example, we'll extend the standard TextBox control to alter its appearance when user input is disabled. We will be altering the functionality of the ReadOnly and BackColor properties.

When we wish to stop user input in a textbox, we can set its ReadOnly property to true. This has several advantages over setting the Enabled property to false: when the ReadOnly property is true, the user cannot change the contents of the textbox via input, but the program can still change the value of the Text property. Also, the textbox's contents can still be selected and copied to the clipboard, but clipboard contents cannot be pasted into the textbox.

Another reason we may not want to completely disable the textbox is that when we do, the font is automatically changed to such a light color that it is barely readable. Setting the ReadOnly property to true does not cause the textbox to lose its original font color, but it would be helpful if there was some visual change to indicate that editing was no longer allowed. In this example we will cause the textbox's background color to change to gray.

First we need to create and setup the project in Visual Studio .NET. These steps will obviously differ depending on the IDE, or if you are using the command-line compiler. Start by creating a brand new Class Library project in Visual Studio .NET. Then follow the following steps:

❑ Choose **Project | Properties** and change the **Assembly Name** and **Default Namespace** to `ExtendedTextBox`.

❑ Add references to `System.Windows.Forms.dll` and `System.Drawing.dll` – the regular class library project does not contain references to the forms and graphics namespaces we will need to use. Do this by selecting **Project | Add Reference** , and then looking for the filenames on the .NET tab of the **Add Reference** screen:

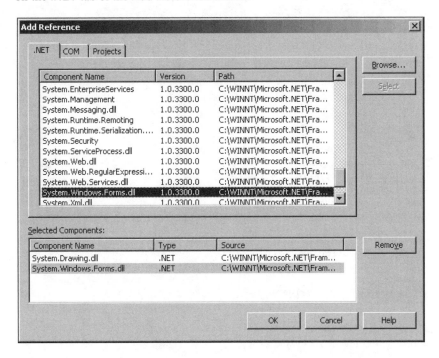

❑ Change the name of the class from `Class1` to `ExtTextBox`.

Now we can start on the code. In Visual Studio .NET some of this will have been done for you, but change the code so that it reads as follows:

```
using System;
using System.Drawing;
using System.Windows.Forms;

namespace ExtendedTextBox
{
  /// <summary>
  /// Simple extension of a standard Windows Forms TextBox
```

```
    /// </summary>

public class ExtTextBox : System.Windows.Forms.TextBox
{
  private Color mHoldColor;

  public ExtTextBox()
  {
  }

  new public bool ReadOnly
  {
    get
    {
      return base.ReadOnly;
    }
    set
    {
      if (base.ReadOnly != value)
      {
        if (value)
        {
          // Push BackColor to hold color
          // before actually changing
          mHoldColor = base.BackColor;
          base.BackColor = SystemColors.Control;
        }
        else
        {
          // Pop BackColor from hold color
          base.BackColor = mHoldColor;
        }
      }
      base.ReadOnly = value;
    }
  }

  public override Color BackColor
  {
    get
    {
      return base.BackColor;
    }
    set
    {
      if (base.ReadOnly)
      {
        // Push Color value to hold color since
        // ReadOnly BackColor should stay LightGray
        mHoldColor = value;
      }
      else
      {
        // We are free to actually change the color
```

```
            base.BackColor = value;
        }
    }
  }
 }
}
```

Note that this line tells the `ExtTextBox` class to inherit the `TextBox` class:

```
public class ExtTextBox : System.Windows.Forms.TextBox
```

We change the code for two properties, `ReadOnly` and `BackColor`.

If `ReadOnly` is being set to true, we store the control's background color `mHoldColor`, then change the control's background color to `SystemColors.Control` – by default a shade of gray. If `ReadOnly` is being set to false, we want to set the background back to its original color. Note that we only do either of these things if the property is changing from its previous value – otherwise we want to leave `BackColor` and `mHoldColor` as they are.

Finally, regardless of what action was taken above, we call the base class's `ReadOnly` property – which will do everything that changing the `ReadOnly` property of a `TextBox` would normally do.

We also want to prevent the control's consumer from changing the `BackColor` property while the control is in read-only mode. We can do this by simply intercepting the property set and storing the color in `mHoldColor` for possible later use if the `ReadOnly` property is set to false.

The `ReadOnly` property is declared as new public, whereas the `BackColor` property is declared as `public override`. Let's look at the reason for this.

Because the `BackColor` property of our `TextBox` base control was itself an overridden property from its parent class (`System.Windows.Forms.TextBoxBase`), we can happily override it again here in our `ExtendedTextBox` class.

However we cannot `override` the `ReadOnly` property because the property is not marked as `virtual`, `abstract`, or `override` in the `TextBox` base class – we can find this out by looking in the Object Browser or .NET documentation. Because of this we use a feature called 'hiding' with the `ReadOnly` property by preceding our declaration with the new keyword and abandoning the `override` keyword:

```
new public bool ReadOnly
```

Finally, just because we are implementing new versions of these properties in our extended control, we don't have to completely reinvent them. We can still use the functionality of the base class (`System.Windows.Forms.TextBox`). As you see, after all our color trapping/swapping logic, we finally call the base class property `get` and `set` accessors:

```
return base.ReadOnly;        // called in get

base.ReadOnly = value;       // eventually called in set
```

```
base.BackColor = value;      // sometimes called in get

return base.BackColor;       // called in get
```

Now, build the ExtendedTextBox project. The default build configuration is debug mode so the DLL will be placed in the \bin\debug directory under the project (we'll need to know this in the next project). If this were a final version of the control for deployment, however, we would want to change the build configuration to release instead of debug. One way to do this is to:

❑ Highlight the solution line in the Solution Explorer

❑ Select Project | Properties, which will display the configuration settings for each project in the solution.

❑ Change the configuration of the project from Debug to Release and then build.

Now, let's start a new Windows Application project to put our ExtTextBox control through its paces. When we built our control project, we created an assembly called ExtendedTextBox.dll. It is possible to simply add a reference to the DLL in our new project and then begin using ExtendedTextBox.ExtTextBox in code. But wasn't one of the points of a control that it could be hosted in the visual designer's Toolbox where we could use it like standard controls?

After creating a new C# Windows Application, right-click on the Windows Forms tab in the Toolbox and select Customize Toolbox. Now, in the Customize Toolbox window, select the Browse button and find the file ExtendedTextBox.dll in the \Bin\Debug directory of the earlier ExtendedTextBox project. Once selected, ExtTextBox appears in the list:

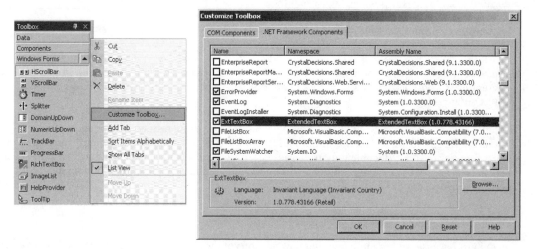

Click OK and now our ExtTextBox control is conveniently located in the Toolbox on the Windows Forms tab.

The full source for this example is in the frmMain.cs file of the ExtendedControlTest folder in the code download.

Add the following controls to the main form:

- ❑ One `ExtTextBox` control – called `myExtendedTextBox`

- ❑ Two `Button` controls – one called `btnWhite` and one called `btnBlue`

- ❑ Two `CheckBox` controls – one called `chkEnabled` and one called `chkReadOnly`

Arrange the controls as shown, changing properties as appropriate. Change the `BackColor` property of `btnColorWhite` to white, and `btnColorBlue` to a shade of blue. Apart from the `Name` properties given above, the other properties can be set to anything we like:

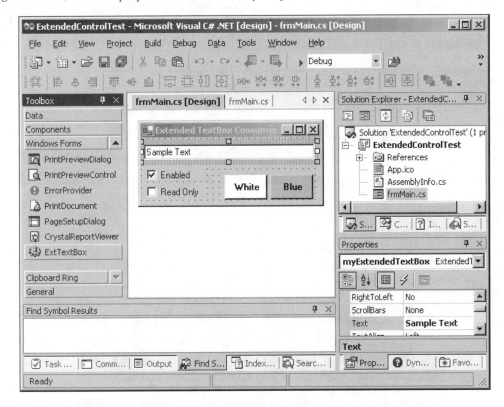

Next, add the following to the form's constructor:

```
public frmMain()
{
  // Required for Windows Form Designer support
  InitializeComponent();

  this.chkEnabled.CheckedChanged
          += new System.EventHandler(ToggleEnabled);
  this.chkReadOnly.CheckedChanged
          += new System.EventHandler(ToggleReadOnly);
```

```
   this.btnBlue.Click
           += new System.EventHandler(ChangeBackColor);
   this.btnWhite.Click
           += new System.EventHandler(ChangeBackColor);
}
```

and having done that, add the following methods:

```
private void ToggleEnabled(object sender, System.EventArgs e)
{
   myExtendedTextBox.Enabled = ((CheckBox)sender).Checked;
}
```

```
private void ToggleReadOnly(object sender, System.EventArgs e)
{
   myExtendedTextBox.ReadOnly = ((CheckBox)sender).Checked;
}
```

```
private void ChangeBackColor(object sender, System.EventArgs e)
{
   myExtendedTextBox.BackColor = ((Control)sender).BackColor;
}
```

The code in this form is not complicated. Remember that the calls to the `ReadOnly` and `BackColor` properties of `myExtendedTextBox` will be executing the custom properties we implemented in the `ExtTextBox` project.

Now build and run the project. We can see that selecting the **Read Only** box will gray out the `ExtTextBox`'s background, while leaving a nice, legible black font. Clicking the blue button will change the textbox's background color, provided the textbox is not in read-only mode. If the textbox is in read-only mode then color changes will take effect once read-only is turned off:

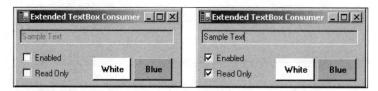

We can see that extending an existing control, especially when making small changes as we did here, is a relatively easy task. To effectively extend classes, we need to know the declaration for members in our base class. Even though we are talking about visual controls here, everything is ultimately just another class. The standard .NET rules of inheritance still apply.

Composite Controls

Extending existing controls is fine for the case of a single control, but what if we wanted to combine several controls and treat them like one ? An address control consisting of Street, City, State, and Postal Code textboxes or a name control – which we will build here – containing First, Middle, and Last name textboxes are simple examples.

Like the `Form` class, `UserControl` derives from `System.Windows.Forms.ContainerControl`. They can both act as containers for other controls. We've seen several examples of adding controls and components to forms, and adding controls to a `UserControl` is similar. Much like a `Form`, a `UserControl` presents a surface in the Visual Studio .NET designer where we can populate it with controls and components.

Start a new **Windows Control Library** project and name it `CompositeControl`. Add three standard textboxes and three standard labels, arranged similar to the following screenshot. Name the textboxes `txtFirstName`, `txtMiddleName`, and `txtLastName`. Name the labels `lblFirstName`, `lblMiddleName`, `lblLastName`:

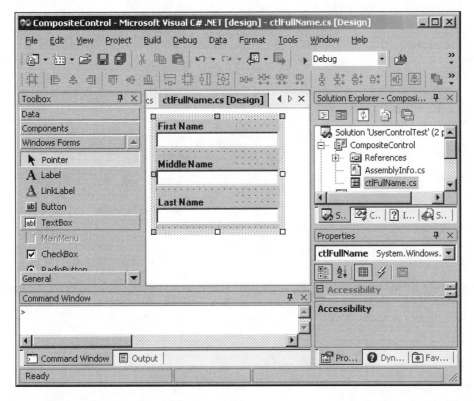

The source code listing that follows omits the `Designer Generated Code` region. The exact positioning and size of the textboxes and labels is not vital to the proper function of the sample. As long as you have created the appropriate number of textboxes and labels and named them as instructed, the following code should be sufficient – modify the code in Visual Studio .NET until it looks like this:

```
using System;
using System.Collections;
using System.ComponentModel;
using System.Drawing;
using System.Windows.Forms;

namespace CompositeControl
```

```
{
/// <summary>Simple Composite Control Sample</summary>
public class ctlFullName : System.Windows.Forms.UserControl
{
  private System.Windows.Forms.Label lblFirstName;
  private System.Windows.Forms.Label lblMiddleName;
  private System.Windows.Forms.Label lblLastName;
  private System.Windows.Forms.TextBox txtFirstName;
  private System.Windows.Forms.TextBox txtMiddleName;
  private System.Windows.Forms.TextBox txtLastName;

  /// <summary>Required designer variable.</summary>
  private System.ComponentModel.Container components = null;

  public ctlFullName()
  {
    // This call is required by the Windows.Forms Form Designer.
    InitializeComponent();
  }

  [Category("Appearance"),
   Description("The text contained in the First Name field.")]
  public string FirstName
  {
    get
    {
      return txtFirstName.Text;
    }
    set
    {
      txtFirstName.Text = value;
    }
  }

  [Category("Appearance"),
   Description("The text contained in the Middle Name field.")]
  public string MiddleName
  {
    get
    {
      return txtMiddleName.Text;
    }
    set
    {
      txtMiddleName.Text = value;
    }
  }

  [Category("Appearance"),
   Description("The text contained in the Last Name field.")]
  public string LastName
  {
    get
    {
```

```
            return txtLastName.Text;
        }
        set
        {
            txtLastName.Text = value;
        }
    }

    [Category("Appearance"),
     Description("The font used to display the labels in the control.")]
    public System.Drawing.Font LabelFont
    {
        get
        {
            return lblFirstName.Font;
        }
        set
        {
            lblFirstName.Font = value;
            lblMiddleName.Font = value;
            lblLastName.Font = value;
        }
    }

    public override string ToString()
    {
        return (txtFirstName.Text + " "
                + txtMiddleName.Text.Trim() + " " + txtLastName.Text).Trim();
    }

    /// <summary>Clean up any resources being used.</summary>
    protected override void Dispose( bool disposing )
    {
        if( disposing )
        {
            if( components != null )
                components.Dispose();
        }
        base.Dispose( disposing );
    }

    #region
        Omitted Component Designer generated code
    #endregion
    }
}
```

The full source, including the designer generated code region, can be found in the ctlFullName.cs file of the CompositeControl project in the chapter example downloads.

By implementing the `FirstName`, `MiddleName`, and `LastName` properties, we provide access to the contents of each of the `TextBox` controls that make up the heart of our control. We also provide the `LabelFont` property to control the fonts of all the labels at once. The attributes in brackets above each of our custom properties provide information to the Visual Studio .NET forms designer. We'll see these in action in our next example, which consumes our composite control.

Finally, we override the `ToString()` method. If we simply allowed our control to inherit the `ToString()` functionality of the base control (`System.Windows.Forms.UserControl`), then the method would return the namespace and control name. This isn't very helpful – we use `ToString()` to provide a string representation of the value of the object. In this case, we have several name values, so we put them together, with spaces, into a meaningful full name.

Consuming the Composite Control

Let's consume our name control by creating a new **Windows Application** project called `UserControlTest`. Right-click on the **Windows Forms** tab in the **Toolbox** and select **Customize Toolbox**. Now, in the **Customize Toolbox** window, select the **Browse** button and find the file `CompositeControl\Bin\Debug\CompositeControl.dll`. Once selected, `ctlFullName` appears in the list:

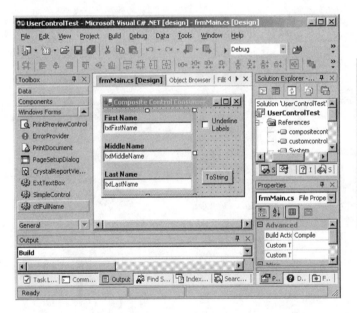

Select `ctlFullName` from the toolbox and drop it on the form. Now, change the control's `Name` property value from `ctlFullName1` to `NameControl`.

Look at the `FirstName`, `MiddleName`, and `LastName` properties in the **Properties** window – the description we gave to each property will appear in the pane at the bottom of the window, as shown above right.

Add a `CheckBox` named `chkUnderline` and set its `Text` property to `Underline Labels`. Finally, add a `Button` named `btnToString` and set its `Text` property to `ToString`.

Once again, we've omitted the Windows Form Designer generated region in the following code listing. The previous screenshot shows the desired layout of controls on our form – the exact size, location, and other properties of these controls are not important.

Now modify the form's code so that it reads as shown:

```
using System;
using System.Drawing;
using System.Collections;
using System.ComponentModel;
using System.Windows.Forms;
using System.Data;

namespace UserControlTest
{
  /// <summary>
  /// Composite Control Consumer Form for testing ctlFullName
  /// </summary>
  public class frmMain : System.Windows.Forms.Form
  {
    private CompositeControl.ctlFullName NameControl;
    private System.Windows.Forms.Button btnToString;
    private System.Windows.Forms.CheckBox chkUnderline;

    /// <summary>Required designer variable.</summary>
    private System.ComponentModel.Container components = null;

    public frmMain()
    {
      // Required for Windows Form Designer support
      InitializeComponent();

      // Hookup this Consumer test Form's Button and CheckBox events
      // to our EventHandlers
      btnToString.Click += new System.EventHandler(ShowToString);
      chkUnderline.CheckedChanged
                      += new System.EventHandler(ToggleUnderline);

      // Demonstrate properties by setting some initial values
      NameControl.FirstName = "Horace";
      NameControl.MiddleName = "Beam";
      NameControl.LastName = "Piper";
    }

    /// <summary>Clean up any resources being used.</summary>
    protected override void Dispose( bool disposing )
    {
      if( disposing )
      {
        if (components != null)
        {
          components.Dispose();
        }
```

```
        }
      base.Dispose( disposing );
   }

   #region Omitted Windows Form Designer generated code #endregion

   /// <summary>
   /// The main entry point for the application.
   /// </summary>
   [STAThread]
   static void Main()
   {
      Application.Run(new frmMain());
   }

   private void ShowToString(object sender, System.EventArgs e)
   {
      MessageBox.Show(NameControl.ToString(),
                      "NameControl's Custom Implementation");
   }

   private void ToggleUnderline(object sender, System.EventArgs e)
   {
      if (((CheckBox)sender).Checked)
      {
         NameControl.LabelFont = new Font(NameControl.LabelFont,
                                    FontStyle.Bold |
                                    FontStyle.Underline);
      }
      else
      {
         NameControl.LabelFont = new Font(NameControl.LabelFont,
                                    FontStyle.Bold);
      }
   }
   }
   }
}
```

Build and run the project. Setting the FirstName, MiddleName, and LastName properties of NameControl in the constructor gives the fields some initial values (see image opposite left). If you click the **ToString** button, the ShowToString() event handler method will display the return value of the NameControl.ToString() method in a message box.

Checking the **Underline Labels** box will invoke the ToggleUnderline() event handler method. This method uses the custom LabelFont property we created earlier. The style is changed from bold to bold and underline as appropriate:

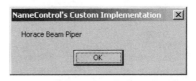

It is easy to see the appeal of encapsulating several related controls into a single unit. The consumer of the control only has to deal with the interface of the single entity, and is not concerned with the rules governing the coordination and behavior of the contained individual controls.

Custom Controls

Unlike a composite control, a custom control renders its own graphical representation. You should try to utilize existing controls if possible, but if nothing meets your needs then it is nice to know you can create a control with a completely custom appearance.

In this section we will look at creating a simple control by inheriting from System.Windows.Forms.UserControl. In the real world, we would not want to make a custom control to implement the functionality of the following simple example since we could achieve better results by using a standard Label control and passing it the desired Text property. For our purposes, however, it will illustrate how to implement our own rendering logic by overriding the OnPaint event.

Lets start by creating a brand new Class Library project in Visual Studio .NET. Choose Project | Properties and change the Assembly Name and Default Namespace to CustomControl. Add references to System.Windows.Forms.dll and System.Drawing.dll using the .NET tab of the Add Reference dialog box.

We will be using the UserControl class as our base class, but since our control will not be composed of other controls, there is really no visual representation for the designer other than the blank canvas of the UserControl. The complete code listing follows:

```
using System;
using System.Collections;
using System.ComponentModel;
using System.Drawing;
using System.Data;
using System.Windows.Forms;

namespace CustomControl
{
    /// <summary>Summary description for SimpleControl</summary>
    public class SimpleControl : System.Windows.Forms.UserControl
    {
        /// <summary>Required designer variable.</summary>
        private System.ComponentModel.Container components = null;

        public SimpleControl()
        {
```

127

```
      // This call is required by the Windows.Forms Form Designer.
      InitializeComponent();
    }

    /// <summary>Clean up any resources being used.</summary>
    protected override void Dispose( bool disposing )
    {
      if( disposing )
      {
        if( components != null )
          components.Dispose();
      }
      base.Dispose( disposing );
    }

    #region Component Designer generated code
    /// <summary>Required method for Designer support</summary>
    private void InitializeComponent()
    {
      // SimpleControl
      this.Name = "SimpleControl";
      this.Size = new System.Drawing.Size(128, 24);
    }
    #endregion

    protected override void OnPaint(PaintEventArgs e)
    {
      base.OnPaint(e);
      SolidBrush myBrush = new SolidBrush(base.ForeColor);
      Font myFont = new Font(base.Font, FontStyle.Bold);
      e.Graphics.DrawString(Environment.UserName, myFont, myBrush, 1, 1);
    }
  }
}
```

The .NET Framework provides GDI+ (Graphics Device Interface) classes, which make even advanced graphics functions easier to use than ever.

The Graphics property of the PaintEventArgs object e is a GDI+ drawing surface representing our control. We use the simple DrawString() method on our graphics surface to render a string. Our call fetches the current user's name from Windows and then renders it at the (x,y) coordinates (1,1) of our control using the font specified in our control's Font property. We specify a solid brush of the color specified in our control's ForeColor property.

We'll need to build our CustomControl project so we can then test it in a form. Let's test our control by creating a new Windows Application project named CustomControlTest. We'll need to add our SimpleControl control to the Windows Forms tab of the Toolbox as we've done for other controls in previous chapter examples.

The source for the custom control consumer is in the frmMain.cs *file of the* CustomControlTest *project in the code download.*

Site a `SimpleControl` on the form and name it `mySimpleControl`. Change the control's `Font` property to about 16 point Arial. Change the control's `Forecolor` property to `White` and its `BackColor` property to `Black`.

This was a very rudimentary control, but you should now be familiar enough with the concept to see the possibilities and begin experimenting with your own custom creations.

Visual Inheritance

Creating a standard form that can then be extended for use elsewhere is a noble and long desired goal. In languages like Visual Basic we can get some way towards this by creating a template form, then copying it several times and making the required modifications. However if we then realize we got something wrong in the template, or the requirements change, we need to change every 'child' form individually.

The beauty of visual inheritance is that standard changes can be made in the base form and all the derived forms can receive changes automatically. Let's take a look at a simple example that provides OK, Cancel, and Help buttons in the base form.

Start a new Windows Application project and name it `BaseForm`. Now go to the **Properties** window of the project and change the **Output Type** from **Windows Application** to **Class Library**. Rename `Form1` to `frmBase`. Add three buttons to `frmBase`: `btnOK`, `btnCancel`, and `btnHelp`. Set the `Modifiers` property of both `btnOK` and `btnCancel` to `Private`, but set the `Modifiers` property of `btnHelp` to `Protected`. Position the buttons as shown:

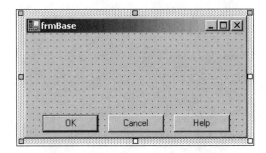

Add the following lines to the constructor of `frmBase`:

```
public frmBase()
{
  // Required for Windows Form Designer support
  InitializeComponent();
```

```
      this.btnHelp.Click += new System.EventHandler(BaseHelp);
      this.btnOK.Click += new System.EventHandler(BaseButtonClick);
      this.btnCancel.Click += new System.EventHandler(BaseButtonClick);
   }
```

and give the `frmBase` class the handler methods to be triggered by these events:

```
   private void BaseButtonClick(object sender, System.EventArgs e)
   {
     MessageBox.Show("Base Form Event Handler",
                   ((Button)sender).Name + " Clicked");
     this.Close();
   }

   private void BaseHelp(object sender, System.EventArgs e)
   {
     MessageBox.Show("Base Form Event Handler",
                   ((Button)sender).Name + " Clicked");
   }
```

Close this project and start a new Windows Application project named `InheritedForm` (rename `Form1` in this project to `frmInherited`). Next, add the `BaseForm` project to the solution via the **File | Add Project | Existing Project** option. Finally, the `InheritedForm` project needs to contain a reference to the `BaseForm` project (accomplished via the **Project | Add Reference** menu option and selecting `BaseForm` from the **Project** tab. Now that the `InheritedForm` project knows about the `BaseForm` project, we can actually change `frmInherited`'s base class by simply replacing:

```
   public class frmInherited : System.Windows.Forms.Form
```

with:

```
   public class frmInherited : BaseForm.frmBase
```

`frmInherited` should now show the visually inherited buttons with a small graphic in the top-left corner to indicate their inherited status. Selecting all the buttons at once should give you the following visual results:

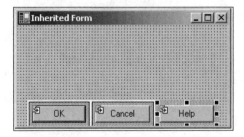

The **OK** and **Cancel** buttons were marked as `Private` in `frmBase` so they are now surrounded by a solid selection border that is not resizable. A quick glance at the **Properties** window for these buttons reveals that the properties are grayed and cannot be modified. The **Help** button, however, was marked as **Protected** in `frmBase` and has the normal selection border with sizing handles, and most of the properties for the **Help** button *can* be modified.

Now, build the solution (both projects) and run it. Although we've written no code yet in frmInherited, clicking on the buttons will execute the event handlers in our base form.

Rather than just customizing some design-time properties for the Help button, let's take a quick look at some events. Add the following event delegate assignment to the constructor of frmInherited:

```
public frmInherited()
{
   // This call is required by the Windows Form Designer.
   InitializeComponent();

   this.btnHelp.Click += new System.EventHandler(InheritedHelp);
}
```

Note that we can only add a delegate to btnHelp because btnOK and btnCancel are declared as private – we cannot change their properties, events, or methods from frmInherited. If we did want to access them from frmInherited, we would need to declare them as protected in the base class.

Next, add the event handler we will call to the frmInherited class:

```
private void InheritedHelp(object sender, System.EventArgs e)
{
   MessageBox.Show("Inherited Form Event Handler (InheritedHelp)",
                   ((Button)sender).Name + " Clicked");
}
```

Build the solution and run it. When we click on the help button, we should see the following messages, one after the other:

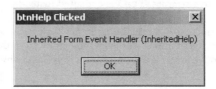

Earlier in the frmInherited constructor we associated the InheritedHelp() handler method with the btnHelp.Click event. Note that this will *not* override the handler in the base form – it adds the second delegate to execute after the first one.

> **Adding a handler to an event using the += operator adds the handler to a list of handlers. Handlers added in the parent class will execute *before* handlers added in the child class.**

If we really want to override an event handler for an inherited control such as this button, we need to make some allowances for this in the design of our base form. An obvious way would be to go back to frmBase and change our BaseHelp() handler method declaration, replacing the access modifier private with protected and adding the virtual keyword – meaning that it can now be overridden:

```
    protected virtual void BaseHelp(object sender, System.EventArgs e)
    {
      MessageBox.Show("Base Form Event Handler",
                      ((Button)sender).Name + " Clicked");
    }
```

Now we can override the `BaseHelp()` handler method in `frmInherited`. This means that we no longer need to assign a new handler to the event – we will just override the existing one – so comment out the handler assignment:

```
    public frmInherited()
    {
      // This call is required by the Windows Form Designer.
      InitializeComponent();

      //this.btnHelp.Click += new System.EventHandler(InheritedHelp);
    }
```

and override the `BaseHelp()` handler method by adding the following code in the `frmInherited` class:

```
    protected override void BaseHelp(object sender, System.EventArgs e)
    {
      MessageBox.Show("Inherited Form Event Handler (Overriden BaseHelp)",
                      ((Button)sender).Name + " Clicked");
    }
```

Rebuild the solution and run it. We can now see that when the **Help** button is clicked, the `BaseHelp()` handler method in `frmInherited` is executed instead of the one from `frmBase`.

That's a brief introduction to visual inheritance. Just because of the added 'visual' moniker, we shouldn't be surprised or confused at how it works (maybe giddy from the power and convenience though!). In .NET, everything is about classes. If a form is just a rich class, why shouldn't we expect and deserve inheritance?

Windows Forms Menus

The Windows Forms menu designer in Visual Studio .NET is a very welcome replacement for previous versions found in Visual Basic.

To add a menu to a form, drag the `MainMenu` component onto the form. This creates a non-visual-component icon in the tray below the form. When you select this icon, the properties of the menu component become visible in the **Properties** window, and the menu appears at the top of the form. The best part, however, is that you can add menu and submenu items by typing directly into the menu at the top of the form design surface, as indicated below:

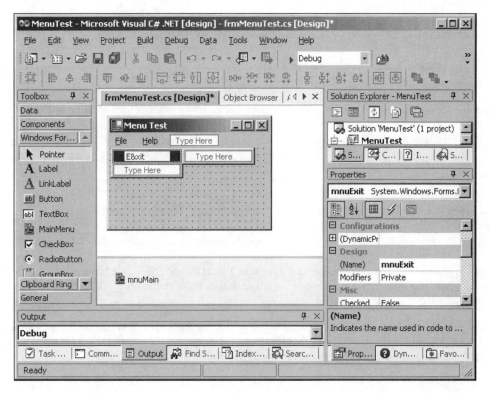

After creating a new option by keying in the text, it would be wise to give that option a meaningful name (instead of `MenuItem1` and so on) to avoid confusion with event handlers.

Entering an "`&`" symbol into a menu item's `Text` property makes the following character a tag for keyboard access. (For example, `E&xit`, will cause the *x* key to be mapped to the Exit option when the File menu is open.) Also note that the `Shortcut` property enables you to specify direct (no need for the menu to be open) keyboard shortcuts such as *Alt-F4* or *Ctrl-N*.

The designer will automatically add `MainMenu` and `MenuItem` declarations to the form's code:

```
private System.Windows.Forms.MainMenu mnuMain;
private System.Windows.Forms.MenuItem mnuFile;
private System.Windows.Forms.MenuItem mnuHelp;
private System.Windows.Forms.MenuItem mnuExit;
```

These declare the menu bar itself, and the items that it holds. Menu items are assigned to the `MainMenu.MenuItems` collection in the form's `InitializeComponent()` method – here we see the File and Help menus being assigned to the menu bar:

```
this.mnuMain.MenuItems.AddRange
    (new System.Windows.Forms.MenuItem[]
    {this.mnuFile, this.mnuHelp});
```

We also need to add the **Exit** menu item to the **File** menu. `MenuItem` provides its own `MenuItems` collection to allow this – in this way we can have several levels of submenu:

```
this.mnuFile.MenuItems.AddRange
        (new System.Windows.Forms.MenuItem[] {this.mnuExit});
```

Double-clicking on a menu option in the designer will insert an empty event handler method in code:

```
private void mnuExit_Click(object sender, System.EventArgs e)
{

}
```

and assign the handler to the `Click` event of the appropriate `MenuItem` object:

```
this.mnuExit.Click += new System.EventHandler(this.mnuExit_Click);
```

That's how easy it is to provide menus for a form in Visual Studio .NET. We have seen the code that Visual Studio .NET creates when we edit menus at design time, and we can use these coding techniques to manipulate menus at run time.

We've had a quick look at some of the technologies and concepts behind Windows forms, and seen how they bring together strengths from Microsoft's previous programming models. Now let's take an even quicker look at some of the other Windows forms possibilities.

Data Binding

There have been many improvements to the way .NET handles databases, and we can take advantage of these with Windows forms data binding. We will see examples of data binding to controls in Chapter 5.

Briefly, data binding refers to having a particular property of a control automatically populated from a data source. In .NET this is usually an in-memory data source such as a `DataSet`. As we move to different records in the `DataSet`, the control's property changes. If we data-bind to a property that the user can edit (say the `Text` property of a `TextBox`) then changes the user makes will be reflected back to the `DataSet` automatically.

In .NET we can data-bind to virtually any property of a control. In Visual Basic we were generally limited to a few properties, such as the `Text` property, and only a few controls supported data binding. In .NET, we have far more flexibility.

The main thing to remember about using Windows forms to write database clients is that a .NET application can cache large amounts of data in memory in a `DataSet`, disconnect from the data source, allow the user to manipulate the data in the `DataSet`, and then merge the changes back to the database in one operation. This has clear implications for the point-of-sale system we mentioned at the start of the chapter – the database server, or the client's connection to it, can stop working without stopping the operation of the client app.

MDI Applications

Multiple Document Interface applications consist of a main (or parent) form that acts as a container for one or many subordinate (or child) forms. Microsoft no longer recommends this style of application – the MS Office products are moving away from MDI interfaces in favor of independent document windows. However many users are familiar with, and even love, this way of working – and Windows Forms can support it.

The only change we are absolutely required to make to the parent form of the application is to set the `IsMdiContainer` property to true. Once we've done that, use the following simple code snippet in the parent form's code to generate a child form:

```
Form myNewForm = new Form();
myNewForm.MdiParent = this;
myNewForm.Show();
```

If you have special menu items that only have context for child windows, then create them within a `MainMenu` component in the child form itself. If a child form with a menu is activated, then its menu items are merged with the menu of the parent window.

Consuming Web Services

Web Services are driving rich clients back to popularity. They enable us to expose methods on a standard web server, and then call them from within an application as if they were a local method. For example, Web Services could provide a middle tier between a Windows client and a database. This can lead to far more efficient systems, because the client does not need to maintain a resource-intensive link with the database, or even know what the data source is.

Windows forms and web services make a formidable team. We will learn more about creating and using web services in Chapter 7.

The .NET Compact Framework

The .NET Compact Framework is Microsoft's latest development initiative for smart devices, especially those running Windows CE and the forthcoming Windows CE .NET. The Compact Framework is modeled after the desktop version of the full .NET Framework so it will be a familiar programming experience for .NET developers. While adhering to the full-fledged .NET Framework as much as possible, the Compact Framework is designed to make the most efficient use of resources on devices with memory limitations.

The .NET Compact Framework is similar to the Windows CE Toolkit for Visual Basic 6.0 and Visual C++ 6.0. Developers will be able to use Visual Studio .NET and the .NET Compact Framework to target supported devices.

Supported devices and operating systems will include Pocket PC 2000, Pocket PC 2002, and Windows CE .NET. Eventually they will also include smart phones, set-top boxes, and Windows CE for Automotive. Like the CE Toolkit, the Compact Framework Smart Device Extensions (SDE) includes a Pocket PC emulator for testing applications.

Summary

We've covered a lot of ground in this chapter, including:

❑ How to create robust Windows Forms applications with the .NET Framework

❑ Using existing .NET components and controls as a starting point for our own

❑ How to benefit from visual inheritance when designing sets of forms in an application

❑ Visual Studio .NET's Windows Forms menu designer, and how it improves on the one in Visual Basic 6.0

❑ Some of the other .NET developments that our client software can benefit from, enabling us to build clients that are rich but not fat

.NET will make Windows applications and rich clients fashionable again. It's an exciting time to be a Windows developer.

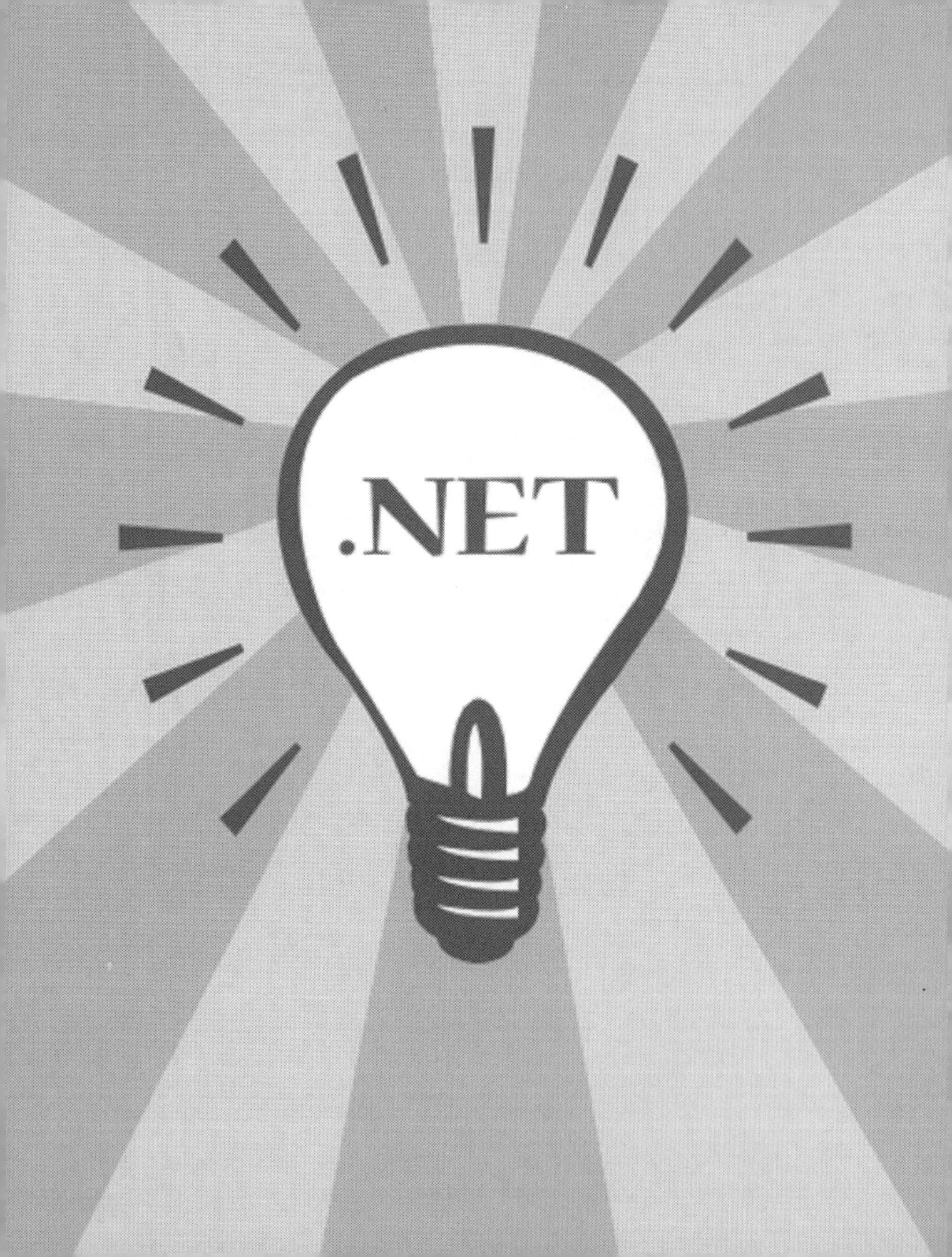
.NET

5

Working with Data

In this chapter we will look at how .NET works with data sources. We will look at three types of data source, and the facilities .NET offers for each one:

❑   Relational data – handled with ADO.NET

❑   XML data – handled with the XML classes in the `System.XML` namespace, among others

❑   Flat-file data – handled with the `System.IO` namespace

We will discuss how the .NET features work, the aims behind the design, and how the .NET features relate to existing data-access technologies. We will also discuss how successful .NET's data handling features are in meeting their aims.

Along the way, we will look at the data-handling features of a simple Web Application called `BookStacks`. This application is a front-end to the `BookStacks` book catalogue, providing ways to view and edit the data, and import data from flat-file and XML sources.

We will only look at relevant snippets from the application's code, although the full application is available in the code download.

Types of Data Explained

Before diving into the .NET Framework's data handling, let's quickly review the nature of each type of data listed above. If you already have a good understanding of each, then there's no point in reading this section, and you can skip to the section headed *Relational Data in .NET*.

Relational Data

Relational data is usually stored in a Relational Database Management System (RDBMS) such as Microsoft Access, Micorosoft SQL Server, or Oracle. The data consists of tables, which in turn consist of fields and records. Each field represents a property of the class of items stored in the table, while each record represents a specific item in the class. So a Books table might contain fields for ISBN, title, and author. Each record will store these properties for a single book.

Relational data can link items from two tables together based on a particular field. The author field for our Books table could have the same content as the author name field in an Authors table. We could then establish a relationship between the two tables.

XML Data

XML stands for eXtensible Mark-up Language. It is a method for structuring data that is readable by humans and machines. It is good for two types of data:

❑   **Hierarchical data**, where an item has properties, which in turn have sub-properties. For example, an author would have a name, an age, and a set of books they have written. The set of books will consist of several books, and each will have a title, an ISBN, and so on.

❑   **Semi-structured data**, where the data is a stream of text, but with some metadata embedded in it. XHTML, a more rigorous form of HTML, is a good example of this. The content is basically human-readable text, but with browser-interpreted tags embedded in it.

As far as the XML is concerned, they are both hierarchical, but conceptually they are quite different. Anything represented in XML will fit somewhere between a precise, repetitive hierarchy, and a stream of text with a few machine-readable tags.

An e-mail message is a good example of semi-structured data. We know that an e-mail message will have To, CC, and BCC fields – each containing a number of recipients. We also know that there will be a subject field – a single line of plain text. Finally there will be the body of the message, which is unstructured. In circumstances like this XML is a great way to store the data.

The Internet has lead to a massive increase in the amount of semi-structured data stored on computers. We now need to exchange information that contains lots of unstructured information for humans, as well as data that the machine uses to organize and transmit the data correctly.

In the Web's earlier days, one of the great things about HTML was that a human could read it and modify it in a text editor, as well as with a browser or WYSIWYG editor. It was great, and many people started to wish that all the documents they ever worked with were in HTML. From this vision, XML was born. XML uses HTML-style tags to structure data. Here is a fragment from an XML file – it is easy to get a fairly good idea what the data means:

```
<titles>
 <title>
  <titleID>0</titleID>
  <publisherID>0</publisherID>
  <categoryID>0</categoryID>
  <title>Professional ADO.NET Programming</title>
```

```
<releaseDate>2001-12-01T00:00:00.000</releaseDate>
<isbn>186100527X</isbn>
<mediaType>S</mediaType>
<price>49.99</price>
<pageCount>700</pageCount>
<referenceURL>http://www.wrox.com/ACON11.asp?ISBN=186100527X</referenceURL>
<imageURL>http://www.wrox.com/Images/Covers/527X.gif</imageURL>
<inStock>2</inStock>
<onOrder>true</onOrder>
<reorder>10</reorder>
<status>A</status>
<description>
<P>ADO.NET is Microsoft's latest data access technology and, as an integral part
of the .NET Framework, is far more than simply an upgrade of previous incarnations
of ADO. ADO.NET provides an extensive set of .NET classes that facilitate
efficient access to data from a large variety of sources, enable sophisticated
manipulation and sorting of data, and forms an important framework within which to
implement inter-application communication and XML Web Services.</P>
<P>This book provides a comprehensive guide to using ADO.NET, with plenty of
practical code examples, extensive technical information, and a detailed case
study. Whether you are developing Web Applications using ASP.NET, Windows Forms
applications, or XML Web Services, this book will show you how to utilize .NET's
data access technology to maximum effect.</P>
</description>
</title>
</titles>
```

However, XML is stricter than HTML. XML must meet these criteria:

❑   It must be well formed, for example having exactly one root element (`<titles>` in the previous example)

❑   It must be valid

Being well formed means that XML follows syntax rules that are true for *all* XML documents. Being valid means that the XML contains an appropriate set of tags for the type of data that it represents. To ensure that XML is valid we define **schemas** that describe the structure of any XML document to which they apply. We will learn more about schemas later. For now, it's enough to know that they exist and that if an XML document does not obey its schema it is not valid, even if it is well formed. The requirement for only one root allows structuring an XML document as a tree when working with it in memory.

Technically, an XML document is a series of entities. Each of these entities falls into one or more classes, such as elements, attributes, processing instructions, or comments. For us as developers, elements and attributes will be of the most importance as these are the containers of data. Each element may have zero or more attributes and zero or more sub-elements. Attributes are commonly used to contain static data specific to a given element, while sub-elements are utilized when a variable amount or structure is part of the current element. The first element of the XML Document is commonly known as the **Root Node**, while subsequent elements are simply called **nodes**.

That is a fairly dense definition of exactly what an XML document is. For a more detailed explanation of this topic, please visit: **http://www.w3c.org/TR/2000/REC-xml-20001006#sec-logical-struct**

The .NET Framework uses XML throughout. It is very easy to read XML data in .NET. If data can be usefully represented as XML, .NET development will become far easier.

Flat-File Data

Flat-file refers to data sources that .NET does not have built-in features to support. .NET presents the data to us as a sequence of characters, and we need to interpret it ourselves. Because .NET perceives no structure, we consider the file to be 'flat'. We call the sequence of characters a **stream**.

Flat-file data can contain virtually anything. If we need to read and write plain text files, or character-delimited files, then streams are the way to go. Here's an example file that we would read in this way:

```
0|ADO
1|XML
2|Flash
```

This is a list of book categories, with an associated ID number. If this were represented in XML, we'd be able to figure that out for ourselves, but this format is less intuitive. A newline character separates each category, and a | separates a category's ID from its name. The .NET Framework does not have a built-in facility for this data format, so we need to open the file as a stream and write our own interpreter.

Relational Data in .NET

The primary .NET technology for working with relational data is ADO.NET. ADO.NET conveniently breaks down into three sections:

- ❑ Data provider classes – these interface with the database. They provide the services for establishing connections with a database and running SELECT, INSERT, UPDATE, and DELETE commands against them.

- ❑ Data consumers – these allow us to manipulate relational data, even without an open connection to the database. They provide us with an in-memory representation of tables and relationships. They interface with the data provider classes, allowing us to synchronize the consumer classes with the database.

- ❑ Data-bound controls – these allow us to display our data on windows and web forms easily, by binding the content of a control to the content of a data-consumer object.

These map very naturally onto the n-tier software architecture. We use the provider classes in the data tier, the consumer classes in the business tier, and the data-bound controls in the presentation tier.

ADO.NET is the technology of choice for working with information in databases in .NET applications. To understand ADO.NET, we need to understand how and why it has come about, and how it differs from previous technologies.

Understanding ADO.NET

A good way to understand ADO.NET is to look at the changes it makes from its predecessor, ADO (now known as 'classic ADO') and the reason for these changes.

Since classic ADO's release, data-handling requirements have changed significantly. Microsoft has risen to the challenge by adding to ADO in subsequent versions, but with .NET Microsoft has taken the opportunity for a thorough redesign.

A major difference between ADO and ADO.NET is the division of the data and business tiers. Classic ADO basically provided a front-end to the database. With ADO.NET data-consumer classes we can now fully manipulate data in-memory, without being connected to the database. We can even pass data consumer objects between machines, so the client can manipulate the object and pass it back to the server once the changes are complete.

Putting the .NET in ADO.NET

To understand ADO.NET, it is important to understand its predecessor – plain old ADO. When Microsoft first released ADO, it was the culmination of Microsoft's other data access technologies: Remote Data Objects (RDO), Open Database Connectivity (ODBC) and Data Access Objects (DAO).

From Client-Server to N-Tier

Classic ADO makes it easy to write client-server applications. The database sits on the server, and ADO on the client accesses the database remotely. Aside from the database itself, including stored procedures, there is no application logic on the server:

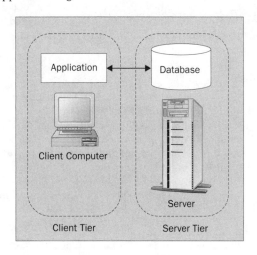

Because so little processing is done on the server, large amounts of data are passed between the client and the server frequently. This is OK in high-bandwidth LANs, but over large and slow networks such as the Internet, it can become inefficient. Also, as the number of client machines increase the stress on the server itself becomes greater. It must maintain many open connections at once, and each of these eats into its resources.

Resolving this was a key motivation behind the development of the n-tier architecture. However, ADO does not cope well with n-tier. While it can pull data from a database server and manipulate it, it's not very good at then sending the manipulated data on to another separate machine. Modern systems have many clients working with many different middle-tier servers and databases spread over multiple servers. Instead of being directly connected to a common network, the client and middle-tier servers tend to be connected over the Internet using HTTP:

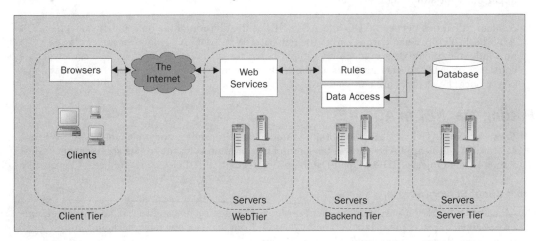

Modifications were made to ADO to make it better – enabling snapshots of data to be taken and passed between machines, for example. However, the networking protocols required to support ADO on the client tier in such a model proved to be incompatible with the security needed on the Internet. With ADO.NET, Microsoft has built a data access technology specifically designed for n-tier, disconnected architectures.

Handling Semi-Structured Data

Around the same time that Microsoft added features to ADO to help it function better in distributed applications, it also started adding features allowing ADO to work better with semi-structured data. One of the first developments was the addition of the Save method to an ADO RecordSet. In ADO, a RecordSet represents the results of a query performed against the data source. The Save method persists a RecordSet to an XML file. The Open method could then reload the data into a new RecordSet. However, a few quirks presented themselves along the way:

❑   The XML generated by Save was rather specific to the needs of the ADO RecordSet – it wasn't very suitable for use as a general-purpose XML file

❑   There were also some significant restrictions placed on what state the RecordSet needed to be in before it could be saved – particularly for a shaped/hierarchical RecordSet

❑   The XML needed to be in a specific format before it could load with the Open method, and the requirements of this format were not well documented

So yet again, a better solution was needed. ADO.NET is that solution, because of its principal object – the DataSet. The DataSet readily serializes to a general XML format that conforms to current schema standards. It also makes it much easier to express what might normally be shaped data as related DataTables. Finally, the DataSet can intelligently infer a schema from an XML file, so it can easily work with generally formatted XML files as well.

Understanding Relationships

One critical shortcoming of ADO is that while it was designed to work with Relational Databases, it offered very little support in terms of relating database objects to each other. Instead, ADO focused on working with query results in an optimal way. Programmers who needed to associate records from one RecordSet with records from another were left to their own devices and programming expertise.

The ADO.NET DataSet can contain several tables, and the relationships between those tables. The DataSet is a crucial component in ADO.NET, and we will see more about it later in this chapter.

The Data-Provider Classes

The key difference between ADO and ADO.NET at this level is that ADO.NET supports different data providers. Classic ADO always interfaced with OLE DB. In turn, OLE DB supported drivers for many different data sources. ADO.NET provides its own support for different data sources, removing the need for an additional bridge.

So much for the principle. In practice, the .NET Framework includes only two data providers:

❑ SqlClient – provides direct access to SQL Server 7.0 and 2000. For earlier versions of Microsoft SQL Server, use the OLE DB .NET Data Provider with the SQL Server OLE DB Provider (SQLOLEDB).

❑ OleDb – provides access to OLE DB. We can then access any data source supported by OLE DB.

Microsoft also provides an ODBC (Open DataBase Connectivity) driver for separate download. The download includes documentation on the classes that make up the ODBC .NET Data Provider. As .NET gains acceptance, more data providers will appear.

All .NET data providers must provide support for the following:

❑ **Connections** – A Connection object represents the connection to a given data source (defined with a ConnectionString). We open, run commands against, and close the connection as needed.

❑ **Transactions** – Transactions enable us to group commands together so that all succeed or all fail. The classic example is transferring funds between bank accounts – we need to remove the money from one account *and* add it to another. We cannot let the first command execute without the second also executing. We use transactions to control this.

❑ **Commands** – We use Command objects to issue commands against the data source – these are usually SQL SELECT, INSERT, DELETE, or UPDATE commands, or calls to stored procedures.

❑ **Parameters** – We use Parameter objects to pass parameters to stored procedures.

- ❑ **DataReaders** – The `DataReader` provides us with a read-only, forward-only view of data returned from a `Command`. We can only use it while the `Connection` is still open – it allows us to avoid the data consumer classes, because we can obtain the results of a query directly from a reader. We can even bind a `DataReader` directly to a `DataGrid`.

- ❑ **DataAdapters** – The `DataAdapter` provides the bridge between the data provider classes and the data consumer classes. The `DataAdapter` loads information returned from a `Command` into a `DataSet`. It can also write changes to a `DataSet` back to the database, by generating appropriate `INSERT`, `UPDATE`, and `DELETE` commands.

The .NET Framework defines the interfaces that a .NET data provider must expose. By adhering to the standards, vendors can create .NET data providers for any kind of data source. This means that eventually we will be able to bypass OLE DB, and therefore improve the performance of our database applications. .NET also provides enough flexibility for vendors to add features to their data providers that are specific to a particular data source.

To use the `SqlClient` data provider, you would include the `System.Data.SqlClient` namespace. All of the major objects will have a `Sql` prefix: to declare a connection you would use the `SqlConnection` class, `SqlCommand` for a command, and so on. To use the `OleDb` data provider (for instance to access a Microsoft Access database), you would need the `System.Data.OleDb` namespace. You would also use `OleDbConnection` and `OleDbCommand`. Although the names are different, all .NET data providers work in a very similar way.

Well, actually, it is not always that simple. In at least two well known cases, some extra work is needed. The first is nested transactions. The other case is where SQL provides slightly different data types from those used by OLE DB. For example, a `SqlDataReader` reading through a result set in SQL Server will extract fields using SQL-specific functions based on SQL data types. An OLE DB-based program will read through the same result set using an `OleDbDataReader` extracting fields based on OLE DB-based data types.

Using .NET's `SqlClient` instead of standard ADO and OLE DB to access SQL Server databases results in improved performance. This is because classic ADO involves so many 'wrappers', each one converting the data to its own format. `SqlClient` takes data straight from SQL Server, and packages it in a form suitable for .NET in one step. Microsoft has reported that using .NET's `SqlClient` can be as much as ten times faster than using ADO and OLE DB. Of course, we can't expect that level of performance increase from `OleDb`-based applications since they still have use to an OLE DB driver. But even here, Microsoft has done some effective work in help ADO.NET perform better with these drivers.

Realizing that there are many data source providers in active use today that are based on the ODBC standard, Microsoft has introduced an `IDataProvider` based class for working with these.

> **The ODBC.NET Data Provider is not provided "out-of-the-box." If you are interested in using it, you will need to download it from:**
> http://msdn.microsoft.com/downloads/default.asp?url=/downloads/sample.asp?url=/msdn-files/027/001/668/msdncompositedoc.xml

We mentioned that each provider has its own `DataAdapter` class. This provides the bridge between the provider and consumer classes, which we will go on to discuss now.

The Data-Consumer Classes

The data-provider classes enable us to issue commands against the database, and view the results. The data-consumer classes enable us to take data from the database, store it in memory, edit it, and then re-connect to the database to perform updates.

The main data-consumer class is the DataSet. The DataSet stores tables, the relationships between tables, and data constraints, in memory. We can change the values in a DataSet, and then update the source database with all the changes in one go.

Working in this way has several advantages. The first is that it provides a conceptual break between the data tier and the business tier of an application. We can have one component or set of components that deal with obtaining data (the data tier). We can have another set of components that manipulate it (the business tier). The business tier does not need to worry whether the data came from a SQL Server database, an Access database, or an XML file. Breaking things up in this way makes software much easier to program and maintain.

Things become more interesting when there is more than a conceptual break between the tiers. A DataSet object can be passed over a network very easily. Let's say that we have a central database, with several client machines all using data from it. In .NET, we could work this way:

❑   The client requests a DataSet from the data tier on the server.

❑   The data tier on the server opens a connection to the database, uses a DataAdapter to fill a DataSet, and closes the database connection. It then sends the DataSet back to the client.

❑   The client enables the user to make any changes they like to the DataSet. When the changes are complete, the client sends the modifications back to the server.

❑   The server opens a database connection, and uses a DataAdapter to update the database.

Working in this way means that there is little stress on the database server – there are only two connections established, and each one is for a short time. A relatively large amount of data may be sent from the server to the client in one go, but we avoid the overhead of opening several new connections between the client and the data tier, and between the data tier and the database.

All this magic is thanks to the DataSet. The DataSet is really an in-memory database engine. It has the following collection properties:

❑   Tables – objects that in turn consist of Rows, Columns, and Constraints

❑   Relations – objects that represent database relationships

When we pass a DataSet over a network, it is converted to XML. We can also save a DataSet to disc as XML using the WriteXml method, or load a saved DataSet back into memory using the LoadXml method. We can even convert a DataSet to an XML String using the GetXml method.

We have seen how the data providers map to the data tier, and the DataSet maps to the business tier. To complete the picture, we need ways for users to interact with the data. There are a variety of data-bound controls that we can bind directly to a DataSet, DataTable, or to a specific Row and Column in a DataTable. We will look at these now.

Data-Bound Controls

Many Windows and web controls can bind to a DataSet, or to a specific part of a DataSet. In fact, we can bind data to almost all properties of many controls. This makes it easy to build a rich presentation tier to your data-centric applications.

The simpler controls, such as the TextBox, simply allow us to bind a property to a specific column in a DataTable. If we were to bind to the Text property, it will always display that column from the DataTable object's selected row. When the selected row changes, the Text property changes. We can also use data binding to modify the DataSet – changes to the Text property can be reflected in the DataSet.

Other controls, such as the DataGrid, offer more complex data binding. We can present a whole DataSet in a DataGrid, and if the DataSet contains multiple Tables and Relations, the users can navigate between them.

The best way to visualize these controls is through examples. In the next section we will see examples of using ADO.NET in the data, business, and presentation tiers.

Using ADO.NET

We've talked about how ADO.NET is tailor-made for n-tier software architectures. Let's have a look at a fairly simple example that exploits these features. This example is based on a SQL Server database named BookStacks, which contains information about a number of books, and which we'll use for several examples in this chapter. Because we're illustrating the value of ADO.NET in an n-tier environment, this example is a bit more complex than the average client-server sample, but the extra work is definitely worthwhile!

The full code for this short example, and a SQL script to create the database, can be found on the Wrox web site at http://www.wrox.com. Note that some error-handling code has been omitted from the code listing for reasons of clarity and space.

The example has three components:

- ❑ A data-tier component that performs the actual data access and updates; this class acts as a wrapper for a DataSet object that contains the selected data. Except for the assumption that every table will have a single GUID primary key column (and the fact that it uses the SqlClient provider), this component will be independent of the data source, and can be used to connect to any SQL Server database.

- ❑ A business-tier object that encapsulates the business logic and provides methods for manipulating the data in the disconnected DataSet.

- ❑ A presentation layer consisting of an ASP.NET page that allows us to control the inventory of active titles in the database by buying or selling individual titles.

The Data-Tier Component

The first component we'll look at is the data tier. This consists of a C# class library containing just one class – our data access component. As we noted above, this class essentially acts a wrapper for a disconnected DataSet object. Each instance of the DataTierComponent class represents one connection to the data source, and has one DataSet, which can contain several DataTable objects. The class has three private member variables:

```csharp
using System;
using System.Data;
using System.Data.SqlClient;
using System.Collections;

namespace Wrox.UnderstandingDotNet.Chapter05.AdoNetExample
{
  public class DataTierComponent
  {
    private string source;
    private DataSet ds;
    private Hashtable sqlCmds = new Hashtable();
```

The source represents the connection string used by the class instance to connect to the database, and ds is the internal DataSet used to store the data retrieved from the database. The final field, sqlCmds, is a hashtable that we'll use to store the SQL command for each DataTable in our DataSet. Each DataTable will be populated by a different command, so we use the field to store the commands for all the DataTables. The DataTable name is used as the key for each value, so we can easily retrieve the command for any named DataTable.

The source and ds fields are initialized in the class's constructor:

```csharp
public DataTierComponent(string SqlConnection, string DataSetName)
{
  if (SqlConnection.Length == 0)
    throw new NoNullAllowedException(
            "The SQL Connection string must be provided.");

  source = SqlConnection;
  ds = new DataSet(DataSetName);
}
```

Access to the private DataSet is permitted from outside the class by exposing it as a read-only property:

```csharp
public DataSet DataSet
{
  get { return ds; }
}
```

We also provide public methods for retrieving and setting individual values within the DataSet. These take parameters that specify the name of the DataTable we want to access or update, the primary key of the specific row we want to access, and the name of the field. The SetFieldValue method also has a fourth parameter, of type Object, for the new value to assign to the cell:

```
public object GetFieldValue(string TableName, Guid PKID, string FieldName)
{
  DataRow row;
  row = ds.Tables[TableName].Rows.Find(PKID);
  if (row == null)
     throw new RowNotInTableException(PKID.ToString() +
           " was not found in " + TableName + " primary key values.");
  return row[FieldName];
}

public object SetFieldValue(string TableName, Guid PKID, string FieldName,
                            object NewValue)
{
  DataRow row;
  row = ds.Tables[TableName].Rows.Find(PKID);
  if (row == null)
     throw new RowNotInTableException(PKID.ToString() +
            " was not found in " + TableName + " primary key values.");
  row[FieldName] = NewValue;
  return row[FieldName];
}
```

The last two methods are perhaps the most complicated, but this is where the advantages of ADO.NET start to be apparent. These methods are where we create and populate a new DataTable within our DataSet, and where we reconnect to the data source and update it with any changes made in the client copy of the DataSet.

The first method, LoadAndAddTable, takes three parameters – the name of the new DataTable we're going to create, the SQL statement we'll execute to populate the data source, and the index position of the primary key column. We start off by declaring and initializing some local variables:

❑ The SqlConnection object. The connection string is taken from the source private field.

❑ A SqlDataAdapter for populating the DataTable. We initialize this object with the SQL statement passed into the method and our SqlConnection object.

❑ A new DataTable to add to the DataSet.

❑ A one-element array of DataColumn objects to represent the primary key column of the table.

```
public void LoadAndAddTable(string TableName, string SqlStatement,
                                      int PrimaryKeyColumnIndex)
{
   // Declare and initialize the local variables
   SqlConnection cn = new SqlConnection(source);
   SqlDataAdapter da = new SqlDataAdapter(SqlStatement, cn);
   DataTable NewTable = new DataTable(TableName);
   DataColumn[] PKColumns = new DataColumn[1];
```

Next (within a `try` block), we open the connection and populate the `DataSet`:

```
try
{
    // Open the connection and populate the DataTable
    cn.Open();
    da.Fill(NewTable);
```

That's basically all there is to it! We've already provided the information for the connection in our `SqlConnection` object, and specified the data we want to retrieve in the SQL statement, and passed these both into the data adapter, so this one line is now enough to populate the new `DataTable` with data from the database. And because the `DataSet` and its child objects are disconnected by definition, we don't need to fiddle about setting the `ActiveConnection` to `Nothing`. The only tidying up we have to do is to tell the data table which the primary key column is (this is a very powerful feature, as it lets us define relationships between our tables, even though they're completely disconnected from the database), add the table to the `DataSet`, and add the command to our hashtable. Lastly, we use the `finally` clause to ensure that the connection will be closed even if an exception is thrown:

```
    PKColumns[0] = NewTable.Columns[PrimaryKeyColumnIndex];
    NewTable.PrimaryKey = PKColumns;

    ds.Tables.Add(NewTable);
    sqlCmds.Add(TableName, SqlStatement);
}
catch (Exception exc)
{
    throw exc;
}
finally
{
    if (cn.State != ConnectionState.Closed)
        cn.Close();
}
}
```

The last method updates the database from the local copy of a `DataTable` in the `DataSet`. The only parameter is the name of the `DataTable`. Again, we start by declaring some local variables. As well as the `SqlConnection` and `SqlDataAdapter` objects (as in the previous method), we also need three more objects:

❑ A `SqlCommandBuilder` object. ADO.NET needs an appropriate SQL command to perform any inserts, updates, or deletes. Although we can define these manually, it's much easier to get ADO.NET to do the work for us. To do this, we simply create a new `SqlCommandBuilder` object, initializing it with the data adapter. This automatically creates the relevant INSERT, UPDATE, and DELETE commands for use with that data adapter. Of course, if we're using stored procedures to handle these operations – as we probably would in the real world – then we'll have to create the commands manually.

❑ A `SqlTransaction` object. We can take advantage of SQL Server's (or other database systems') built in transaction support very easily in ADO.NET using a `SqlTransaction` (or `OleDbTransaction`) object. We're making the update transactional because we need to call the data adapter's `Update` method three times (once each for updates, inserts, and deletes), and we want to make sure that if one operation fails, none of the changes are actually made.

❑   A SqlCommand object. The SqlTransaction object has to be associated with a specific command object, so we'll retrieve the command for this DataTable from our sqlCmds hashtable. We'll also use this to initialize our data adapter.

```
public void UpdateDBFromTable(string TableName)
{
   SqlConnection cn = new SqlConnection(source);
   SqlDataAdapter da;
   SqlCommandBuilder cmdBuilder;
   SqlTransaction trans = null;
   SqlCommand cmd;

   if (ds.Tables[TableName] == null)
      throw new NullReferenceException(TableName +
                 " does not exist in the current DataSet.");
```

After checking that the DataTable we're using to update the database really does exist, we open the connection and start the transaction. We do this by calling the SqlConnection's BeginTransaction method. This returns a SqlTransaction object, which we assign to our local variable, and which we'll use later to commit or roll back the transaction:

```
try
{
   cn.Open();
   trans = cn.BeginTransaction();
```

Next, we initialize our command, data adapter, and command builder objects, retrieving the command string from the sqlCmds hashtable. Hashtables aren't strongly typed, so we need to cast this value to a string before we can pass it into the SqlCommand's constructor. Once we've got these three objects, we associate the command with our transaction by setting its Transaction property:

```
cmd = new SqlCommand((string)sqlCmds[TableName], cn);
da = new SqlDataAdapter(cmd);
cmdBuilder = new SqlCommandBuilder(da);
cmd.Transaction = trans;
```

Now, we can get down to the real business and call the Update method on the data adapter. As mentioned above, we need to call this three times; in each case, we'll pass in a new DataTable object containing a subset of the affected data – inserted rows, updated rows, and deleted rows. We retrieve these by calling the GetChanges method of the DataTable, passing in a DataRowState enum value to indicate which rows we want in the new table. Before we pass the new tables into the Update method, however, we need to check that they aren't null, since calling Update with a null value generates an exception:

```
DataTable dtAdded =
           ds.Tables[TableName].GetChanges(DataRowState.Added);
if (dtAdded != null)
   da.Update(dtAdded);

DataTable dtModified =
```

```
                    ds.Tables[TableName].GetChanges(DataRowState.Modified);
          if (dtModified != null)
            da.Update(dtModified);

          DataTable dtDeleted =
                    ds.Tables[TableName].GetChanges(DataRowState.Deleted);
          if (dtDeleted != null)
            da.Update(dtDeleted);
```

If all went well, we can now commit the transaction; otherwise we rethrow any exceptions that occurred, and finally close the connection:

```
          trans.Commit();
        }
        catch (SqlException sqlExc)
        {
          trans.Rollback();
          throw sqlExc;
        }
        catch (Exception exc)
        {
          trans.Rollback();
          throw exc;
        }
        finally
        {
          if (cn.State != ConnectionState.Closed)
            cn.Close();
        }
      }
    }
  }
```

The Business-Tier Component

That's the worst part of the code over with, and the only part that connects directly to the data source. We haven't yet written any code to manipulate our data – in fact, we haven't really written any data-specific code at all. This code resides in our business-tier component; however, this is less specific to ADO.NET, and we'll go through it much faster.

Like the data component, the business component is a class library consisting of a single C# class. Unlike the data component, however, our business component is designed specifically for working with the BookStacks database. It has two private fields; the first, dataTier, is an instance of our data-tier component. The second, editTable, is a DataTable object used to store a local copy of the data we retrieve from the data tier – information about the number of copies in stock of all the active book titles in the database. We expose this as a public property:

```
using System;
using System.Data;
using System.Collections;
```

```
namespace Wrox.UnderstandingDotNet.Chapter05.AdoNetExample
{
  public class BusinessTierComponent
  {
    private DataTierComponent dataTier;
    private DataTable editTable;

    public DataTable EditTable
    {
      get { return editTable; }
      set { editTable = value; }
    }
```

The constructor of the class instantiates the data component, and creates and populates the `DataTable` with data from the data-access component:

```
public BusinessTierComponent(string SqlConnStr)
{
  try
  {
    dataTier = new DataTierComponent(SqlConnStr, "InventoryList");
    dataTier.LoadAndAddTable("InventoryLevels",
        "SELECT TitleID,Title,InStock FROM TITLES WHERE STATUS = 'A'", 0);
    CreateEditTable();
    PopulateEditTable();
  }
  catch (Exception exc)
  {
    throw exc;
  }
}
```

The `CreateEditTable` method demonstrates creating a `DataTable` object programmatically (much like we'd create a programmatic recordset in ADO). This emphasizes the point that the `DataSet` and its child objects are by nature disconnected from the data source. Again, notice that we can set a primary key column, even though this `DataTable` has never been connected to a data source:

```
private void CreateEditTable()
{
  DataColumn[] PKColumns = new DataColumn[1];
  editTable = new DataTable("EditTable");
  editTable.Columns.Add(new DataColumn("TitleID", typeof(Guid)));
  editTable.Columns.Add(new DataColumn("Title", typeof(string)));
  editTable.Columns.Add(new DataColumn("InStock", typeof(byte)));
  editTable.Columns.Add(new DataColumn("Delta", typeof(int)));

  PKColumns[0] = editTable.Columns[0];
  editTable.PrimaryKey = PKColumns;
}
```

The `PopulateEditTable` method simply reads data from our data-access component and uses it to populate the local `DataTable` that we've just created:

```
private void PopulateEditTable()
{
  editTable.Rows.Clear();

  foreach (DataRow sourceRow in dataTier.DataSet.Tables
                                        ["InventoryLevels"].Rows)
  {
    DataRow newRow = editTable.NewRow();
    newRow[0] = sourceRow[0];                    // TitleID
    newRow[1] = sourceRow[1];                    // Title
    newRow[2] = sourceRow[2];                    // InStock
    newRow[3] = 0;                  // Delta
    editTable.Rows.Add(newRow);
  }
}
```

We'll also define some methods for setting the inventory level of particular titles. Because it's important that this data is kept completely up-to-date, we'll execute these methods directly against the data access component, rather than against the local `DataTable`.

The first of these methods is `ChangeInStockCount`, which is publicly accessible from outside the class. This takes the ID of the title to update and the number of units change (positive or negative). Here, we simply check that the new value is valid, and if so call a private method:

```
public int ChangeInStockCount(Guid TitleID, int Delta)
{
  int proposed;

  try
  {
    proposed = (int)(GetInStockCount(TitleID)) + Delta;
    if (proposed > byte.MaxValue)
      throw new OverflowException(
                   "Change results in too many copies in inventory!");

    if (proposed < byte.MinValue)
      throw new OverflowException(
                   "Change results in too few copies in inventory!");

    return SetInventoryLevel(TitleID, (byte)proposed);
  }
  catch (Exception exc)
  {
    throw exc;
  }
}
```

The private `SetInventoryLevel` method just calls the `SetFieldValue` method on the data tier component:

```
private byte SetInventoryLevel(Guid TitleID, byte SetTo)
{
  try
  {
    return (byte)(dataTier.SetFieldValue("InventoryLevels", TitleID,
                                "InStock", SetTo));
  }
  catch (Exception exc)
  {
    throw exc;
  }
}
```

In order to calculate the proposed new inventory level, we need to know the current level. We do this in the private `GetInStockCount` method, which – as you've probably guessed – just calls `GetFieldValue` on the data-tier component:

```
private byte GetInStockCount(Guid TitleID)
{
  try
  {
    return (byte)(dataTier.GetFieldValue("InventoryLevels", TitleID,
                                "InStock"));
  }
  catch (Exception exc)
  {
    throw exc;
  }
}
```

Next, if any changes are made in the local `DataTable`, we'll need to propagate these back to the data component. We provide an `Update` method for this purpose. This method simply iterates through each row in our `DataTable`, reads the value from each of the four columns, and calls the `SetFieldValue` method on the data-tier component:

```
public void Update()
{
  byte inStock, delta;
  Guid PKID;

  foreach (DataRow editRow in editTable.Rows)
  {
    PKID = new Guid(editRow[0].ToString());
    inStock = Convert.ToByte(editRow[2]);
    delta = Convert.ToInt32(editRow[3]);
    dataTier.SetFieldValue("InventoryLevels", PKID, "InStock",
                        inStock + delta);
    editRow[3] = 0;
  }
}
```

Finally, we provide two (very short) methods for committing changes back to the data source and for refreshing the local `DataTable` from the data tier. The first of these just calls the `UpdateDBFromTable` method; the second just acts as a public alias for the `PopulateEditTable` method:

```
public void Commit()
{
  try
  {
    dataTier.UpdateDBFromTable("InventoryLevels");

  }
  catch (Exception exc)
  {
    throw exc;
  }
}

public void Refresh()
{
  PopulateEditTable();
}
}
}
```

The Presentation Layer

The last piece in the puzzle is the presentation layer. This consists of an ASP.NET page containing a datagrid which is bound to the `EditTable` property of our business object. This allows users to work with the data locally, and to commit any changes made to the data when they've finished.

Because this isn't an ASP.NET chapter, we're only going to look at this page (and its code-behind class) very quickly, and we're going to keep the functionality as simple as possible (sorry – no fancy images!):

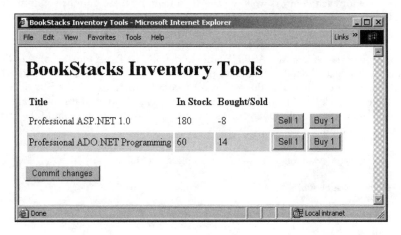

The bulk of the code is in the code-behind file, so the ASP.NET page itself just includes the tags for the server-controls:

```
<form id="Form1" method="post" runat="server">
  <h1>BookStacks Inventory Tools</h1>
  <P><asp:datagrid id="DataGrid1" BorderWidth="0" CellSpacing="3"
                CellPadding="3" AutoGenerateColumns="False" runat="server">
    <AlternatingItemStyle BackColor="#e0e0e0" />
    <EditItemStyle BackColor="#ffff99" />
    <HeaderStyle Font-Bold="True" />
    <Columns>
      <asp:BoundColumn DataField="TitleID" HeaderText="ID" ReadOnly="True"
                Visible="False" />
      <asp:BoundColumn DataField="Title" HeaderText="Title" ReadOnly="True" />
      <asp:BoundColumn DataField="InStock" HeaderText="In Stock"
                ReadOnly="True" />
      <asp:BoundColumn DataField="Delta" HeaderText="Bought/Sold"
                ReadOnly="False" />
      <asp:ButtonColumn ButtonType="PushButton" Text="Sell 1"
                CommandName="Sell" />
      <asp:ButtonColumn ButtonType="PushButton" Text="Buy 1"
                CommandName="Buy" />
    </Columns>
  </asp:datagrid></P>
  <P><asp:button id="Button1" runat="server" Text="Commit changes"
                Width="121px"></asp:button></P>
</form>
```

The actually binding for the datagrid is performed manually, when the page loads for the first time. However, we'll bind each column in the datagrid to a column in our DataTable, so we use the DataField attribute on each of the <asp:BoundColumn> elements to specify which column we want to bind to. We also add two columns containing buttons, which allow the user to increase or decrease the inventory level for each item. As we'll see shortly, including these buttons within the datagrid means that when a button in a specific row is clicked, our event handler will be able to access the other data in that row.

We won't go through the code in the ASP.NET file in detail – we'll just look at some of the most important points. The actual databinding takes place in the Page_Load event. Since this event is fired every time the page is posted back to the server (for example, when one of the Buy or Sell buttons is clicked), we have to check that this is the first time the page has loaded. If it is, we create a new instance of our business component, set the DataGrid's DataSource property to point to the EditTable, and call its DataBind method:

```
private void Page_Load(object sender, System.EventArgs e)
{
  if (!Page.IsPostBack)
  {
    business = new BusinessTierComponent("Persist Security Info=True;" +
                "Initial Catalog=BookStacks;Data Source=MyServer;" +
                "User ID=UserName;Password=password");
```

```
      DataGrid1.DataSource = business.EditTable;
      DataGrid1.DataBind();
    }
  }
```

The next important piece of code is the event handler for our **Buy/Sell** buttons. When the user clicks on either of these bound buttons, an `ItemCommand` event is raised. The `DataGridCommandEventArgs` object passed into this method has a property named `Item`, which gives our event handler access to the row in the grid for which the user clicked one of the buttons. Within this method, we just increase or decrease by one the value in the **Bought/Sold** column of the datagrid. Note that we don't make any changes to the business object at this point, as that goes out of scope when the page is reloaded. The beauty of databinding in ASP.NET is that we can manipulate the page's local cache of the data, without needing to reconnect to the server until we want to commit our changes.

```
private void DataGrid1_ItemCommand(object source,
            System.Web.UI.WebControls.DataGridCommandEventArgs e)
{
  DataGridItem item = e.Item;
  Guid itemId = new Guid(e.Item.Cells[0].Text);

  int delta = Convert.ToInt16(item.Cells[3].Text);

  if (e.CommandName == "Buy")
    item.Cells[3].Text = (delta + 1).ToString();
  else
    item.Cells[3].Text = (delta - 1).ToString();
}
```

The last bit of code we need to write is executed when the user has finished editing the data, and clicks on the **Commit Changes** button. As the business object will have gone out of scope at this point we need to create a new instance, and update its `EditTable` with the values from the `DataGrid` (we do this in a method named `UpdateEditTable`). Now we propagate the changes back to the data-tier component by calling the business object's `Update` method. This may seem like a wasteful repetition of effort, but it allows the business and data components to run on different physical machines, and – more importantly – allows us to abstract the ASP.NET page completely from our data component. Finally, we commit the changes to the database, refresh the business object's `EditTable`, and reset the `DataGrid`'s databinding:

```
private void Button1_Click(object sender, System.EventArgs e)
{
  if (business == null)
  {
    business = new BusinessTierComponent("Persist Security Info=True;" +
                 "Initial Catalog=BookStacks;Data Source=MyServer;" +
                 "User ID=UserName;Password=password");
  }

  UpdateEditTable();
  business.Update();
  business.Commit();
```

```
    business.Refresh();

    DataGrid1.DataSource = business.EditTable;
    DataGrid1.DataBind();
}
```

And that's it! It may seem like a lot of work for a simple application, but there are many advantages to this completely disconnected approach. The data-tier component doesn't need to know the precise format of the data it's used to retrieve, and can actually be used to access many different data sources. This means we only have to write our data-access code once. The business-tier component calls the generic methods provided by the data tier, and abstracts the methods we need for working specifically with the BookStacks database. Finally, the presentation layer uses databinding to store a local copy of the data, so that users can work with this without needing to connect back to the data source every time they make a change to the data.

ADO.NET Summary

So far, we have learned that ADO.NET provides solutions for the problems that classic ADO could not address. If you ponder for a moment, these improvements seem rather natural because these are the features that we always wanted to see in ADO technology! Let's recap the salient features of ADO.NET before we move on to the next section.

❑   A major difference between ADO and ADO.NET is the division of the data and business tiers. ADO.NET fully supports disconnected data handling.

❑   ADO.NET is deeply integrated with XML.

❑   Using ADO.NET, handling relational data is more intuitive because you can represent relationships in disconnected mode – you use DataSets for that purpose.

❑   ADO.NET supports many data sources through its OLEDB provider. Not only that, but SqlDataProvider comes fully optimized for SQL Server data operations.

❑   Data-Consumer and Data-Bound Controls provide more control over data in disconnected mode.

Now let's move on to look in more detail at XML Data.

XML Data in .NET

The .NET Framework introduces a new standards-based API for XML. The new API provides innovative solutions to handle XML data to achieve better performance. Although the System.Xml namespace provides improved functionality and performance compared to its predecessor, MSXML, in many ways it is a natural evolution of the MSXML API.

The .NET XML namespace is System.Xml, and it contains the following child namespaces:

❑   System.Xml – the parent namespace provides classes for basic I/O such as creating, reading, updating and persisting XML Documents.

❑   System.Xml.XPath – provides classes for navigating XML Documents using the XPath language

- ❑ System.Xml.Xsl – provides classes to transform XML Documents into other forms such as HTML

- ❑ System.Xml.Schema – provides classes to handle the XSD types for XML Documents

- ❑ System.Xml.Serialization – provides classes for serializing XML objects to streams or files and for deserializing them

In this section, we will examine the above namespaces to find out how System.Xml can provide us with the suite of APIs that we need to process XML data in .NET.

XML Processing Models

In .NET, there are two main ways to process an XML Document. These two models stem from the way we perceive the XML Document.

We can think of XML as a hierarchy of nodes, with attributes and sub nodes. In this model we can traverse through the XML Document using the hierarchy. Since this model supports traversing the document in many directions, the entire XML Document needs to be loaded into the memory. This object-oriented way of processing XML is the **Document Object Model**, or DOM.

We can also think of XML as a sequence of tags. In this model, we work through a stream of nodes from the beginning to the end of the file. This model allows forward-only traversal, so we don't have to load the whole document into memory. Because of this simplified model, the **stream-oriented** way of processing XML Documents proves to be more efficient. This model is also known as the **pull model** in the .NET Framework.

Although the above model sounds similar to the well known **Simple API for XML** or **SAX**, it is fundamentally different. A SAX parser raises an event when particular nodes are encountered, but in the pull-model we request each node one at a time as we traverse the file, and then interrogate it to find out what sort of node it is. SAX is often called the push model, because we do not request each node – the parser 'pushes' particular nodes to us.

Now let's take a look at how to implement the above models programmatically using the .NET Framework.

Stream-Oriented XML I/O

In this model the XML Document processing is done using the XmlReader and XmlWriter classes. These two classes are the members of the System.Xml namespace. Both XmlReader and XmlWriter are implemented based on the streaming adapters such as System.IO.Stream in the .NET Framework, which we will be looking at later.

The XmlReader class is an abstract base class that provides a forward-only, read-only cursor for reading a stream of XML data. The XmlWriter is an abstract base class that provides an interface for producing streams of XML data. As we have discussed before, neither class caches the XML Document in memory.

Most of the other class implementations in the System.Xml namespace are in one way or another built using the above two types. Since the above two classes are the abstract base classes, if you want to use XmlReader or XmlWriter you have to implement classes that inherit from them.

The .NET Framework provides a set of classes that implement the above base classes for our use.

XmlReader Implementations

The XmlReader class is implemented in different forms according to different needs. The basic implementations that you find in .NET Framework are:

- ❑ **XmlTextReader** – This is the canonical XmlReader implementation. This class reads XML Documents one node at a time.

- ❑ **XmlNodeReader** – Using this class you can read an XML DOM sub-tree, rather than a whole XML file. But still this is a forward-only and non-cached reader.

- ❑ **XmlValidatingReader** – This class provides a reader that can validate XML Documents.

Now let us consider a simplified version of the titles XML that we have seen earlier in this chapter. This time the titles XML is going to be simple, as shown below:

```xml
<titles>
  <title>
    <name>Professional ADO.NET Programming</name>
    <isbn>186100527X</isbn>
    <price>49.99</price>
    <pageCount>700</pageCount>
    <description>
      This is a great reference for ADO .NET!
    </description>
  </title>
</titles>
```

Of course this file could contain several books. Let's say that we want to find the price for *Professional ADO.NET Programming*, by ISBN. Here's one way we could do it (we would need to import the System.Xml and System.IO namespaces):

```vb
Dim ReadStream As FileStream
Dim File As File
Dim MyXmlReader As XmlTextReader
Dim price As String

'Open the Title.xml file
ReadStream = File.Open("Titles.xml", FileMode.Open)

MyXmlReader = New XmlTextReader(ReadStream)

'Work through each node sequentially
While MyXmlReader.Read()
  'If we reach an ISBN element
  If MyXmlReader.NodeType = XmlNodeType.Element And _
```

```
                                    MyXmlReader.Name = "isbn" Then

     'Move on to the next 'node' (i.e. the element's CDATA -
     'the ISBN number)

     MyXmlReader.Read()

     'And if we have the correct ISBN
     If MyXmlReader.Value = "186100527X" Then
       'Continue reading until we get to an Element with the name "price"
       MyXmlReader.Read()
       While MyXmlReader.NodeType <> XmlNodeType.Element And _
                                    MyXmlReader.Name <> "price"

         MyXmlReader.Read()
         Console.WriteLine(MyXmlReader.NodeType.ToString)
       End While

       'When we do, move to the next node (which is the actual price)
       MyXmlReader.Read()

       'And display that value
       Console.WriteLine(MyXmlReader.Value)
     End If
   End If
End While
```

When we're using this parser, just about everything is a "node". Before satisfying the

```
If MyXmlReader.NodeType = XmlNodeType.Element And _
                                    MyXmlReader.Name = "isbn" Then
```

condition, we have already had a Read step for:

- ❏ The <titles> element
- ❏ Some whitespace
- ❏ The <title> element
- ❏ More whitespace
- ❏ The <name> tag
- ❏ The CDATA inside the <name> element – "Professional ADO.NET Programming"
- ❏ The </name> end-tag

The cursor is now hovering over the <isbn> element, but to read what the ISBN number is we need to move on one more step. If it isn't the ISBN we want, we'd just carry on reading each node until we meet the next <isbn> element.

If it is the ISBN that we want, then we need to find the price. So once again we start reading the document until a condition is satisfied – this time, to find a <price> element. Again after we've found it we move on again to get the price itself, and then display it.

The way that we've done this, we read every single node. If the XML file contained 10,000 books and we only wanted the price for one of them, we would not want this overhead.

Using the Skip method, we can skip the current node and all of its child nodes. So calling MyXmlReader.Skip while the reader is positioned on the <title> element will jump right over name, ISBN, price, page count, and description. If we knew the book's ISBN without needing to drill down past the <title> element, we could benefit from this. Let's make this small change to the XML:

```xml
<titles>
  <title isbn="186100527X">
    <name>Professional ADO.NET Programming</name>
    <price>49.99</price>
    <pageCount>700</pageCount>
    <description>
      This is a great reference for ADO .NET!
    </description>
  </title>
</titles>
```

We now have ISBN as an **attribute** of the <title> element. We could now process the XML using this, far more efficient, code:

```vb
Sub Main()
   Dim ReadStream As FileStream
   Dim File As File
   Dim MyXmlReader As XmlTextReader
   Dim price As String

   'Open the Title.xml file
   ReadStream = File.Open("Titles.xml", FileMode.Open)

   MyXmlReader = New XmlTextReader(ReadStream)

   MyXmlReader.MoveToContent()

   ' Get to the first <title> element
   While Not (MyXmlReader.NodeType = XmlNodeType.Element _
                                   And MyXmlReader.Name = "title")

      MyXmlReader.Read()
   End While

   ' Work through each title, checking the ISBN
   While Not (MyXmlReader.NodeType = XmlNodeType.EndElement _
                                   And MyXmlReader.Name = "titles")
      If MyXmlReader.GetAttribute("isbn") = "186100527X" Then
         MyXmlReader.Read()
         While Not (MyXmlReader.NodeType = XmlNodeType.Element _
                                   And MyXmlReader.Name = "price")

            MyXmlReader.Skip()
         End While
         MyXmlReader.Read()
         Console.WriteLine(MyXmlReader.Value)
```

```
      Else
         MyXmlReader.Skip()
      End If
   End While
   Console.ReadLine()
End Sub
```

We're introducing a number of new `XmlTextReader` methods here:

- ❏ `MoveToContent`
- ❏ `Skip`
- ❏ `GetAttribute`

Let's go through how this snippet works, and how we use these methods. The first 'new' line is `MyXmlReader.MoveToContent()`. This method takes us to the next available 'content' node. Content nodes are nodes of type `Element`, `Entity`, `CDATA`, `EndElement`, or `EndEntity`. Calling `MyXmlReader.MoveToContent` moves over any document definitions, comments, processing instructions, or whitespace at the start of our document – positioning the cursor over the <titles> tag. However once the cursor is positioned on a content node, `MoveToContent` will do nothing.

So we are now positioned over the <titles> tag. We now call Read() until we reach the first <title> tag – this will move us through the whitespace between <titles> and <title>.

Here's where we start benefiting from the changes we made to the XML. We can now obtain the ISBN number without moving the cursor beyond the <title> tag – using `GetAttribute`. If the ISBN number is *not* the one that we want, we can call Skip(), which will jump over every child element for that <title>, and leave the cursor over the whitespace immediately following the </title> end-tag. We then Read() until we get to the next <title> (which usually just means passing over the whitespace).

If the ISBN number we found *is* the one we want, we call Read() to move past the <title> element. We then Skip() until we reach the price. The reason for calling Read() first is that otherwise we would skip over all of the child elements for that <title>. Once we reach the price, we display it, and then continue on through the XML file (although since ISBNs should be unique, we could exit the loops at this stage).

If you want to validate your XML against a pre-defined schema before you process/read, then you have to use the `XmlValidatingReader` class. This class supports schema types DTD, XDR, and XSD, and the validation of data type information is performed during parsing.

We've seen a general overview of how `XmlReader` classes work in .NET. With this in mind, the .NET documentation covers many of the details.

XmlWriter Implementations

The .NET Framework provides an implementation for the `XmlWriter` base class: `XmlTextWriter`. This is the `XmlWriter` implementation for writing XML to an output stream. This class supports different stream types and formatting options. The code shown overleaf demonstrates how to write an XML file using the `XmlTextWriter` class:

```
Sub Main()
  Dim WriteStream As FileStream
  Dim File As File
  Dim MyXmlWriter As XmlTextWriter

  Try

    WriteStream = New FileStream("CopyTitles.xml", FileMode.Create)

    MyXmlWriter = New XmlTextWriter(WriteStream, Text.Encoding.UTF8)

    MyXmlWriter.Formatting = Formatting.Indented
    'Start Writing the Docuemnt
    MyXmlWriter.WriteStartDocument(True)
    'Write a Comment
    MyXmlWriter.WriteComment("This is a sample Title XML")
    'Begin the Root - titles Element
    MyXmlWriter.WriteStartElement("titles")
    'Begin the title Element
    MyXmlWriter.WriteStartElement("title")
    MyXmlWriter.WriteString("Professional ADO.NET Programming")
    'End the title Element
    MyXmlWriter.WriteEndElement()
    'End the titles Element
    MyXmlWriter.WriteEndElement()
    'End the Document
    MyXmlWriter.WriteEndDocument()

    'Now spit the stream into the file
    MyXmlWriter.Flush()

  Catch Xmle As XmlException
    'Handle the XML Exception

  Catch IOe As IOException
    'Handle the I/O Exception

  Finally
    'Clean-up
    WriteStream.Close()

  End Try
End Sub
```

When executed, the above code will result in XML like this:

```
<?xml version="1.0" encoding="utf-8" ?>
<!-- This is a sample Title XML -->
<titles>
  <title>
    <title>Professional ADO.NET Programming</title>
  </title>
</titles>
```

It's all pretty simple really. We can also write attributes, whitespace, and processing instructions using similar techniques – the details are in the .NET documentation.

Document Object Model

Under this processing model, an entire XML Document is loaded into memory and represented in a hierarchical structure. The XML DOM is conceptually similar to the HTML DOM, which you may have already worked with. In both cases the document is represented as objects and properties rather than a sequence of tags.

Because this approach loads the entire document into memory, it makes finding any given node and reordering elements in an XML Document fairly easy. The downside of this approach is that unless the XML document is small, the model consumes a significant amount of memory. As the size of the XML document grows, it can easily exhaust the available memory of the computer.

Let's consider the task we did in the Stream Oriented XML I/O section once again. We need to access the price from the titles XML. Here is how to do it using the DOM model:

```
Sub Main()
   Dim XmlDom As New XmlDocument()
   Dim price As String

   Try

      XmlDom.Load("Titles.xml")
      'Access the price
      price = XmlDom.SelectSingleNode _
            ("titles/title[@isbn='186100527X']/price ").InnerText()
      Console.WriteLine(price)

   Catch Xmle As XmlException
      'Handle the XML Exception

   Catch IOe As IOException
      'Handle the I/O Exception

   Finally
      'Clean-up
      XmlDom = Nothing
      Console.ReadLine()

   End Try

End Sub
```

Here is what we do. We load the entire titles XML file into memory for processing using the load method. We then pass some **XPath** to the SelectSingleNode method of the DOM document, specifying that we want to access the first occurrence of a price node where its parent title node has an ISBN attribute equal to 186100527X. The method returns a node that matches the expression and we access the value via the InnerText property. We will see more on XPath in the next section.

As we have seen from the above example, .NET offers a simple interface that is familiar to experienced DOM developers for manipulating XML. But under the hood DOM is built on the `XmlReader` to load the document!

In summary, the .NET implementations of XML I/O make it easy to work with XML data. But remember to leverage the innovative pull model in your applications wherever you can to gain performance!

XPath

Officially known as the XML Path Language, **XPath** expresses queries that search, locate, and filter the elements and text of XML documents. XPath can also manipulate strings and numbers. For example, to access the price node in the previous example we have used a hierarchical path like that below:

```
price = XmlDom.SelectSingleNode("titles/title/price").InnerText()
```

The string pattern `titles/title/price` is nothing but an XPath expression.

In .NET XPath could be used to navigate the XML Documents in two ways:

1. Traditional DOM – The most common direct use of XPath is the DOM Document's `SelectSingleNode` and `SelectNodes` methods. Each of these methods requires an XPath parameter. `SelectSingleNode` returns the first node matching the XPath statement, while `SelectNodes` returns an `XmlNodeList` containing all matching nodes.

2. `XPathNavigator` – This is an abstract class that models navigating a tree of nodes. If you don't want to deal with the XPath expressions by yourself, then you have to use this class. You can find this class in the `System.Xml.XPath` namespace. Not only does the XPathNavigator class encapsulate XPath 1.0, it also provides an optimized in-memory tree for navigation. `XPathNavigator` provides methods like `MoveToRoot`, `MoveToFirstChild` etc. that make it easy to navigate the XML Document.

So the .NET Framework supports XPath 1.0 in the above two models to navigate the XML Documents.

Transformations

XSLT (Extensible Stylesheet Language Transformation) provides a way to easily convert XML to another format, like HTML.

> You can find more on XSLT 1.0 specifications at **www.w3.org/TR/XSLT.**

In .NET, the `XslTransform` class manages XSLT 1.0 transformations. You can find this class in the `System.Xml.Xsl` namespace. The `Transform` function will transform an XML Document loaded into an `XPathNavigator` based on a pre-defined stylesheet. The `XslTransform` class supports multiple output types such as `XmlReader`, `XmlWriter`, `TextWriter`, and `Stream`.

Schemas

XSD Schemas are a critical part of the XML suite of standards because of its omnipresence. You feel the need of schemas when you work with applications that either emit language mappings or need dynamic type information, or when you need to validate XML Documents.

> The specification for XML schemas is available online. Visit
> http://www.w3.org/TR/xmlschema-1/ for Schemas for Structures and
> http://www.w3.org/TR/xmlschema-2/ for Data types.

With the System.Xml.Schema namespace, .NET provides a type-safe model. In addition to that, the schemas are presented in the DOM model in .NET, so the traversal is really made easy. One important class that you most likely are going to use from the System.Xml.Schema namespace is the XmlSchema class. Using this class, you can programmatically generate schema documents and validate XML Documents against them.

Since we deal with Schemas in everyday .NET life, let us consider a small example on how to validate an XML Document against a dynamically generated schema.

Say for example you need to validate an element called price, which is supposed to be a decimal by definition. You can generate the required XSD schema using the XmlSchema class as shown below:

```
Dim Xs As New XmlSchema()
Dim ElementPrice As New XmlSchemaElement()

ElementPrice.Name = "price"
ElementPrice.SchemaTypeName = New XmlQualifiedName("decimal",
"http://www.w3.org/2001/XMLSchema")
Xs.Items.Add(ElementPrice)
```

Now, with the above code, you have built an XSD document that looks like this:

```
<xs:schema xmlns:xs="http://www.w3.org/2001/XMLSchema">
    <xs:element name="price" type="xs:decimal" />
</xs:schema>
```

Sounds cool right? Wait, there is more. You can even compile the schema using the compile method of the XmlSchema class. By compiling the schema document you are not only making sure that you have built a valid schema document, but can also gain better performance while parsing the XML Documents against this schema.

XML Serialization

XML serialization converts (serializes) the public fields and properties, parameters, and return values of methods into an XML stream that conforms to a specific XML Schema definition language (XSD) document. Why do we need it? The serialization process bridges the gap between the CLR types and the XML types.

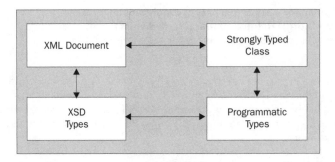

> **The XML type system is based on XSD types, while the CLR type system is based on programmatic types.**

Through the XML serialization one can serialize strongly typed classes with public properties and fields to an XML document to save it as a file or to transmit over the wire. The process if obtaining classes from the serialized XML streams is called **Deserialization**

.NET provides base classes that are needed for the serialization and deserialization process in the namespace System.Xml.Serialization. If you are thinking of XML Serialization, the class that you cannot miss in this namespace is XmlSerializer. This class provides two important methods, Serialize and Deserialize. The Serialize method generates XML streams for objects and the Deserialize method generates classes from XML streams.

Apart from the base classes that are needed for the Serialization process, the System.Xml.Serialziation namespace also provides attributes to control the XML serialization process at a granular level.

.NET leverages the Serialization and Deserialization processes heavily in two areas: Remoting and Web Services. In Remoting, CLR types are serialized into XSD types, and XSD types are deserialized into CLR types. However, in Web Services, the serialization process generates types that are SOAP 1.1-conformant.

XML Summary

In this section we have seen how the .NET Framework supports different processing models for XML Documents. We have learned that .NET's new Pull Model yields better performance when compared to the DOM or the SAX Push Model. We have also seen how the .NET Framework supports XML-related technologies such as XPath, XSL, and XSLT.

As you can imagine by this time, Schemas and Serialization are the most important XML-related technology members that are deeply integrated into .NET Framework.

Flat-File Data in .NET

Over time, application-level I/O has changed dramatically. Now we are talking about exchanging application data using XML Documents over the Internet using Web Services technology. But there is one format of data that we are bound to see if we are working with data – Flat Files. Even today, Flat Files are heavily used to import and export data, such as loading a database with a csv file!

In this section let's see how the .NET Framework supports Flat-File data management.

.NET provides the System.IO namespace to handle all file-related data manipulations.

A flat file can be viewed as a sequence of bytes. The System.IO namespace defines an abstract base class, Stream, that provides a sequence of bytes of data from files. Having said that, streams can be classified into three categories:

1. Sequence of bytes – System.IO namespace defines a set of classes, StreamReader/StreamWriter, that provide methods to handle this type of data

2. Sequence of characters – System.IO namespace defines a set of classes, TextReader/TextWriter, that provide methods to handle this type of data

3. Sequence of primitive data – System.IO namespace defines a class, BinaryReader/BinaryWriter, that provide a sequence of primitive data such as binary data and character data with specific encoding

You need to choose your reader/writer classes according to the file type.

> Use **StreamReader** for reading lines of information from a standard text file as it defaults to UTF-8 encoding.

Using Streams with .NET

With this background, let's take a look at an example on how to copy a text file to another text file using the .NET Framework.

Since the text files are nothing but a sequence of bytes, we need two streams to handle the data flow:

```
Stream readStream, writeStream;
```
Now open the input file to create an input stream:

```
readStream = File.Open
    (@"c:\in.txt", FileMode.Open, FileAccess.Read, FileShare.Read);
```

And open the output file to write the contents to create the output-stream:

```
writeStream = File.Open
                    (@"c:\out.txt", FileMode.Create, FileAccess.Write);
```

As we are handling two text files here, we need a `StreamReader` and a `StreamWriter` class to read from and write to text files respectively:

```
reader = new StreamReader(readStream);
writer = new StreamWriter(writeStream);
```

Now, we are all set. All that we need to do is to read the contents of the input file and write it into the output file. This can be done as shown below:

```
writer.Write(reader.ReadToEnd());
```

Then close the reader and writer to free up the resources:

```
reader.Close();
writer.Close();
```

Of course the above code is a much-simplified version. When you implement this kind of functionality, you need to provide exception handling to catch exceptions such as `IOException` and `OutOfMemoryException`.

Summary

We started this chapter by looking at ADO.NET and its architectural aspects. We have learned that the classes provided in ADO.NET can be classified into Data Providers, Data Consumers and Data-Bound Control classes. ADO.NET simplifies the way we pass data between tiers. For the first time Microsoft has separated the SQL Data Provider from the generic OLE DB provider. So the SQL Data Provider in .NET comes with highly optimized communication protocols for SQL Server (such as TDS – Tabular Data Streams).

We have looked at the key classes within the `System.Xml` namespace in this chapter. XML is important in .NET because you will see a strong coupling between ADO.NET and XML, Web Services and XML, and Remoting and XML. It is not an overstatement to say that almost all of the .NET technologies are built around XML and related technologies.

The .NET Framework comes in very handy not only when handling sophisticated relational data and semi-structured XML data, but also when handling raw file I/O. In this chapter we have seen how to handle a text file using the .NET Framework.

Finally, handling data in .NET Framework is not only efficient for building high-performance, enterprise-ready applications, but is also simple and intuitive.

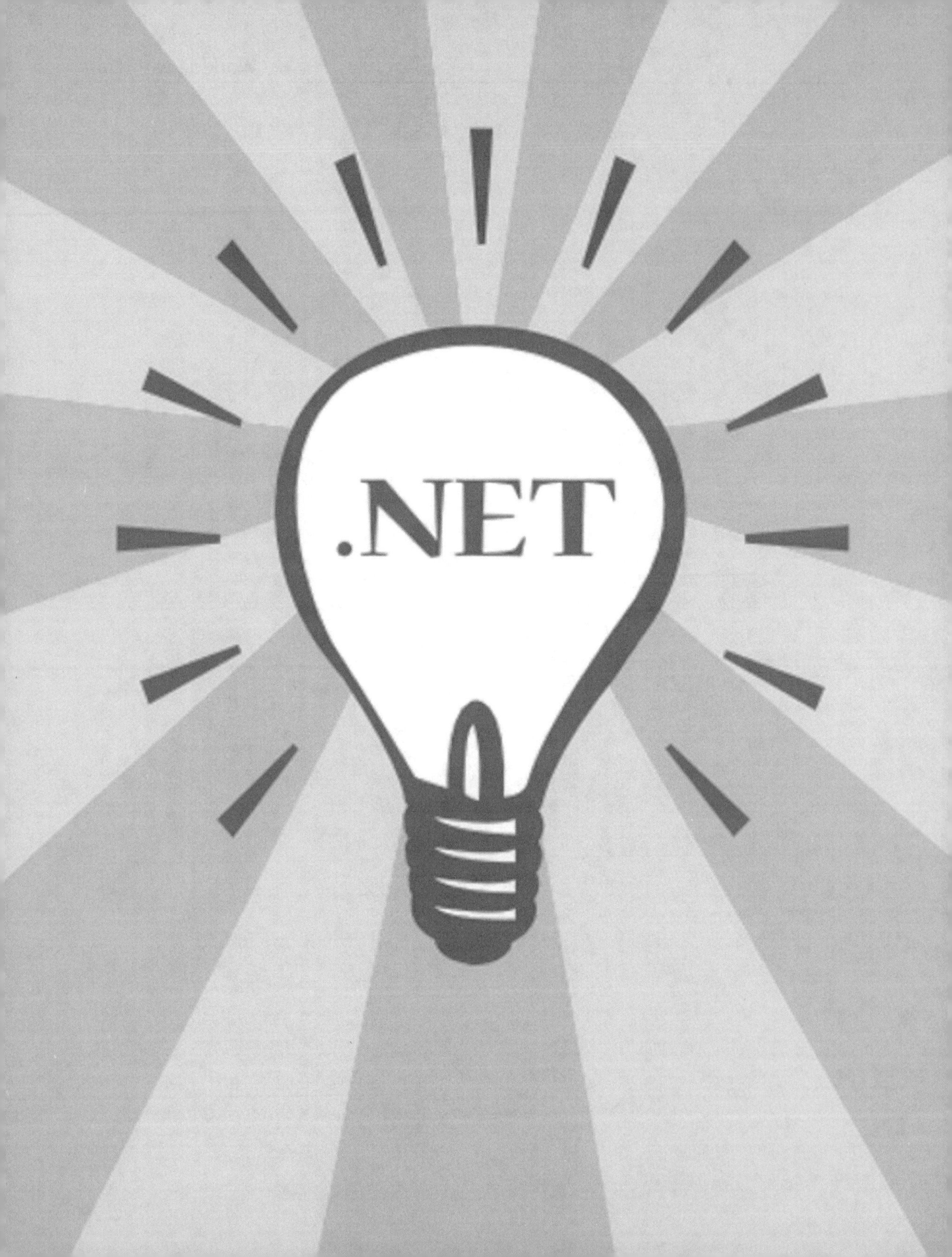
.NET

6

Legacy and Enterprise Systems

Developing enterprise-level applications has traditionally taken a significant amount of time, largely spent on developing infrastructure such as:

❑ Administrative features

❑ Client-server capabilities

❑ Communications libraries

❑ The ability to run as a Windows service

❑ Logging and performance measurement

❑ Object pooling and thread management

❑ Transaction handling across multiple data sources

Thrown in among this potpourri of tasks is usually a requirement to interface with legacy software and systems. Formerly, no developer has wanted to be the one assigned to get the new system talking with the old one.

The .NET Framework has been designed to let developers worry about their applications' business-related features, and let the framework worry about the things listed above. This includes interoperability with legacy APIs and COM components.

This chapter presents an overview of the features .NET provides for legacy and enterprise development.

We will start by looking at accessing old-style DLLs, such as those found in the Windows API, using the `System.Runtime.InteropServices` namespace. This namespace provides a feature called 'platform invoke', which enables .NET applications to access old, non-COM DLLs.

We will then look at interoperating with COM DLLs. We will see how to 'wrap' COM components so that they can be used in .NET applications, and how to wrap .NET libraries so that they can be treated as COM components. We will also look at COM marshaling, error handling, and performance in .NET.

As we will see, a lot of thought and work has gone into making .NET interface with legacy systems smoothly and easily. .NET is far better at interoperating with legacy systems than its predecessors, but it still has its complications. Over the course of the chapter we will discuss some of those complications and how to overcome them.

In addition to legacy access, the .NET Framework also provides a straightforward mechanism for accessing and utilizing COM+ services, also known as Enterprise Services. Enterprise Services are made available through the `System.EnterpriseServices` namespace. Using this namespace, components created with .NET can participate in COM+ applications and take advantage of services such as transaction management, object pooling, and just-in-time activation. .NET components can also utilize the role-based security used in COM+. These .NET components, which are derived from the `System.EnterpriseServices.ServicedComponent` class, are called Serviced Components. From the perspective of a .NET class, a serviced component is no different from any other .NET class. Likewise, COM components view serviced components hosted in a COM+ application as just another COM component. We will discuss how this happens later in the chapter.

Additionally we will discuss .NET Remoting. The .NET remoting system is an architecture designed to simplify communication between objects living in different application domains, whether on the same computer or not, and between different contexts, whether in the same application domain or not. You can even use remoting to enable your application to interface and communicate with applications running on different operating systems. Remoting is an abstract approach to inter-process communication, and provides a number of services such as activation and lifetime control, as well as security in the form of encoding and decoding communication messages.

This chapter discusses all of the above technologies and provides examples showing how to get started using them.

Accessing Legacy Functions

Before the era of COM/DCOM, DLLs ruled the world and DLLs exposed functions. DLLs were developed by third-party vendors and in-house, and included in the Win32 API. The Win32 API is still useful because even though the .NET Framework is thorough, it doesn't do everything. There are some instances where we need to drop below the .NET Framework and access Win32 functions. We may also at times need to call functions from old third-party DLLs.

The `System.Runtime.InteropServices` namespace exposes the `DllImportAttribute` class to provide access to old-style DLLs. This class allows the functions exposed by an unmanaged (non-.NET) DLL to be a called by a managed (.NET) application. `DllImportAttribute` identifies a method of a .NET class that corresponds to a legacy function exposed by unmanaged code. The method we specify becomes a member of the class we create it in, but we do not specify an implementation – calls are routed straight to the DLL.

The following snippet creates a static method called `GetCurrentThreadId` method, which routes calls to the `GetCurrentThreadId` function in `Kernel32.dll`:

In C#:

```
[DllImport("Kernel32.dll")]
public static extern int GetCurrentThreadId();
```

A reason to do this is that .NET's `Thread` class does not provide access to a thread's ID. The `DllImport` attribute provides a conduit to platform invoke, which in turn provides a mechanism where managed code can call unmanaged functions. The criteria required to perform this task are:

❑ The `DllImport` attribute must apply to a method identified as `static extern` in C# or simply `Shared` in VB.NET. It doesn't matter whether the method is `public`, `private`, or `protected`.

❑ The return and parameter types declared must match the return and parameter types in the underlying legacy function.

VB.NET can also take advantage of `DllImportAttribute` or it can use `Declare` in conjunction with the `Lib` keyword. This matches the VB 6 method of accessing DLLs more closely. Here is an example of legacy function interoperability using `Declare`:

```
Declare Function GetCurrentThreadId Lib "Kernel32.dll" () As Integer
```

Mapping between managed and unmanaged types is not quantum physics. The MSDN article *Platform Invoke Data Types* provides each specific mapping. If you have MSDN installed, you can access the article here:

ms-help://MS.VSCC/MS.MSDNVS/cpguide/html/cpconplatforminvokedatatypes.htm

The .NET type `IntPtr` maps to a C-style `void*` or Windows `HANDLE` type. Here is a C# method that uses this type to access `CloseHandle`, the function used to close Windows handles:

```
[DllImport("Kernel32.dll")]
public static extern bool CloseHandle(IntPtr handle);
```

The reason we use `IntPtr` and not a data type fixed at 32-bits is so this field can expand. Right now there is a tremendous amount of Win32 code using 32-bit handles, but in the future Win64 will become more common. The intermediate language provided by .NET enables `IntPtr` to use 32-bit or 64-bit handles, depending on the platform on which the code is running.

Accessing Legacy Structures

When we're only using simple types, calling old DLLs in .NET is easy. Moving structures and buffers from managed to unmanaged space and vice-versa is more complicated.

> **Passing structures to legacy DLLs requires the use of pointers. .NET considers
> pointers 'unsafe'. This means that they cannot be used in VB.NET. One way to work
> around this would be to write a wrapper for the DLL function in C#, and call that
> from a VB.NET application.**

We will look at the `QueryServiceConfig` function found in `Advapi32.dll` on Windows NT, 2000, and XP as an example. This function takes as a parameter a pointer to a QUERY_SERVICE_CONFIG structure defined in the `Winsvc.h` header file:

```
typedef struct _QUERY_SERVICE_CONFIG { // qsc
    DWORD dwServiceType;
    DWORD dwStartType;
    DWORD dwErrorControl;
    LPTSTR lpBinaryPathName;
    LPTSTR lpLoadOrderGroup;
    DWORD dwTagId;
    LPTSTR lpDependencies;
    LPTSTR lpServiceStartName;
    LPTSTR lpDisplayName;
} QUERY_SERVICE_CONFIG, LPQUERY_SERVICE_CONFIG;
```

Why would a managed application need to access the `QueryServiceConfig` Windows function? Because .NET does not provide a way to change a Windows service's start type (automatic, manual, or disabled) without completely reinstalling the service. Using the Windows `QueryServiceConfig` Windows function it is possible to query the start type and then call the `ChangeServiceConfig` function to change the value of a service's start type.

Creating a Managed Structure

The first step in the process of passing a structure from managed code to unmanaged code is to declare a managed class or structure that mirrors the Windows legacy structure. This managed type will also be called QUERY_SERVICE_CONFIG and its layout will parallel its Windows counterpart. The names of this type's members are not important – values are passed based on the member's *order*, not name. However, it makes the program easier to read if we use the same names:

```
[StructLayout(LayoutKind.Sequential, CharSet=CharSet.Unicode)]
public class QUERY_SERVICE_CONFIG
{
    public uint serviceType = 0xFFFFFFFF;
    public uint startType = 0xFFFFFFFF;
    public uint errorControlType = 0xFFFFFFFF;
    public string lpBinaryPathName = null;
    public string lpLoadOrderGroup = null;
    public uint dwTagId = 0;
    public string lpDependencies = null;
    public string lpServiceStartName = null;
    public string lpDisplayName = null;
}
```

Notice the use of the `StructLayout` attribute before the class declaration. This attribute ensures that the `QUERY_SERVICE_CONFIG` class is laid out sequentially, in the same way as the original Windows structure. Setting the `CharSet` property to `CharSet.Unicode` means that the Unicode version of the `QUERY_SERVICE_CONFIG` structure will be used. Windows NT, 2000, and XP use Unicode internally. Since only these versions of Windows include the DLL we'll be using we can safely use Unicode here.

Creating the Method and Configuring for 'Unsafe' Code

Before declaring the `QueryServiceConfig` method, we need to do some project configuration. The `QueryServiceConfig` function takes as a parameter a `void*` (generic pointer) corresponding to the `QUERY_SERVICE_CONFIG` structure. .NET considers pointers to be unsafe, which means we need to set this project to use unsafe code. We do this by right-clicking on the project in the Solution Explorer, selecting **Properties** and then opening the **Configuration Properties** folder. From here we select the Build sub-folder and set the option **Allow unsafe code blocks** to true.

When the `QueryServiceConfig` method is declared it must also be specified as `unsafe`:

```
[DllImport("Advapi32.dll", CharSet=CharSet.Unicode, SetLastError=true)]
unsafe private static extern
    bool QueryServiceConfig(IntPtr hService,
    void *pServiceConfig, // QUERY_SERVICE_CONFIG pointer
    int lBufSize,
    int *pBytesNeeded);
```

The `DllImport` attribute specifies that the underlying `QueryServiceConfig` method is implemented in `Advapi32.dll`.

Setting the `SetLastError` property to `true` indicates that this function will set the Windows per-thread error variable. If anything goes wrong with the call, we can then get information about the error from the `System.Runtime.InteropServices.Marshal.GetLastWin32Error` method.

Using the Method

To use the `QueryServiceConfig` method we need to:

1. Call the unmanaged function `OpenSCManager` to retrieve a handle to the Windows Service Control manager.

2. Call the unmanaged function `OpenService`, passing in a handle to the Service Control manager. This function returns a handle to the specific service to be accessed.

3. Call `QueryServiceConfig`, passing in the service-specific handle and a zero-length buffer. The function will return the size of the buffer required to hold the `QUERY_SERVICE_CONFIG` structure.

4. Allocate the buffer required to hold the `QUERY_SERVICE_CONFIG` structure.

5. Call `QueryServiceConfig`, passing in the service-specific handle and the buffer allocated in Step 4.

6. Call the unmanaged function `CloseServiceHandle` in order to close the service-specific handle.

7. Call the unmanaged function, `CloseServiceHandle`, in order to close the handle to the service control manager.

Creating the .NET methods for Steps 1, 2, 6, and 7 is a two-minute task (we have seen how to access simple unmanaged functions above). The difficult bit is allocating the buffer from an unmanaged heap, calling `QueryServiceConfig`, and moving the contents of the unmanaged buffer into the `QUERY_SERVICE_CONFIG` .NET class. Here are Steps 1 – 5 in more detail:

❏ Call `QueryServiceConfig` passing in the service-specific handle and a zero-length buffer. Calling the function in this way will write the size of the buffer required to hold the `QUERY_SERVICE_CONFIG` structure to the `size` parameter:

```
int size;
bool result;
result = QueryServiceConfig(serviceHandle, null, 0, &size);
```

❏ Allocate the buffer required to hold the `QUERY_SERVICE_CONFIG` structure. This buffer can be allocated using the `Marshal` class's `AllocCoTaskMem` method. This method allocates memory from an unmanaged source – the unmanaged heap used by COM applications. The buffer corresponds to an unmanaged `void*`, so we use a .NET `IntPtr`:

```
IntPtr buffer = Marshal.AllocCoTaskMem(size);
```

> Remember that **AllocCoTaskMem** allocates unmanaged memory. We need to manually clean this memory up because it is out of the garbage collector's reach. Use the **Marshal** class's **FreeCoTaskMem** method to free this memory.

❏ Call `QueryServiceConfig` passing in the service-specific handle and then the unmanaged buffer we just allocated:

```
result = QueryServiceConfig(serviceHandle, buffer.ToPointer(), size, &size);
```

❏ Create an instance of the `QUERY_SERVICE_CONFIG` class:

```
QUERY_SERVICE_CONFIG serviceConfig = new QUERY_SERVICE_CONFIG();
```

❏ Call the `Marshal` class's `PtrToStructure` method, which maps the unmanaged buffer into the managed class of type `QUERY_SERVICE_CONFIG`. This step is significant – it represents the transition from unmanaged to managed code courtesy of the `StructLayout` attribute associated with the `QUERY_SERVICE_CONFIG` class:

```
Marshal.PtrToStructure(buffer, serviceConfig);
```

❑ Call `Marshal.FreeCoTaskMem` in order to free the unmanaged buffer:

```
Marshal.FreeCoTaskMem(buffer);
```

Once `QueryServiceConfig` retrieves the service-related information we can modify it and then call the `ChangeServiceConfig` legacy function to update the service configuration. We could not do this using .NET alone.

The code required to retrieve the legacy `QUERY_SERVICE_CONFIG` structure takes a lot more Win32 knowledge than it does .NET knowledge. This code in its entirety is found in the `SWPLegacyAPI` class library in the code download. The following snippet of the code demonstrates moving an unmanaged buffer into a managed type, leaving out the trivial stage of opening and closing the service-related handles:

```
unsafe public static int
    SWPQueryServiceConfig(string serviceName,
    out QUERY_SERVICE_CONFIG serviceConfig)
{

    serviceConfig = null;
    IntPtr scmHandle = new IntPtr(0);
    IntPtr serviceHandle = new IntPtr(0);
    IntPtr buffer = new IntPtr(0);
    bool result;

    try
    {
        // Open scmHandle using OpenSCManager
        // and open serviceHandle using OpenService here
        int lastError;
        int size = 0;

        result = QueryServiceConfig(serviceHandle, null, 0, &size);
        if (!result)
        {
            lastError = Marshal.GetLastWin32Error();
            if ((int)WinError.ERROR_INSUFFICIENT_BUFFER == lastError)
            {
                buffer = Marshal.AllocCoTaskMem(size);
                if (null == buffer.ToPointer())
                {
                    return Marshal.GetLastWin32Error();
                }

                result = QueryServiceConfig(serviceHandle,
                            buffer.ToPointer(), size, &size);
                if (!result)
                {
                    return Marshal.GetLastWin32Error();
                }

                serviceConfig = new QUERY_SERVICE_CONFIG();
                Marshal.PtrToStructure(buffer, serviceConfig);
            }
```

```
            else
            {
                return lastError;
            }
        }
    }

    finally
    {
        // serviceHandle and scmHandle handles closed here using
        // CloseServiceHandle
        if (null != buffer.ToPointer())
        {
            Marshal.FreeCoTaskMem(buffer);
        }
    }

    return 0;
}
```

Clearly the above code is not trivial, but it is far easier than pre-.NET approaches to accessing legacy code.

COM Interoperability

There are literally millions of lines of COM code used in production systems around the world. For this reason Microsoft put great effort into .NET-to-COM and COM-to-.NET interoperability. The result of this effort is great simplicity in developing .NET applications that can access COM components or be accessed by COM components.

In many respects working with COM objects in C# or VB.NET is easier than working with COM objects using Visual C++ 6.0, Visual Basic 6.0, and legacy scripting languages such as VBScript or JScript. The following code snippet, from WXCOMInteropDemo in the code download, demonstrates this. Here we will use C# to access an ADO Connection object:

```
ADODB.Connection conn = new ADODB.ConnectionClass();

conn.Open("PROVIDER=sqloledb;DATABASE=NorthWind;UID=sa;PWD=sa", null,
                    null, (int)ADODB.ConnectModeEnum.adModeUnknown);
// work with connection here and access data
conn.Close();
```

The code above is very similar to code dealing with COM objects in non-.NET languages, and demonstrates how readable .NET code that accesses COM objects is. Additionally if you're using Visual Studio .NET, setting up a project to access such code is a matter of few quick steps (from the **Project** menu select **Add Reference**, and then from the dialog displayed, select the reference to **adodb** under the **.NET** tab). This step means our project now references an assembly that is typically found in the following location:

```
C:\Program Files\Microsoft.NET\Primary Interop Assemblies\adodb.dll
```

`adodb.dll` is not the COM DLL used to access ADO – the actual COM DLL is typically `msado15.dll` – `adodb.dll` is runtime-callable wrapper: an assembly that bridges the managed world of .NET and the unmanaged world of COM.

A runtime-callable wrapper provides the necessary information for the managed environment of .NET to understand the members (methods, properties, events, and so on) that are encapsulated in the COM object. This wrapper is built using the COM server's type library. A COM Server (EXE or DLL) is generally associated with a type library that is either included directly in the COM server or located in a separate file (a TLB file). A type library describes what the COM server implements, although not as thoroughly as a .NET assembly's metadata.

To build the runtime-callable wrapper we can use the `TlbImp.exe` utility that comes with the .NET SDK, or Visual Studio .NET's built-in facilities for effortless creation of runtime-callable wrappers. This step was not required in the ADO example above because `adodb.dll` is a ready-made runtime-callable wrapper for ADO that ships with the .NET Framework. The .NET Framework comes with runtime-callable wrappers for a few other key COM libraries.

Let's look at how Visual Studio .NET can generate a runtime-callable wrapper. To add a reference to a COM component, select **Project | Add Reference** and then click the **COM** tab:

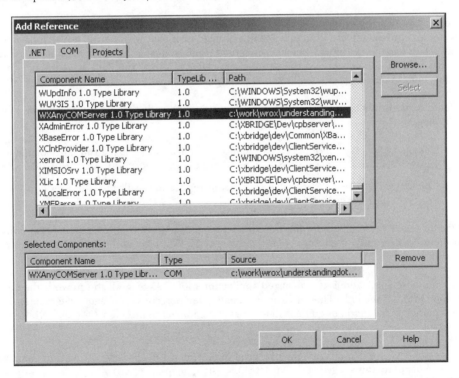

In the previous screenshot we have selected the **WXAnyCOMServer** (a COM DLL developed for this chapter). After **OK** is clicked, a runtime-callable wrapper is created named `Interop.WXAnyCOMServer.dll` and placed in the project's `Obj` folder. A reference is automatically added to the project.

The following screenshot shows the WXAnyCOMServer COM server referenced by the WXCOMInteropDemo project, as if it were a .NET assembly:

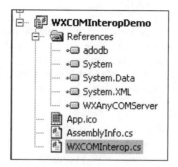

COM Interoperability Performance

If .NET-COM interoperability is so easy, what is the catch? Clearly there will be performance overheads in transition environments (managed .NET applications to/from unmanaged COM applications).

An overhead is incurred every time we call the COM component. A single method that computes the payroll for an entire company would incur the overhead once, but we'd hardly notice it because it was so small relative to the execution time of the method itself. Repeated calls to a method, or using a COM object that exposes zillions of properties (sometimes called a "chatty interface"), would incur a noticeable penalty.

In order to demonstrate the cost of COM interoperability, the code that can be downloaded includes the following:

❑ Managed WXCOMInteropDemo.exe (console application) calls the runtime-callable wrapper, interop.wxanycomserver.dll, which calls the WXAnyCOMServer.dll COM server.

❑ Unmanaged WXAnyCOMClient.exe (console application) calls the COM server, WXAnyCOMServer.dll COM.

Both the managed (WXCOMInteropDemo.exe) and unmanaged (WXAnyCOMClient.exe) console applications create a million instances of the WXChatty COM object and then call ten methods for this object.

When I ran these applications, the managed application took 5.25 seconds to run while the unmanaged application took 4.7 seconds. There was approximately ten percent performance degradation. This is hardly a perfect benchmark, but it does demonstrate the impact of mixing COM and .NET – significant, but workable.

The same projects also demonstrate the overhead in passing a 100-character string from managed code (a managed heap) to unmanaged code (an IMalloc–style heap).

When I tried this, passing the string in the unmanaged arena (WXAnyCOMClient project) took 4.7 seconds while passing the string in the managed arena (WXCOMInteropDemo project) took 5.4 seconds – giving a performance differential between the managed and unmanaged scenarios of twelve percent.

Error Handling

Error handling in COM is accomplished by COM methods returning HRESULTs – specific error values describing the error. Handling these errors in COM requires interrogation of the HRESULTs and calling specific code based on the type of error that has occurred. The .NET Framework takes a different approach by using exception handling as the standard mechanism for error handling. These two different error-handling methods present a unique circumstance when it comes to COM interoperability.

The Exception class in .NET exposes an HResult property for use when developing .NET classes targeting COM interoperability. The HResult property of the Exception class is defined as follows:

In VB.NET:

```
Protected Property HResult As Integer
```

In C#:

```
protected int HResult {get; set;}
```

In most cases, the .NET Framework handles this interoperability challenge automatically. When we are accessing a COM component from a .NET client, the Framework converts COM HRESULTs into .NET exceptions – with the COM HRESULT value being passed as the HResult property of the exception.

When we are accessing a .NET component from a COM client, HRESULTs are returned when errors occur in the .NET component's execution. For this to work, we must set the HRESULT property on our exception object – otherwise .NET will not know the HResult value to return. Here is an example of how we'd set up our .NET component to do this:

```
public class WXIForgot : Exception
{
    public WXIForgot()
    {
        const int E_OUTOFMEMORY = unchecked((int)0x8007000E);
        this.HResult = E_OUTOFMEMORY;
    }
}
```

Now that we've seen how a .NET component can throw COM style errors back to a COM client, how do we react to COM errors in our .NET clients? Fortunately there is a way to generate a specific exception given a specific HRESULT. The Marshal class provides the ThrowExceptionForHR method. This method throws specific exceptions based on the HRESULT value passed to it as a parameter. For example, the following code snippet ends up throwing an exception of type NotImplementedException, given that the HRESULT passed to ThrowExceptionForHR was E_NOTIMPL (represented numerically as 0x80004001):

```
Marshal.ThrowExceptionForHR(unchecked((int)0x80004001));
```

The HRESULT values that cause the ThrowExceptionForHR method to generate these exceptions can correspond to the familiar HRESULT values found in winerror.h or to new HRESULT values generated by the core .NET assemblies. Some of these HRESULT values and their corresponding exceptions are as follows:

❑ E_NOTIMPL – causes `ThrowExceptionForHR` to throw `NotImplementedException`

❑ COR_E_NOTSUPPORTED – causes `ThrowExceptionForHR` to throw a `NotSupportedException` exception

❑ COR_E_NULLREFERENCE, E_POINTER – causes `ThrowExceptionForHR` to throw a `NullReferenceException` exception

❑ COR_E_OUTOFMEMORY, E_OUTOFMEMORY – causes `ThrowExceptionForHR` to throw an `OutOfMemoryException` exception

For a complete mapping of HRESULT values to the corresponding .NET exception, see the MSDN article entitled, *HRESULTs and Exceptions* found at:

ms-help://MS.VSCC/MS.MSDNVS/cpguide/html/cpconhresultsexceptions.htm

The mapping between HRESULT and exception provided by the previous link is certainly not complete. If a particular HRESULT does not correspond to a specific exception then user-defined exception classes can be created that take advantage of the HResult property of the Exception base class, as demonstrated in the previous code snippet.

Unmanaged Code Accessing .NET Assemblies

We have already seen how a COM type library is used to generate metadata in a runtime-callable wrapper. A .NET assembly can also be used to generate a type library. To get .NET assemblies ready to be accessed from COM applications we need to:

❑ Create and register the type library using the `RegAsm.exe` utility and its `/tlb` option. This step also registers the assembly as a COM server. In order for a COM client to use type libraries, the type libraries must be registered (as is demonstrated below in the following excerpt from the `WXToCOM.bat` batch file):

RegAsm /tlb WXAnyDotClassLibrary\bin\Debug\WXAnyDotClassLibrary.dll

While this step acheives our goal of exposing our .NET assembly as a COM server, there is one notable limitation. By default the various members of our assembly are not included in the created COM type library. This does not prevent us from calling those members from COM clients, but it does mean that we need to know about those members first. To get around this situation all we need to do is add some COM interoperability-specific directives into our .NET assembly code:

❑ Specify the `System.Runtime.InteropServices` namespace's `ClassInterface` attribute for each class, structure, or interface to be exported for access by COM clients. An example of this is as follows for the managed `WXClassLibrary`:

```
[ClassInterface(ClassInterfaceType.AutoDual)]

public class WXManagedClass

{

}
```

`WXManagedClass` is an example of a managed class that is to be exposed as a COM object. This class is implemented as follows, where the return values of each method are not of type `HRESULT`. Note that each method is specified as `public` so it can be exposed by a COM method:

```csharp
using System;
using System.Runtime.InteropServices;

namespace WXClassLib
{
    [ClassInterface(ClassInterfaceType.AutoDual)]
    public class WXManagedClass
    {
        public void WXNoReturnValue()
        {
        }

        public int WXReturnValueInt()
        {
            return 3261;
        }

        public string WXReturnValueString()
        {
            return "You've gotta have Faith";
        }
    }
}
```

The type library generated from the previous code (via `RegAsm` / `tlb`) can be viewed like any type library using Visual Studio .NET's **OLE/COM Object Viewer** found under the **Tools** menu. The **File** menu of this utility enables us to view type libraries and save them as IDL. An excerpt from the IDL associated with the `WXManagedClass` is as follows:

```
interface _WXManagedClass : IDispatch {
    [id(00000000), propget,
      custom(54FC8F55-38DE-4703-9C4E-250351302B1C, 1)]
    HRESULT ToString([out, retval] BSTR* pRetVal);
    [id(0x60020001)]
    HRESULT Equals([in] VARIANT obj,
                   [out, retval] VARIANT_BOOL* pRetVal);
    [id(0x60020002)]
    HRESULT GetHashCode([out, retval] long* pRetVal);
    [id(0x60020003)]
    HRESULT GetType([out, retval] _Type** pRetVal);
    [id(0x60020004)]
    HRESULT WXNoReturnValue();
    [id(0x60020005)]
    HRESULT WXReturnValueInt([out, retval] long* pRetVal);
    [id(0x60020006)]
    HRESULT WXReturnValueString([out, retval] BSTR* pRetVal);
};
```

187

Notice that the methods inherited from `System.Object` (`Equals`, `ToString`, and so on) are also exposed via IDL in addition to the methods explicit to the `WXManagedClass`. Notice that each method returns `HRESULT` and that the method's original return value is now the last parameter of the method.

To understand this, recognize that the C# prototype, `public string WXReturnValueString()`, became the following in IDL:

```
HRESULT WXReturnValueString([out, retval] BSTR* pRetVal);
```

We can now use our .NET assembly as we would any COM assembly. The client application is not aware that it is accessing a .NET component – to the client it is just a COM object.

Clearly the .NET to COM and COM client to managed code scenarios presented here are fairly basic. There are lots of more complicated situations that could arise with respect to marshaling to/from COM, handling apartments, and creating objects using Program IDs (`ProgID`) rather than `GUID`'s. These complicated situations are the exception and not the norm. Most developers will find that accessing COM from .NET and .NET from a COM client is a straightforward process.

Serviced Components

While the .NET Framework has introduced many new and enhanced features for enterprise development, there is continued need for the enterprise services provided by COM+ such as Transaction Support, Object Pooling, and Shared Property Management. A serviced component is the mechanism that enables context sharing between COM+ and .NET Framework classes. Using the `System.EnterpriseServices` namespace and COM+ interoperability, you can develop components that co-exist in harmony with existing COM+ components, and develop new .NET-only applications that use COM+ services.

Formerly we have used tools such as Visual Basic 6.0 to build components, and install those components in Windows 2000 Component Services (COM+ Services) or Windows NT Server 4.0's Microsoft Transaction Server (MTS) in order to use core services such as transactions, just-in-time activation, and object pooling. With .NET we are able to develop components using tools such as Visual Studio .NET and install them in Windows 2000 Component Services to gain access to those services.

Before continuing, let's review what COM+ is and what makes up a serviced component.

COM+ Services

COM+, introduced with Windows 2000, is a set of DLLs, COM interfaces, methods, and tools created to provide special development and administrative services for enterprise-level applications and the components of those applications. COM+ is one of the primary technologies used in developing enterprise-level applications for the .NET platform.

It is important to understand the true nature of COM+. Because of its name, it is easy to mistakenly think that COM+ is dependent on the COM component architecture. This is not true since the component model used is irrelevant. COM+, which is the evolution of Microsoft Transaction Server (MTS), is a services architecture, and provides complementary services for .NET components and COM components.

COM+ is automatically installed and configured as part of the Windows 2000 and Windows XP operating systems. Under Windows 2000 and Windows XP, COM+ exists as un-managed code, whereas with the introduction of Windows .NET Server, COM+ is a hybrid of managed and un-managed code in order to more tightly integrate with the .NET Framework. Future versions of COM+ may be migrated completely into 100% managed code, providing complete managed services.

Using the Component Services administrative tool we can configure component and application behavior such as transaction participation and security configuration. Other COM+ services include connection pooling, thread pooling, process isolation, and message queuing.

In addition to providing enterprise services needed for today's enterprise-class applications, COM+ Services also make it possible to create components with less code. Less code to create, test, debug, and maintain, means quicker, simpler, and more effective application development.

What is a Serviced Component?

A serviced component is a .NET class that is hosted in a COM+ application in order to take advantage of various COM+ services such as automatic transactions and object pooling. In order for a class to be hosted by COM+, it must be specially configured in the code of the class itself. The first and most basic configuration is that the class must be derived directly or indirectly from the `System.EnterpriseServices.ServicedComponent` class. This class provides the core functionality to communicate with COM+ services. Additional configuration information is provided below.

From the perspective of a .NET class, a serviced component is no different from any other .NET class. Likewise, COM components view serviced components as just another COM component.

.NET and COM+ Interoperability

Components written in .NET and hosted in a COM+ application are available to COM clients, just as if the component were created using VB 6. Although there are some special considerations when building .NET components that you plan to consume from COM clients (such as type handling), the application of these is fairly straightforward.

Any considerations for COM interoperability does not apply if the consumer of your component is also written in managed code. In other words, although COM+ is used to provide enterprise services to your components, full fidelity continues to exist between managed objects. This means that you can write type-specific code and still utilize COM+ enterprise services, so long as the client is also written in .NET.

Following is a summary of the COM+ services accessible through .NET. All of these services are accessed through the `System.EnterpriseServices` namespace, which is described later in this chapter:

❑ Automatic Transaction Processing – One of the most widely used services, enabling configuration of a class at design time to participate in a transaction at run time

❑ Bring Your Own Transaction (BYOT) – Allows components to use a preexisting Microsoft Distributed Transaction Coordinator (DTC) or Transaction Internet Protocol (TIP) transaction

- ❑ COM Transaction Integrator (COMTI) – Allows components to participate in IBM CICS and IMS system transactions

- ❑ Compensating Resource Managers (CRMs) – A CRM is a COM+ service that allows us to include non-transactional objects in a DTC transaction

- ❑ Just-In-Time-Activation (JIT) – JIT activation allows you to create an inactive, context-only object that remains inactive until the runtime creates the full object.

- ❑ Loosely Coupled Events – Provides support for late-bound events and method calls

- ❑ Object Construction – Allows us to specify initialization and construction information externally

- ❑ Object Pooling – Allows pooling pre-created objects for immediate reuse

- ❑ Private Components – Allows creation of private (sometimes called helper) components accessible to your application, but not publicly accessible

- ❑ Queued Components – Provides support for invoking and executing components asynchronously

- ❑ Role-based Security – Provides a mechanism for applying security permissions to objects and methods based on security roles

- ❑ SOAP Services – Enables us to take an existing component in COM+ and expose it as a SOAP Service

- ❑ Synchronization – Handles concurrency and synchronization support

- ❑ XA Interoperability – Enables us to access databases that support the X/Open transaction-processing model

The System.EnterpriseServices namespace provides the infrastructure for developing enterprise-level applications that participate in COM+ services. All serviced components are derived directly or indirectly from the System.EnterpriseServices.ServicedComponent class.

When building serviced components, most interaction with the System.EnterpriseServices namespace will be in the form of setting attributes related to COM+ services. While we can directly call and access the various System.EnterpriseServices classes, it is not necessary to do so in order to implement the simplest level of COM+ services support.

Configuring and Deploying Serviced Components

Now that we have established what a serviced component is, let's take a look at how to configure an existing .NET component as a serviced component, and discuss the deployment of that component.

Consider the following code:

```
using System;

namespace WXChameleonClassLib100
{
    public class WXServicedComponentABC
    {
        public int ProcessID()
        {
```

```
            return Process.GetCurrentProcess().Id;
        }
    }
}
```

In order to configure this class as a serviced component, allowing it to take advantage of the COM+ services discussed above, we must:

❑ Have the project reference the System.EnterpriseServices assembly (Project | Add Reference, then the .NET tab from the Add Reference dialog).

❑ For C# applications add using System.EnterpriseServices at the top of the source file, or for VB.NET put Imports System.EnterpriseServices at the top of source file. While this step is not mandatory, it does make accessing the types exposed by the System.EnterpriseServices namespace simpler and produces cleaner code.

❑ Derive the class to become a serviced component from the ServicedComponent base class.

With these additions, the above code now looks like this (notice the additions made in bold):

```
using System;
using System.EnterpriseServices;

namespace WXChameleonClassLib100
{
    public class WXServicedComponentABC : ServicedComponent
    {
        public int ProcessID()
        {
            return Process.GetCurrentProcess().Id;
        }
    }
}
```

The last step, which in most cases is optional, is to give the assembly a strong name. Giving an assembly a strong name is required if you wish to place the assembly in the Global Assembly Cache (GAC) – required when running a .NET assembly as a Windows Service. The GAC is where assemblies shared by multiple applications on the machine are deployed.

A strong name provides a unique way to identify an assembly and hence the assembly can be placed in the global repository (the GAC) without causing a duplicate name conflict. To provide an assembly with a strong name recall that each assembly project created under Visual Studio .NET comes with an assembly information file (AssemblyInfo.cs under C# and AssemblyInfo.vb under VB.NET). The attributes in this file support the creating of a strong named assembly. The steps required to make a strong named assembly are as follows:

❑ Run the sn.exe command-line utility as follows:

```
sn -k sgKey.snk
```

The sn utility generates a public-private key pair required by an assembly. Run in the previous context, this utility places the public-private key in a file called, sgKey.snk.

❑   Specify the key in the assembly info file (`AssemblyInfo.cs` under C# and
`AssemblyInfo.vb` under VB.NET) using the `AssemblyKeyFile` attribute:

```
[assembly: AssemblyKeyFile(@"WXChameleonClassLib100\sgKey.snk")]
```

We can also configure this information in the assembly's property pages within Visual Studio
.NET.

Building a class derived from `ServicedComponent` using Visual Studio .NET dynamically configures
the component as a serviced component on the machine on which you build the component. A serviced
component can also be installed manually, as we will see later.

We expose methods from a serviced component in the normal way. For our example,
`WXServicedComponentABC`, we specify a method called `ProcessID`. This method returns the ID of
the process in which the serviced component is executing. The reason for this is to demonstrate when
the serviced component runs as a DLL or within a separate executable. The implementation of the
`ProcessID` method is as follows (where the `Process` class is used to retrieve the process ID):

```
public class WXServicedComponentABC : ServicedComponent
{
    public int ProcessID()
    {
        return Process.GetCurrentProcess().Id;
    }
}
```

Developing a Client that Accesses a Serviced Component

To demonstrate how to use serviced components, we will develop a console application that uses the
`WXChameleonClassLib100` assembly and its serviced component. The steps required to access this
console application assembly are identical to the steps required to access any class library (add a
reference to the class library and optionally add `using` under C# or `imports` under VB.NET).

The class inside the `WXChameleonClassLib100` assembly that our application will access is
`WXServicedComponentABC`. This class is derived from `ServicedComponent`, so our client (console
application) must also reference the `System.EnterpriseServices` assembly.

The part of our client code that creates and accesses a serviced component is as follows (where the
serviced component is `WXServicedComponentABC` and the sole method exposed by this component
is `ProcessID`):

```
WXServicedComponentABC sComponent = new WXServicedComponentABC();

Console.WriteLine(sComponent.ProcessID());
```

The previous code looks simple, but it is impressive because it represents all the coding required for the
client to access the serviced component when deployed as a DLL, Windows Server, or Windows
Service. The client does not need to know how the serviced component is deployed.

Serviced Component Administration

The administrative application for serviced components is found under Control Panel | Administrative Tools | Component Services. The left panel of this application contains a folder entitled COM+ Applications:

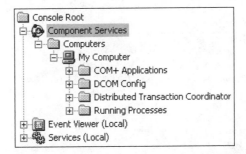

> When developing serviced components, it simplifies matters greatly if each class library developed is prefixed by the same sequence of letters – such as WX indicating Wrox. When the contents of the COM+ Applications folder are viewed, serviced components for the same company and/or application are then clustered together, simplifying administration. This also means that if the class libraries are deployed as services then they will be next to each other when they are managed by the service control manager application.

Displaying the contents of the COM+ Applications folder reveals entries for each COM+ application deployed including the WXChameleonClassLib100 class library. Right-clicking on this entry reveals a context menu from which the Properties menu item can be selected. From the dialog displayed by this action, select the Activation tab:

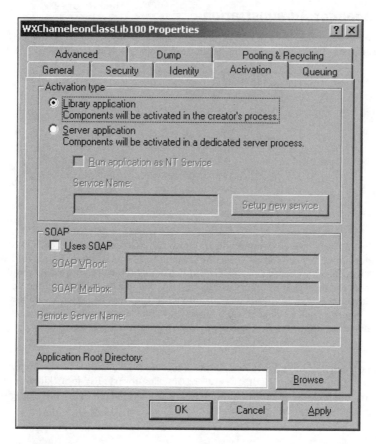

When the Server application option is selected, the Run application as NT Service checkbox becomes enabled. Using this requires that the DLL be strongly named since each .NET implemented Windows Service must exist in the Global Assembly Cache.

Selecting Server Application also enables the textbox labeled Remote Server Name. This allows an administrator to specify a remote instance of the class library containing the component service. The client application need never know that the component is executing remotely. This dialog also allows SOAP to be configured, so a serviced component can be accessed as a Web Service.

> When developing a serviced component that will run as a server application, it is simpler to debug the component when it runs as a library application. Once the majority of the bugs have been removed, the serviced component can be configured to run as a separate executable (a more complicated environment in which to debug).

Installation

Once the Component Services administrative tool has been used to configure a component, a Microsoft installation file (MSI) can be generated. This installation file allows the serviced component assembly to be reinstalled at another location with precisely the same configuration settings. Generating this MSI file is a matter of right-clicking on the service components folder (as show in the following screenshot) and selecting Export from the context menu:

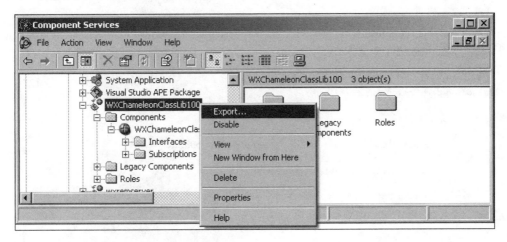

The wizard displayed when Export is selected allows the MSI file to be specified and generated.

Remoting

Before the arrival of .NET remoting, DCOM (distributed COM) was the mechanism used on the Windows platform to allow applications residing on separate machines to communicate. As a technology DCOM was not well suited for the era of the Web, when corporations raised firewalls and typically permitted client-server access over port 80 (the HTTP port).

Unfortunately DCOM was extremely proprietary and did not interface well, and sometimes not at all, with non-Windows platforms. Additionally, the configuration of DCOM was very complicated causing many to abandon efforts and use competing technologies.

.NET provides two alternatives to using DCOM for inter-application development: XML Web Services and Remoting. This section focuses on .NET Remoting – for XML Web Services see Chapter 7.

Remoting works by using encoders to bundle the data for transport and un-bundle the data on the other side. Using Remoting it is also possible to select a variety of transport protocols, which are exposed as channels.

There is a relationship between Remoting and .NET COM+ components (classes derived from `ServicedComponent`). To understand this, consider the base classes from which the class `ServicedComponents` is derived:

```
System.Object
    System.MarshalByRefObject
        System.ContextBoundObject
            System.EnterpriseServices.ServicedComponent
```

The `MarshalByRefObject` and `ContextBoundObject` classes ensure that `ServicedComponents` can transport across application-domain or network boundaries.

In order to demonstrate how remoting works in the context of a class derived from `ServicedComponent`, consider the following class (source file, `WXRemoteServerDemo.cs`) contained in a class library that references `System.EnterpriseServices.dll`:

```
using System;
using System.EnterpriseServices;

namespace WXRemServer
{
    public class WXRemoteServerDemo : ServicedComponent
    {
        public string WXAMethod(int a, int b)
        {
            return "a plus b equals " + (a + b).ToString();
        }
    }
}
```

The above method takes two integers and returns a string based on those integers. The class itself is a serviced component since it is derived from the `ServicedComponent` base class.

This application is configured to use the HTTP channel, so we will need to create a virtual directory using the MMC snap-in found at **Control Panel | Administrative Tools | Internet Information Services**. For the purpose of this exercise the virtual directory will be called UDotNET. The UDotNet directory should contain a `Bin` directory in which the `WXRemoteServerDemo` serviced component should be placed.

The client will attempt to access our component as a URL:

http://SonyasPet/UDotNet/WXRemServer.soap

The specific host where the remoted service is found is `SonyasPet`. The virtual directory UDotNet was discussed previously. The actual service is associated with a Universal Resource Identifier (URI) that corresponds to `WXRemServer.soap`. The previous URL does not quite provide enough information for the client to find our remoted service. What the URL does specify is a path to a configuration file. Like most .NET configuration files, the format is XML. This configuration file (`web.config`) is found in the UDotNet directory. The contents of the `web.config` configuration file describe the services remoted over HTTP (the channel) using SOAP (the encoder). The contents of the `web.config` file are as follows:

```
<configuration>
    <system.runtime.remoting>
        <application>
```

```
    <service>
       <wellknown
          mode="SingleCall"
          displayName="Not the most exciting service in the world"
          type="WXRemServer.WXRemoteServerDemo, WXRemServer"
          objectUri="WXRemServer.soap"
       />
    </service>
   </application>
  </system.runtime.remoting>
</configuration>
```

The basic idea is that Internet Information Server (IIS) is used to activate well-known objects, hence the use of the wellknown element in order to specify remoted objects. The attributes of the wellknown element describe the specific object that has been remoted. The MSDN article *<wellknown> Element (Service Instance)*, available from:

http://msdn.microsoft.com/library/default.asp?
　　　　　url=/library/en-us/cpgenref/html/gnconwellknownserviceinstance.asp

describes fully the behavior of the wellknown element which is defined as follows:

```
<wellknown
   mode="Singleton | SingleCall"
   displayName="name"
   type="type, assembly"
   objectUri="objectUri"
/>
```

Our example specified SingleCall for the mode attribute. This corresponds to the server creating a new object with the invocation of each method. The Singleton attribute means that regardless of the number of clients, only a single instance of the server will be deployed.

.NET Remoting does not use the displayName attribute, but this attribute is used by the Control Panel | Administrative Tools | .NET Framework Configuration utility in order to display list of published server-side objects.

The type attribute specifically identifies the type exposed (namespace.type, assemblyname). For our example (WXRemServer.WXRemoteServerDemo, WXRemServer), the namespace and assembly name were the same – a common occurrence in .NET.

In order to understand the objectUri, recall that the client will specify a URL that ends in WXRemServer.soap. So the URI (objectURI attribute) is used in the client to specifically select the underlying service type (as specified by the type attribute).

The only other caveat with respect to the WXRemoteServerDemo class comes from changing the build location of this class's DLL (the WXRemServer.dll assembly) in Visual Studio .NET. The reason for changing the default location for build output would be to ensure that the assembly resided under UDotNet\bin.

> **There is a big downside to changing the location where a serviced component is built. Namely, when the build location is changed, the class derived from `ServicedComponent` is no longer automatically registered as a COM+ application. Such a class must be manually registered using the Component Services MMC snap-in.**

The steps required to manually register an assembly containing serviced components are as follows:

❑ Right-click on the **COM+ Applications** folder and from the context menu displayed, select **New | Application**:

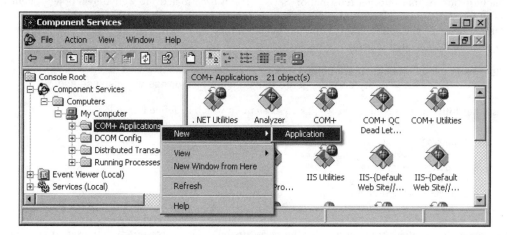

❑ The new application wizard permits **Create an empty application** to be selected. After selecting this option, simply enter the name of the application (such was `WXRemServer`) and chose if it is to be deployed as a DLL or an executable.

❑ Now that the application is created, expand the **COM+ Applications** folder and expand the entry associated with the newly created application. Under the newly created application right-click on the **Components** folder and from the context menu displayed select **New | Component**.

❑ This menu item displays the **Component Install** wizard. Using this wizard select **Install new component(s)** and simply browse for the location where the component resides

Remoting Client Implementation

The `WXHumbleClient` class (contained in a C# console application) is the client for our remoted class. This class needs knowledge of our server-side object so it does reference the project containing the `WXRemoveServerDemo` class. The basic client implementation is as follows:

```
static void WXShowRemote()
{
    HttpChannel hc = new HttpChannel();
    ChannelServices.RegisterChannel(hc);
    WXRemoteServerDemo rc = (WXRemoteServerDemo)
```

```
        Activator.GetObject(typeof(WXRemoteServerDemo),
        @"http://localhost/UDotNet/WXRemServer.soap");
    Console.WriteLine("Secret Message: " + rc.WXAMethod(1, 2));
}
```

The client creates an instance of the `System.Runtime.Remoting.Channels.Http` namespace's `HttpChannel` class. This is an implementation of a sender-receiver channel that uses the HTTP protocol in order to provide messaging between client and server. Another channel type could have been specified such as `TcpChannel`, which corresponds to the sender-receiver channel used by TCP/IP applications.

Once created, the sender-receiver instance is registered with channel services, and the specific object can be created using the `Activator.GetObject` method. `GetObject` creates a proxy referring to an instance of type `WXRemoteServerDemo`. The `GetObject` method of the `Activator` class is aware of the currently registered channel, which is used to create a proxy for the remote object.

With the object proxy set up, the methods associated with the object can be invoked just as the following code demonstrates – as we do in the final line of the example.

All this in just four lines! Clearly, a big aim of the .NET remoting system is simplicity.

Remoting Realities and Complexities

The example presented was extremely simple and straightforward. Remoting is more complex than just this one example.

For example, in our previous example when was the remote instance created? If the instance was created by explicitly instantiating the server object, then the remote instance is considered client-activated. This would be achieved by calling the `Activator` class's `CreateObject` method. This method is overloaded and allows a variety of parameters to be passed to the server object's constructor (the `new` method). When an object is client-activated, the client dictates the lifetime of the object. In client-server terms this is an extremely powerful feature that could be abused by a client.

If the remote instance was created by calling a method, then the instance was server-activated. This later scenario was the type of activation used in our code snippet. Recall that in the `web.config` a choice was made in the area of server activation (`Singleton` versus `SingleCall`). The lifetime of a server-activated instance is controlled by the server. If the instance is exposed as type `Singleton`, then an object is reused and can maintain state between client method invocations. An object of type `SingleCall` is created with each method invocation and is hence stateless.

An application that maintains state is more costly than a stateless application. Furthermore if the server-side object maintains state but expires then the next time the client calls a method, a new instance will be created without the previous state.

Client-side activation incurs an extra network roundtrip because the call to `new` instantiates the server object. On the plus side, client-instantiated objects can have constructors that take parameters (non-default constructors).

The mechanism used under the covers to support remoting is the proxy. A proxy is a client-side representation of the server object. In our example the proxy could be seen in action as `rc.WXAMethod(1, 2)`.

`rc` is a "transparent proxy". By this we mean that it can call methods on the server, but is not outwardly knowledgeable as to how those methods are invoked or where the server resides. The transparent proxy ends up calling the real proxy using methods exposed by the `IMessage` interface. The real proxy ultimately communicates with the remote object.

Communications is over channels such as HTTP and TCP. Channels can be broken down as follows:

❑ Client-side – channels of this type have the ability to send messages from client to server but do not have the ability to receive messages. Such channels implement the `Channel` class's `IChannelSender` interface.

❑ Server-side – channels of this type have the ability receive message from the client but do not have the ability to send messages to the client. Such channels implement the `Channel` class's `IChannelReceiver` interface.

❑ Both – by implementing both the `IChannelSender` and `IChannelReceiver` interfaces it is possible for a channel to both send and received.

The two flavors of channel provided by .NET (HTTP and TCP) indirectly identify the type of data transported (the encoding mechanism used on the data sent in the channel). For the HTTP channel, data is encoded as XML and the default representation is SOAP. When using TCP it is possible to encode data as binary. Binary encoded message will achieve higher performance than an XML encoded message (such as is provided with SOAP). HTTP, although using XML and hence slower, is more readily deployed. As was mentioned early, corporate infrastructures revolve around port 80 and permitting access or denying access to this port. Using the TCP channel, higher performance can be achieved, but along with this performance comes an administrative cost incurred by a customer's MIS department. There is no better way to quash a sale than by explaining to a customer that they will have to open up a new port (for a TCP channel) on each of their thousand-plus firewalls.

The world of remoting is a world of many choices: server versus client invocation, binary versus text encoding, reference versus value, just to name a few. These choices are application-specific and it should be recognized they do add complexity to remoting.

Summary

Nearly every enterprise application requires legacy access, infrastructure, and an ability to be deployed across the enterprise (across multiple machines). This chapter demonstrated legacy access using the `System.Runtime.InteropServices` namespace. We demonstrated both legacy functions (access to C-style functions in DLL's) and COM access. With legacy functions, the `DllImport` attribute provided the key to unlock the legacy code, while with COM `TlbImp.exe` or Visual Studio .NET generated a runtime-callable wrapper using a COM server's type library.

We also demonstrated the scenario of having legacy-style applications access .NET assemblies. In this situation, the legacy applications acted as COM clients and the .NET assemblies appeared to be COM servers. This was all courtesy of the register assembly utility, `RegAsm.exe`.

We also discussed .NET interaction with COM+ services, centring on the `System.EnterpriseServices` namespace's `ServiceComponent` class.

The final topic presented was Remoting. We saw a basic example that demonstrated its simplicity. Clearly there will be a variety of administrative obstacles, performance issues, and deployment issues to consider. The point is that remoting has pushed client-server technology forward, garnished (where needed) with other enterprise enhancement technologies.

In the next chapter we will look at another way to build distributed systems: Web Services.

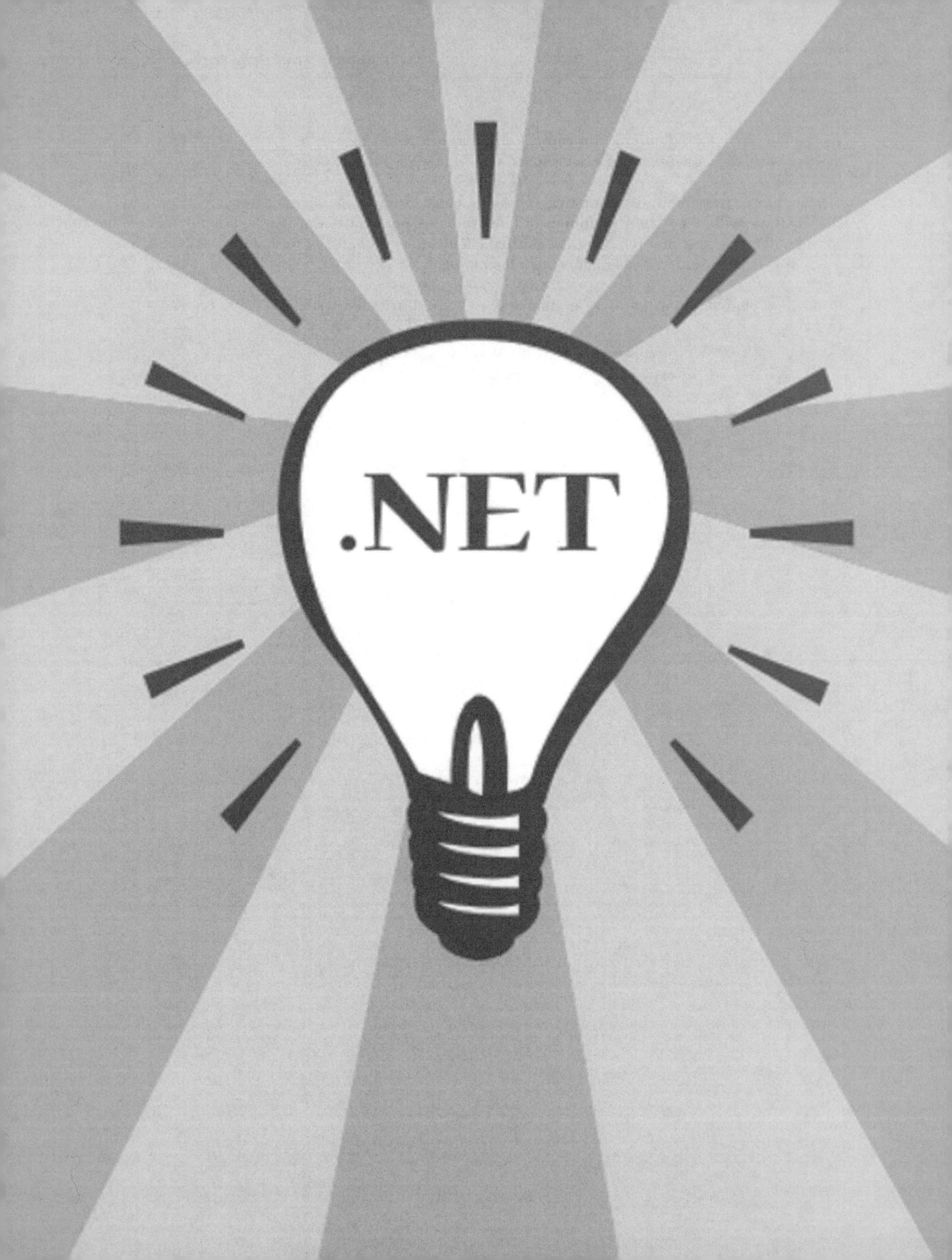
.NET

7

Web Services

What Are Web Services?

Web Services are programmable application logic that is accessible via the Internet using standard protocols such as HTTP, SMTP, FTP, and SOAP. In other words, Web Services allow developers to build applications that are independent of programming languages, operating systems, and even geographic locations. Web Services are gaining such momentum today for two reasons. First, they are based on open standards making them interoperable, and, second the protocols used to implement them are ubiquitous. What makes Web Services ubiquitous is that they combine the best aspects of component-based development and method invocation via the Internet. Like components, Web Services represent black-box functionality that can be reused without worrying about how the service is implemented. Unlike current component technologies, Web Services are not invoked via object-model-specific protocols, such as the Distributed Component Object Model (DCOM), Remote Method Invocation (RMI), or the Object Management Group's CORBA. Instead, Web Services are accessed via simple web protocols such as HTTP, and universal data formats such as eXtensible Markup Language (XML), and Simple Object Access Protocol (SOAP). In addition to that, the Web Services interfaces are exposed in terms of messages. So that any client that can send and receive plain SOAP messages over HTTP can consume Web Services!

Why do we need Web Services? What makes them so important? In a world that is ruled by software vendors, it has always been a problem to be able to connect different software applications from different vendors together and let them communicate with each other. For example, Windows COM applications can speak to each other using DCOM, but other major vendors did not seriously support DCOM. With the advent of Web Services, applications can now be designed that work together regardless of where they reside or how they are implemented. Seamless communication among remote, diverse systems has always been a dream for software developers and software users. Now with the advent of Web Services the dream is a step closer to reality.

In this chapter we are going to cover the following topics:

❑   Web Services Applications – We see where and when Web Services can be used

❑   Architectural aspects of Web Services – We discuss the protocols that Web Services are built on

❑   Building and Consuming Web Services in .NET – We build an interesting, real-world Web Service and a client to 'consume' that Web Service

❑   .NET My Services and future of Web Services – We finish the chapter with a discussion about the future of Web Services and a look at .NET My Services

Let's start our discussion by examining Web Services Applications, looking at where and when Web Services can be deployed.

Web Services Applications

In .NET world, Web Services are the building blocks of distributed computing over the Internet. One could list a huge number of applications where Web Services could be effectively deployed, and we shall look at some examples shortly. However, the most obvious applications will fall into one of the following two categories:

❑   Software-as-Service

❑   Data Integration

Software-As-Service

You might have heard of the term "Software-As-Service" a number of times in the Web Services context by now. Ever wondered what it is? To put it simply, it is nothing but the Web Services in action.

Here is an example: Suppose you'd like to book a flight ticket for your vacation. You can do so using a flight ticket booking Web Service. Here you are using the flight ticket booking Web Service software that is residing on a remote server as a service to book your flight ticket, just as you use your telephone provider's phone systems to make a phone call.

You may be doing that even today using a web browser and web sites that provide flight ticket booking services online. But using Web Services you can automate the process of booking your flight ticket programmatically, instead of using a web browser manually. This flexibility gives you the advantage of integrating the flight booking process into any application you want! You can even develop a program to book flight tickets based on your vacation plan in your Microsoft Outlook Calendar. So Web Services expose the programmatic interfaces of the software applications that reside either on a remote server that is a million miles away or on a server in the room right next to you.

There is no better example in this category than Microsoft Passport Service. Microsoft Passport is an authentication Web Service with over 2 million users today!

> **If you are new to Microsoft Passport, you can read more at http://www.passport.com.**

Data Integration

Data Integration applications can be classified into two categories:

❑   Inter-organization Data Integration

❑   Intra-organization Data Integration

Inter-organization data integration or data integration among various organizations is often called "Business-to-Business" (B2B) integration. Today most of the B2B data integration among diverse platforms is being achieved by developing custom solutions that implement system-specific interfaces. Hence the data integration becomes a complex and tightly coupled solution, which leads to implementation and maintenance problems. However, with Web Services the loose coupling among the diverse systems is the key. Using Web Services the disparate systems speak XML using SOAP, and communicate over the Network using standard and ubiquitous protocols like HTTP. As you can see, the Inter-organization data integration implementation with Web Services is completely independent of the system specifics.

Intra-organization data integration is also known as Enterprise Application Integration (EAI). It is common that the information within an organization is distributed among several different information systems run by different departments and branches. Again, Web Services with the standard communication protocols like HTTP and data formats such as XML/SOAP come to our rescue to connect these diverse platforms.

Let's talk about an example in this category. Let's assume that there is a huge company with two departments: Human Resources and Accounting. The departments' information systems are different: say, an SAP system and an AS400 system. In this case, if you need to make the Human Resources data (from the SAP system) available to the Accounting department (to the AS400 system), you need to implement a complex custom solution. But when you use Web Services to do this the task is much simpler because of the very fact that the building blocks of Web Services technology (HTTP, XML, and SOAP etc.) are not tied to any specific platform or a vendor. That way, Web Services pave the way to connect diverse systems seamlessly and cost-effectively.

With this background, let's move on to learn about the building blocks of Web Services technology.

Building Blocks Of Web Services Technology

As we discussed earlier, Web Services technology is built upon vendor-and platform-independent protocols and standards such as HTTP, XML, and SOAP. But how do they stack up and work together? Take a look at the following Web Services Technology Stack's pictorial representation:

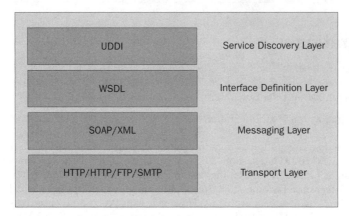

As you can see from the above picture, Web Services are not really dependent on any specific protocol at the Transport layer (HTTP/HTTPS/FTP/SMTP). How is this possible? It is possible because the Messaging layer (SOAP/XML) is transport-independent by nature! Then comes the Interface Definition layer, which you can use to find out the specifics of the service such as what parameters you need to pass to the service and what output you can expect from the service. The topmost layer is the Service Discovery layer, using which you can really find out the service that meets your business needs. We will discuss each of these layers in more detail shortly.

The above Web Services technology stack is also known as the Web Services baseline architecture. Microsoft is building another stack of standards on top of this baseline architecture that is known as Global XML Web Services architecture (GXA). We will discuss the details of GXA later in this chapter when we look towards the future of Web Services.

Now let's take a look at each of the above layers in detail, starting with the Transport layer.

HTTP – The Transport Layer

As you can see, Web Services depend on the standard protocols such as HTTP, FTP, and SMTP at the Transport layer. The next layer is the Messaging layer, where the actual communication to and from a Web Service occurs. The Messaging layer together with the Transport layer is called the "Wire Format". XML is the lingua franca of Web Services communication. At the time of writing, the .NET Framework supports HTTP-GET, HTTP-POST, and SOAP protocols for Web Services.

> **Although SOAP is transport-independent by nature, at the time of writing the .NET Framework provides only HTTP implementation for the SOAP protocol. Hence SOAP on HTTP is nothing but a HTTP-POST with an XML payload.**

SOAP/XML – The Messaging Layer

SOAP is a general application-level protocol that is designed for application-to-application communication over any underlying transport protocol. SOAP defines the XML format for messages – and as we have mentioned before, the Web Services' interfaces are exposed in terms of messages. So if you have a well-formed XML document that conforms to the SOAP protocol specifications, you are ready to communicate with a Web Service!

A SOAP message contains the following parts:

❑   **Envelope** – This is the top-level container representing the message.

❑   **Header** – The optional header part of the SOAP message is usually used to carry data that is not related to the main application itself. For example, authentication information could be sent as a SOAP `Header` in a SOAP message.

❑   **Body** – This is a container for mandatory information intended for the ultimate message receiver.

In the context of Web Services, the SOAP `Body` is the most important part of a SOAP message. So let's take a closer look at the SOAP `Body` element of a SOAP message.

A sample XML document containing stock information embedded in the SOAP `Body` is shown below:

```xml
<?xml version="1.0" encoding="utf-8"?>
<soap:Envelope xmlns:soap="http://schemas.xmlsoap.org/soap/envelope/">
 <soap:Body>
  <GetStock xmlns="http://tempuri.org/">
    <GetStockInfo>
              <ticker>ABCD</ticker>
              <price>65.59</price>
    </ GetStockInfo>
  </ GetStock>
 </soap:Body>
</soap:Envelope>
```

Although the SOAP specification does not strictly outline the formatting of XML messages, there are two sections in the SOAP specification that discuss how to format XML data. Section 5 of the SOAP specification outlines the rules for encoding parameters. According to the specification you can either have your parameters in **Literal** style or **Encoded** style.

> **Literal means that the message must be formatted exactly as dictated by a pre-defined schema. Encoded means the parameters in the messages are always wrapped according to the encoding style defined in Section 7 of the SOAP specification.**

Section 7 of the SOAP specification outlines the rules on how the SOAP `Body` can be formatted. Depending on the application type, you can choose the messaging style. For example, in applications that are intended for data integration, you can use Document/Literal, and in applications that that use SOAP as an RPC protocol to invoke remote objects you have to use RPC/Encoded style. The RPC formatting style only supports the Encoded parameter, while the Document style supports both Literal and Encoded.

> You can read more about the SOAP 1.1 specification at
> http://www.w3.org/TR/SOAP. You can find the working draft of the SOAP 1.2
> specification at http://www.w3.org/TR/2001/WD-soap12-20010709/ .

The stock information SOAP message we have seen previously is an example of a Document-style format. Due to the simplicity of the Document style SOAP messages, Document-style Web Service applications are very flexible when compared to RPC-style Web Service applications.

Below is the same document formatted in RPC style:

```xml
<?xml version="1.0" encoding="utf-8"?>
<soap:Envelope xmlns:soap="http://schemas.xmlsoap.org/soap/envelope">
<soap:Body soap:encodingStyle="http://schemas.xmlsoap.org/soap/encoding/">
    <types:GetStock>
      <GetStockInfo href="#id1" />
    </types:GetStockInfo>
    <types:Stockinfo id="id1" xsi:type="types:Stockinfo">
     <ticker xsi:type="xsd:string">ABCD</ticker>
     <price xsi:type="xsd:double">65.59</price>
    </types:Stockinfo>
</soap:Body>
</soap:Envelope>
```

Microsoft .NET Framework supports these formatting styles using attributes. The table below shows how the different format types can be supported using different attributes.

Attribute	SOAP body style	Parameter encoding
SoapDocumentMethod	Document	Literal/Encoded
SoapDocumentService	Document	Literal/Encoded
SoapRpcMethod	RPC	Encoded
SoapRpcService	RPC	Encoded

The attribute SoapDocumentMethod specifies the Document-style body, but supports both the Literal and the Encoded parameter styles. SoapRpcMethod specifies the RPC-style body, but supports only the Encoded parameter style.

The attributes SoapDocumentMethod and SoapRpcMethod are applied at a method level, while SoapDocumentService and SoapRpcService are applied at a service level, which means the formatting is applied to all methods in the service.

WSDL – The Interface Definition Layer

WSDL stands for **Web Services Description Language**. For our purposes, we can say that a WSDL file is an XML document that describes a set of SOAP messages and how the messages are exchanged. In other words, WSDL is to SOAP what Interface Definition Language (IDL) is to COM. So by looking at a WSDL document, you can understand what methods are exposed as Web Services and how to invoke them by passing right set of parameters.

Now let us look at a simple WSDL document in detail to understand how to decipher the interface definition for a Web Service.

Understanding the Contract

There is a standard structure that every WSDL document it should follow to be able to define a Web Service completely. Since WSDL is XML, it is readable and editable, but in most cases, it is generated and consumed by software with not much human intervention. Having said that, let's talk about an example. Assume that there is a CD Catalogue Web Service that lets you enter the name of a CD and returns information about the CD, such as the list of songs and lyrics. Based on the above requirement for the CD Catalogue Web Service, one can assume that this Web Service should accept a CD name as a string and should return the CD information that contains a list of songs and lyrics.

If such a Web Service existed, the following would be the WSDL document (a simplified version):

```xml
<?xml version="1.0" encoding="utf-8" ?>
<definitions xmlns:http="http://schemas.xmlsoap.org/wsdl/http/">
 <types>
    <s:schema targetNamespace="http://localhost/WroxUnderstandingDotNet/">
       <s:element name="WXFindLyrics">
          . . .
          <s:element name="cdName" type="s:string" />
          . . .
          <s:element name="WXFindLyricsResult" type="s0:WXCDInfo" />
          . . .
       </s:element>
       <s:complexType name="WXCDInfo">
          <s:sequence>
            . . .
          </s:sequence>
       </s:complexType>
          . . .
    </types>
  <message name="WXFindLyricsSoapIn">
     <part name="parameters" element="s0:WXFindLyrics" />
  </message>
  <message name="WXFindLyricsSoapOut">
     <part name="parameters" element="s0:WXFindLyricsResponse" />
  </message>
  . . .
  <portType name="WXCDLookupSoap">
     <operation name="WXFindLyrics">
        <input message="s0:WXFindLyricsSoapIn" />
        <output message="s0:WXFindLyricsSoapOut" />
     </operation>
  </portType>
  . . .
  <binding name="WXCDLookupSoap" type="s0:WXCDLookupSoap">
     . . .
  </binding>
  <service name="WXCDLookup">
     <port name="WXCDLookupSoap" binding="s0:WXCDLookupSoap">
        <soap:address location="http://localhost/WXCDLookup.asmx" />
     </port>
        . . .
  </service>
</definitions>
```

By examining the above document structure, you can see that there are six unique element types under the root node `definitions` (the root node is `definitions` after the fact that WSDL is simply a set of definitions that define a Web Service). They are:

- ❑ Types
- ❑ Message
- ❑ PortType
- ❑ Binding
- ❑ Port
- ❑ Service

So we have a total of six major element types in any given WSDL document.

Let us take a look at each of them to understand what they really are and what we can decipher from them.

Types

The `types` element encloses data type definitions that are relevant for the exchanged messages to and from the Web Service. For maximum interoperability and platform neutrality, WSDL prefers the use of XSD as the canonical type system.

The simplified version of the `types` element from the CD Catalogue Web Service WSDL is shown below.

```
<types>
  <s:schema targetNamespace="http://localhost/WroxUnderstandingDotNet/">
    <s:element name="WXFindLyrics">
      <s:complexType>
        <s:sequence>
          <s:element name="cdName" type="s:string" />
        </s:sequence>
      </s:complexType>
    </s:element>
    <s:element name="WXFindLyricsResponse">
      <s:complexType>
        <s:sequence>
          <s:element name="WXFindLyricsResult" type="s0:WXCDInfo" />
        </s:sequence>
      </s:complexType>
    </s:element>
    <s:complexType name="WXCDInfo">
      <s:sequence>
        <s:element name="error" type="s:string" />
        <s:element name="songs" type="s0:ArrayOfString" />
        <s:element name="lyrics" type="s0:ArrayOfString" />
      </s:sequence>
    </s:complexType>
    <s:complexType name="ArrayOfString">
      <s:sequence>
        <s:element maxOccurs="unbounded" name="string" type="s:string" />
```

```
        </s:sequence>
      </s:complexType>
      <s:element name="WXCDInfo" type="s0:WXCDInfo" />
    </s:schema>
  </types>
```

There are two elements that we need to understand: WXFindLyrics and WXFindLyricsResponse.

The element WXFindLyrics contains an element cdName, which is defined as a string – this will be the input to the CD Catalogue Web Service.

The element WXFindLyricsResponse contains an element WXFindLyricsResult, which is defined as type WXCDInfo. WXCDInfo is a custom complex type that contains three elements: error – as a string, songs – as an array of strings, and lyrics – as an array of strings. So the element WXFindLyricsResult holds the CD information that's being requested.

Message

As we have discussed before messages are the abstract definition of the data being sent to and from a Web Service. One of the message elements from the CD Catalogue Web Service is shown below:

```
<message name="WXFindLyricsSoapIn">
   <part name="parameters" element="s0:WXFindLyrics" />
</message>
```

As you can see, the message element contains one or more logical parts. Parts are a flexible way of describing the logical abstract content of a message, or to put it simply, a part may represent a parameter (or an argument for a method) in a message.

In the above message, the element part contains an element type WXFindLyrics that we have discussed in the *Types* section.

To sum up the relation between the message and the types, we can say that the message with the name WXFindLyricsSoapIn contains a part called parameters of type WXFindLyrics element that is nothing but a string – cdName.

Also there could be many messages present in a service definition. In a typical WSDL document for a .NET Web Service you may see as many as six messages or three pairs of messages. Each pair corresponds to particular protocol types that are supported in Web Services. They are: HTTP-GET, HTTP-POST, and SOAP. Each message within a pair corresponds to a Request and a Response. You might be wondering how these messages are mapped to a specific protocol. We will see that in a moment when we discuss bindings!

PortType

A `portType` is defined as a set of abstract operations that involve messages. The operations are nothing but the transportation primitives that a network endpoint can support, such as a "Request-Response".

```
<portType name="WXCDLookupSoap">
 <operation name="WXFindLyrics">
  <input message="s0:WXFindLyricsSoapIn" />
  <output message="s0:WXFindLyricsSoapOut" />
 </operation>
</portType>
```

If you think of a `portType` as a method that takes input arguments and returns results, the method name is the `operation`, and the input arguments and output results are `messages`.

```
portType = operation + messages
```

Binding

A `binding` defines the message format and protocol details for the operations and messages defined by a particular `portType`.

```
<binding name="WXCDLookupSoap" type="s0:WXCDLookupSoap">
  <soap:binding transport="http://schemas.xmlsoap.org/soap/http" style="document" />
 <operation name="WXFindLyrics">
  <soap:operation soapAction="http://localhost/WXFindLyrics" style="document" />
 <input>
  <soap:body use="literal" />
 </input>
 <output>
  <soap:body use="literal" />
 </output>
 </operation>
</binding>
```

An `operation` element within a `binding` element specifies binding information for the operation specified in that particular `binding`'s `portType`.

The binding information includes

❑ Protocol to be used – In the above case the protocol is SOAP from the `soap:binding` element. Also you can see that in this implementation the SOAP is sitting on top of the HTTP protocol from the `transport` attribute.

❑ SOAP Parameter Encoding – In the above case the Encoding is `Literal`.

❑ SOAP Body style – In the above case the Body style is `Document`.

> **binding = protocol + portType**

Since operation names are not required to be unique, the `name` attribute in the `operation` element might not be enough to uniquely identify an operation. In that case, providing the `name` attributes of the corresponding `input` and `output` elements should identify the correct operation. This is analogous to method overloading in object-oriented programming.

Port

A `port` defines an individual network endpoint (a URL) by specifying a single address for a binding. The `port` element from the above WSDL document is shown below:

```
<service name="WXCDLookup">
  <port name="WXCDLookupSoap" binding="s0:WXCDLookupSoap">
    <soap:address location="http://localhost/WXCDLookup.asmx" />
  </port>
</service>
```

As you can see, the `port` contains the URL (`location` attribute), the network endpoint of the Web Service, and also a reference to the `binding` element (`binding` attribute).

> **port = binding + network address**

Service

A `service` element is a collection of related ports, and each port defines an individual network endpoint by specifying a single address for a binding.

```
<service name="WXCDLookup">
  <port name="WXCDLookupSoap" binding="s0:WXCDLookupSoap">
    <soap:address location="http://localhost/WXCDLookup.asmx" />
  </port>
</service>
```

With this background, we now understand the Web Service contract spelled out in WSDL. To summarize, we can define the CD Catalogue Web Service contract in plain English as follows:

CD Catalogue Web Service:

❑ Accepts an input parameter as string – `cdName`

❑ Returns output parameter as `WXCDInfo`, which is defined as a `complexType` element that contains arrays of songs and lyrics as strings

❑ Can be accessed at the network endpoint http://localhost/WXCDLookup.asmx

With this information, we can post properly formatted SOAP messages to the above service URL to browse the CD Catalogue.

OK, now you know how to understand a Web Service from a WSDL document. But where do you find these WSDL documents for the Web Services that you are looking for? How do you **discover** a Web Service that satisfies your business needs?

That's where the Discovery layer in the Web Services technology stack comes into picture. There are two types of discovery mechanisms for Web services: DISCO – a short form for the term Discovery and UDDI – Universal Description, Discovery, and Integration.

Let's take a look at each of them briefly in the next section.

DISCO and UDDI – The Service Discovery Layer

Let's start our discussion with DISCO. The DISCO protocol, which is developed by Microsoft, allows you to browse Web Services in a free-form model. What it really means is that you can find all the Web Services on a particular web server by browsing a DISCO file that links (actually through hyper-links) to the Web Services or the other DISCO files. As you can see this model is neither structured nor standardized. Also the limitation of DISCO is that you can discover only Web Services that are local to a server.

So we need a better solution for Web Services discovery that is more structured and standard. Of course we also need a discovery mechanism that allows us to find Web Services no matter where they are hosted! That's where UDDI comes into picture.

UDDI – Universal Discovery Description and Integration is the yellow pages of Web Services. As with traditional yellow pages, you can search for a company that offers the services you need, read about the service offered and contact someone for more information. You can, of course, offer a Web Service without registering it in UDDI, but you need UDDI so your customers can find your Web Service. (Of course, you can also depend on your own marketing efforts to reach your customers too!)

> **UDDI is an industry standard that backed by a significant number of technology companies, including Microsoft, IBM, and Ariba. You can find more about UDDI at http://www.uddi.org.**

These registries are run by multiple Operator Sites, and can be used by anyone who wants to make information available about one or more businesses or entities, as well as anyone who wants to find that information.

> **You can find different operator sites at http://www.uddi.org/find.html.**

A UDDI directory entry is an XML file that describes a business and the services it offers. There are three parts to an entry in the UDDI directory. The "white pages" describe the company offering the service: name, address, contacts, etc. The "yellow pages" include industrial categories based on standard taxonomies such as the North American Industry Classification System and the Standard Industrial Classification. The "green pages" describe the interface to the service in enough detail for someone to write an application to use the Web Service. The way services are defined is through a UDDI document called a Type Model or **tModel**. In many cases, the tModel contains a WSDL file that describes a SOAP interface to an XML Web Service, but the tModel is flexible enough to describe almost any kind of service.

The UDDI specifications include definitions for Web Service interfaces that allow programmatic access to the UDDI registry information. The API is divided into two logical parts. These are the Inquiry API and the Publishers' API.

UDDI Inquiry API

The **UDDI Inquiry API** offers three forms of functions/queries to match the needs of software traditionally used with registries. The patterns of queries are:

- The Browse Pattern API
- The Drill-Down Pattern API
- The Invocation Pattern API

The Browse Pattern API

When you start searching for a particular business/service with broad information, this is the API you need to use. The UDDI API specifications accommodate the browse pattern by way of the `find_xx` API calls. Generally these calls return a summary of results with overview information that satisfy the search criteria.

> You can find the UDDI programmer's API specifications and the list of all the functions available at the UDDI specifications page:
> http://www.uddi.org/specification.html.

For example, if you intend to find a business with the name "xyz Inc", you have to start with a call to `find_business`. This call returns a `businessList` result that is overview information matching the name "xyz Inc".

Then you spot the company that you are looking for and you can issue a Drill-Down Pattern API call to obtain the detailed result for that particular business/service.

The Drill-Down Pattern API

If you know the specifics, such as the UDDI-Key (a unique key assigned to each registered business/service in the UDDI registry) of a business/service from the Browse Pattern API call, you can issue a Drill-Down Pattern API call to get the details. The UDDI API specifications accommodate the browse pattern by way of the `get_xx` API calls.

For example, if you have the UDDI-Key for the business "xyz Inc", you can call `get_businessDetail` to retrieve the details of that business.

The Invocation Pattern API

This API is intended for the business/service owners who have published their businesses/services in the UDDI registry. By using this API one can automate the UDDI invocation calls.

For example, if your business has activated a disaster recovery site after a disaster on the main site that is registered with the UDDI, most of the calls from your Web Service users will fail when they try to invoke services at the failed site. By updating the UDDI information with the new address for the service, partners who use the invocation pattern API call (specifically get_bindingDetails call) will automatically locate the new service information and recover without further administrative action.

UDDI Publishing API

The UDDI Publishing API offers programmatic interfaces to publish and update businesses/services in the UDDI registry. The API in this section represents commands that require authenticated access to the UDDI. Each business/service should initially select one Operator Site to host its information. Once chosen, information can only be updated at the site originally selected. UDDI provides no automated means to reconcile multiple or duplicate registrations.

We have seen from the above discussions that the UDDI API calls enable developers to query UDDI to discover Web Services. So how do developers invoke these API functions? Now let's discuss how to invoke the UDDI API functions.

UDDI and SOAP

Since UDDI is built on top of the SOAP protocol, the API functions can be invoked via the Internet using Web Services! For example, to find a company by name "xyz Inc" in the UDDI registry, you can simply send a message to any of the UDDI operator sites as shown below:

```
<find_business generic="1.0" xmlns="urn:uddi-org:api">
  <name>xyz Inc</name>
</find_business>
```

If there is a match for the above query, you will receive the following message as a result of your query:

```
<businessList generic="1.0" xmlns="urn:uddi-org:api"
operator="www.ibm.com/services/uddi" truncated="false">
    <businessInfos>
        <businessInfo usinessKey="782D1783-13BE-4D84-9B55-023030F7DAB2">
            <name>xyz Inc</name>
            <description xml:lang="en">xyz Inc is a company</description>
            <serviceInfos>
                <serviceInfo serviceKey="2B454FAC-C3A3-409D-A166-43D5BA46789D"
                businessKey="782D1783-13BE-4D84-9B55-023030F7DAB2">
                    <name>xyz service</name>
                </serviceInfo>
            </serviceInfos>
        </businessInfo>
    </businessInfos>
</businessList>
```

Microsoft provides the UDDI SDK that encapsulates the UDDI API model into a set of base classes, using which you can perform UDDI operations in your .NET applications.

Now that we have all the necessary theoretical background about Web Services, let's see how to build a Web Service using the .NET Framework.

Building Web Services

Right from the beginning, Microsoft's .NET strategy has been built around Web Services. Because of this Web Services orientation, the .NET Framework offers a complete set of base classes and tools to develop, test, and deploy Web Services.

> The `System.Web.Services` namespace in the .NET Framework consists of the classes that enable you to create Web Services in .NET.

In the .NET world, Web Services are files with an `.asmx` extension. The `WebService` class from the .NET Framework defines the optional base class for Web Services, which provides implicit access to ASP.NET objects such as Application and Session state. However, if you do not need Application or Session state access in your Web Service, you don't need to derive from it.

Now it's time to build a Web Service! Instead of yet another "Hello World" Web Service, let's do something interesting this time. Let's build the CD Catalogue Web Service that we discussed in the WSDL section earlier in this chapter.

Building a CD Catalogue Web Service

If you have .NET Framework installed on your computer, you can even build Web Services using Notepad. However, using Visual Studio .NET greatly simplifies the development of your Web Service, and therefore we will use Visual Studio .NET in this example. Let's begin!

1. From Visual Studio .NET's File menu, select New | Blank Solution.

2. From the New Project dialog, select from Project Types the Visual C# Projects folder. From the Templates listbox select ASP.NET Web Service, as shown overleaf:

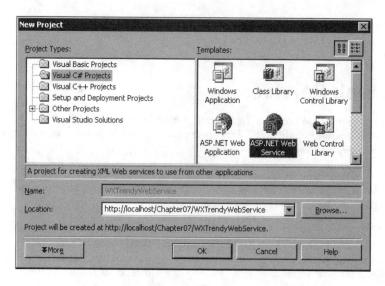

3. After specifying the correct path and name (that is
`http://localhost/Chapter07/WXTrendyWebService`), select **OK** to create your Web
Service. The **Solution Explorer** looks as follows:

As you can see from the above screenshot, the **System.Web.Service** namespace reference is added
by default.

Also, you can see that Visual Studio .NET's project wizard created a file for us, Service1.asmx. This file contains a sample Web Service with a single method, HelloWorld. This method is initially commented out, but after un-commenting the method, the Service1.asmx.cs source file (the code behind Service1.asmx) appears similar to the following:

```
using System;
using System.Collections;
using System.ComponentModel;
using System.Data;
using System.Diagnostics;
using System.Web;
using System.Web.Services;


namespace WXTrendyWebService
{
    public class Service1 : System.Web.Services.WebService
    {
        public Service1()
        {
            //CODEGEN: This call is required by the ASP.NET Web Services
            // Designer
            InitializeComponent();
        }

        // Component Designer generated code

        [WebMethod]
        public string HelloWorld()
        {
            return "Hello World";
        }
    }
}
```

As you can see, the main difference between a usual function and the function in the code shown above is an attribute [WebMethod]. Adding this attribute to a **public** method within a Web Service created using ASP.NET makes the method callable from remote Web Service clients. This attribute corresponds to the WebMethodAttribute class found in the System.Web.Services namespace.

4. Now let's begin implementing the CD Catalogue Web Service. First, change the file name from Service1.asmx to WXCDLookup.asmx. The class name should be changed from Service1 to WXCDLookup as shown below:

Change:

```
public class Service1 : System.Web.Services.WebService
{
    public Service1()
```

To:

```
[WebService(Namespace="http://localhost/WroxUnderstandingDotNet/")]
public class WXCDLookup: System.Web.Services.WebService
{
    public WXCDLookup()
```

The code-behind file will automatically be renamed as WXCDLookup.asmx.cs. This file contains our actual CD Catalogue implementation.

5. What makes this asmx file a Web Service? To understand that let's take a look at the contents of the WXCDLookup.asmx file. To view the contents of this file, select the file from the **Solution Explorer** and right-click to see the Context Menu. From the Context Menu click on the **Open With** option. You will see a window with a set of options. Select **Source Code (Text) Editor**. The WXCDLookup.asmx file should look as follows:

```
<%@ WebService Language="c#" Codebehind="WXCDLookup.asmx.cs"
Class="WXTrendyWebService.WXCDLookup" %>
```

As you can see instead of an @ Page directive, there is an @ WebService directive at the top of the page. So an @ WebService directive at the beginning of an .asmx page will make a Web Service in ASP .NET!

6. Now, let's replace the HelloWorld function with the function below. Since this Web Service is a CD Catalogue Web Service, it should accept any CD name as an input parameter and should return the matching CD information:

```
[WebMethod]
public WXCDInfo WXFindLyrics(string cdName)
{
    WXCDInfo cdInfo = new WXCDInfo();

    switch (cdName.ToLower())
    {
        case "mini":
            // Code to look up songs on album and lyrics to song handled here
            WXFillInMini(cdInfo);
            break;
        default:
            cdInfo.error = "CD not in catalog";
            break;
    }

    return cdInfo;
}
```

In the above code the WXFillInMini function populates the instance of type WXCDInfo with song titles and lyrics. Wondering what the WXCDInfo class is? We are going to take a look at that in a moment!

7. Now let's look at the implementation of the function `WXFillInMini` (the actual function that returns the CD information). To keep it simple we are going to hardcode the songs and lyrics for the CD named "Mini" (from the band "The Wedding Present") as our discussion is to build a Web Service. Add the following code (both the function and the class definition) in the class `WXCDLookup` that we have created in Step *4*.

Note that the only CD in our catalogue is "Mini" and for any other CD Name an error message will be returned. The CD Information that this function returns is a class, `WXCDInfo`, which is shown below (remember the complex type definition from the WSDL discussion earlier in this chapter?):

```
public class WXCDInfo
{
    public string error= null;
    public string [] songs= null;
    public string [][] lyrics= null;
}
```

```
private void WXFillInMini(WXCDInfo cdInfo)
    {
        string [] songs =
        {
            "Drive", "Love Machine", "Go, Man Go", "Mercury",
            "Convertible", "Sports Car", "Sucker"
        };
        string [] lyrics =
        {
            "You drive, no, no, I want you to. " +
                "Because I've only one thing on my mind",
            "You are obscene. " +
                "But I'm not your love machine",
            "By the time you read this. " +
                "I will be a world away",
            "The air is so cold tonight. " +
                "Here, let me put my arm around you",
            "You know that I could make you very happy. . . " +
                "Sure, he said he'd try but he talks. . .",
            "It's okay, I know you've got to go. " +
                "Because he's walked in the room",
            "I knew something wasn't quite right. " +
                "The way you were drinking"
        };

        cdInfo.songs = songs;
        cdInfo.lyrics = lyrics;
    }
```

As you can see the `WXCDInfo` class returns `songs`, and error `lyrics`, as an array of type `string`.

221

8. In order to test the above Web Service from within Visual Studio .NET, make sure that the Web Service project is selected as **Set Startup Project** from the **Project Menu**. From the **Debug** menu, select **Start** and thus launch your web browser. An excerpt from what the browser (Internet Explorer for the following screenshot) displays is as follows:

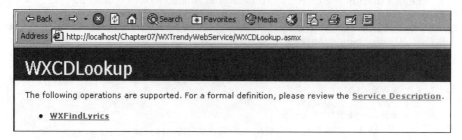

> **As you can see, the URL displayed in the browser corresponds to the location where the Web Service resides; or in WSDL terms, the above URL represents the Network EndPoint in a port definition for this Web Service. This URL is used by the Web Service users to invoke the WXFindLyrics method.**

The .asmx file handlers in the .NET Framework parse through the Web Service and present the methods that are exposed as Web Services on the web browser.

9. In our case the method WXFindLyrics is shown on the browser as a hyperlink. Clicking on this link displays the following:

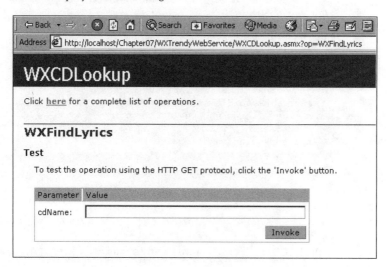

This time you will see a form that is dynamically generated to invoke the Web Service on the Web Browser. The reason why you see this is that the CD Catalogue Web Service supports the protocol HTTP-GET. However, it also supports HTTP-POST, as well as the standard SOAP protocols in this case. If your Web Service does not support HTTP protocol, you will not see a test form, instead you have to send SOAP messages to the Web Service in order to invoke it.

10. Let's enter the CD name Mini as the value for the cdName parameter. Clicking on Invoke displays the following XML in the browser (abbreviated for brevity):

```
<?xml version="1.0" encoding="utf-8" ?>
 <WXCDInfo xmlns:xsd="http://www.w3.org/2001/XMLSchema"
    xmlns:xsi="http://www.w3.org/2001/XMLSchema-instance"
    xmlns="http://localhost/WroxUnderstandingDotNet/">
  <songs>
   <string>Drive</string>
   . . .
  </songs>
  <lyrics>
   <string>You drive, no, no, I want you to. Because I've</string>
   . . .
  </lyrics>
 </WXCDInfo>
```

At this stage the Web Service is ready to be consumed by a Web Service client. Actually, this has already been demonstrated in the above section as we have used a Web Client (web browser) and a form. But is it really ready to be consumed by Web Service users? Then the question arises, how do the users know what to send to this Web Service and how do they know what they will receive? Well, that's where the WSDL document comes into play.

For any .NET Web Service, to view the WSDL document, we just append the query string ?WSDL at the end of the Service URL while viewing it in a web browser.

11. In our case the WSDL document can be viewed by typing the following URL into the web browser:

http://localhost/Chapter07/WXTrendyWebService/WXCDLookup.asmx?WSDL

You should be able to see the following WSDL document in your browser (looks familiar?). Yes, you are right, this is exactly the same WSDL document we have analyzed in the WSDL section of this chapter!

Adding the query string `?WSDL` to an `.asmx` (Web Service source file) file returns the WSDL document for that Web Service.

Now our CD Catalogue Web Service is ready to be consumed by users.

WebMethod Attribute Properties

Before we move on to the next section, there are a few important properties for the `WebMethod` attribute that we may find useful.

BufferResponse

This gets or sets whether the response for this request is buffered. The default value is `true`. But you have to set it to `false` if your Web Service is returning large volumes of data (You don't want your buffer to be filled with one Web Service's output!). This property is set to `false` as shown below:

```
[WebMethod(BufferResponse=false)]
```

CacheDuration

This gets or sets the number of seconds the response should be held in the cache. The default value for this property is 0 seconds. One good example where you can use the caching option is if you have a product catalogue Web Service, where you provide a search facility based on product names; you can cache the output results for a better performance!

EnableSession

Indicates whether session state is enabled for an XML Web Service method. Even if you set this property to `true`, you need to have access to the Session state object in your Web Service in order to access the state. You can achieve this in two ways:

- ❑ By deriving your Web Service from the `WebService` base class to access the `Session` object directly

- ❑ By accessing the `Session` object via the `HttpContext.Current` instance

Also when your client communicates with the Web Service, you need to manually attach the session cookies to the request to maintain a stateful communication. Remember that in .NET, SOAP is being implemented on HTTP protocol, which is stateless by nature! However, it is not recommended that you use the `EnableSession` property, as it will cause some performance overheads.

TransactionOption

Web Services can participate in transactions. However, due to the stateless nature of the HTTP protocol, Web Services can only participate as the root object in a transaction. However, it is always a good idea to leverage SQL built-in transactions or the ADO.NET transactions if needed.

Building Web Services Clients

A Web Service client is a piece of software that remotely invokes the functions of a Web Service. When testing the service above, we've seen the browser being used as a client. A Web Service client is also known as a Web Service Consumer. If you remember from our discussion at the beginning of this chapter, you can make the Application data available anywhere by using a Web Service. To prove this point, let's build a Windows application that invokes the CD Catalogue Web Service for CD Lookup. (As a matter of fact, you could also build a client to invoke this Web Service using Java or Perl, it still works!) This is a classical example of Software-as-Service. The interesting factor is that you can also build a Web Form or a console application to consume the above-mentioned Web Service. However, we thought accessing the Web Service from a desktop would be more fun and effective.

CD Catalogue Web Service Consumer

Let's begin by designing a Windows Form to access this Web Service.

1. Open a new Windows Application project, `WXUnadorned`, by selecting **File|Add Project|New Project** Create a Windows Form as shown overleaf (you will need to drag-and-drop the necessary controls from the VS .NET **Toolbox** to create the form):

Now, since we have the Windows Form ready, let's talk about how a Web Service consumer is going access a Web Service. As mentioned earlier we need to send SOAP messages over the wire to invoke a Web Service. Since our SOAP implementation is based on the HTTP protocol (transport) what we essentially have to do is to post a well-formed XML document to the Web Service URL (network endpoint).

Fortunately, the .NET Framework provides us with a class, SOAPHTTPClientProtocol, that has all the above-mentioned functionality. So we have to build a class that is derived from the above class to access the Web Service. The derived class is known as a **Web Service Proxy**. If you want to send raw SOAP messages from your own homemade SOAP client, you can do so also. But Visual Studio .NET simplifies building the Web Service Proxy by using the above-mentioned class. Let's see how to build a proxy for the CD Catalogue Web Service.

2. Displaying the WXUnadorned project in Visual Studio .NET's **Solution Explorer**, right-click on the **References** folder and select the **Add Web Reference** menu item from the context menu displayed.

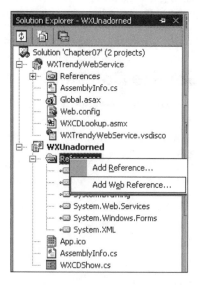

A **Web Reference** is just like any other Assembly Reference that we add to a project. But the difference is that a **Web Reference** creates a Proxy Class locally that references the original Web Service on a remote server via the Web.

3. After Add Web Reference has been selected, the Add Web Reference dialog box is displayed. Enter the CD Catalogue Web Service URL in the Address box. This will associate the WXUnadorned client (a Web Service consumer) with the Web Service residing at the specified URL.

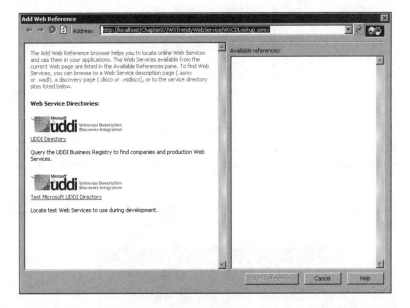

Since you have built this Web Service you know the URL for the Web Service. How does a Web Service User know what URL they should point their **Add Web Reference** dialog box to? That is where UDDI comes into the picture as a Web Service Discovery solution. If you publish your CD Catalogue Web Service in UDDI, consumers should be able to find the Service URL or the WSDL document for your service!

4. Upon hitting *Enter*, you will see that it will display the .asmx page on the left window of the Add Web Reference dialog box and the Add Reference button is activated.

5. If you click on the Add Reference button, a Web Reference will be added to your project.

6. To see what exactly the Add Web Reference dialog box has done to our project by adding a Web Reference, check the Solution Explorer once again. It should look like the screenshot shown below:

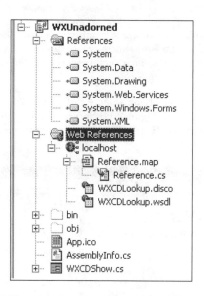

As you can see there is a set of files added under **Web References** with `localhost` as the namespace. The file of interest at this moment is `Reference.cs`. This is the **Proxy Class** that is generated by Visual Studio .NET.

7. To see this file, you may need to turn on the **Show All Files** option of your **Solution Explorer** as shown below:

8. If you open this file to view the contents you should be able to see the following code (abbreviated for brevity):

```
[System.Web.Services.WebServiceBindingAttribute(Name="WXCDLookupSoap",
Namespace="http://localhost/WroxUnderstandingDotNet/")]
    public class WXCDLookup : System.Web.Services.Protocols.SoapHttpClientProtocol
```

```
{

    public WXCDLookup() {
        this.Url =
"http://localhost/Chapter07/WXTrendyWebService/WXCDLookup.asmx";
    }


[System.Web.Services.Protocols.SoapDocumentMethodAttribute("http://localhost/WroxU
nderstandingDotNet/WXFindLyrics",
RequestNamespace="http://localhost/WroxUnderstandingDotNet/",
ResponseNamespace="http://localhost/WroxUnderstandingDotNet/",
Use=System.Web.Services.Description.SoapBindingUse.Literal,
ParameterStyle=System.Web.Services.Protocols.SoapParameterStyle.Wrapped)]

    public WXCDInfo WXFindLyrics(string cdName) {
        object[] results = this.Invoke("WXFindLyrics", new object[] {
                cdName});
        return ((WXCDInfo)(results[0]));

    }
}
```

As you can see from the above code, the WXCDLookup class is inherited from the SoapHTTPProtocol class. The constructor for this class points the url to the Web Service URL. The WXFindLyrics function invokes the Web Method WXFindLyrics of our CD Catalogue Web Service. Now we can use this class in the Windows Form we have created to consume this Web Service.

9. The code below shows how to call the proxy class created in the previous step. This code needs to be added to the button event handler of our form.

```
WXUnadorned.localhost.WXCDInfo _cdInfo

    private void buttonLookup_Click(
            object sender,
            System.EventArgs e)
    {
        try
        {
            WXUnadorned.localhost.WXCDLookup cdLookup =
                new WXUnadorned.localhost.WXCDLookup();

            _cdInfo = cdLookup.WXFindLyrics(textBoxCD.Text);
            if (_cdInfo.error != null)
            {
                throw new Exception(_cdInfo.error);
            }

            if ((_cdInfo.lyrics == null) ||
                (_cdInfo.songs == null) ||
                (_cdInfo.lyrics.Length == 0) ||
                (_cdInfo.songs.Length == 0) ||
                (_cdInfo.songs.Length != _cdInfo.lyrics.Length))
            {
                throw new Exception("Invalid data returned");
            }

            foreach (string lyric in _cdInfo.lyrics)
            {
                if (lyric == null)
                {
```

```
                        throw new Exception("Invalid data returned");
            }
        }

        foreach (string song in _cdInfo.songs)
        {
            if (song == null)
            {
                throw new Exception("Invalid data returned");
            }

            listBoxSongs.Items.Add(song);
        }

        listBoxSongs.SelectedIndex = 0;
        textBoxLyrics.Text =
            _cdInfo.lyrics[listBoxSongs.SelectedIndex];
}
```

The elegance of the code shown above is that the highlighted lines simply look like creating an instance of type WXCDLookup, and then calling the WXFindLyrics method in order to retrieve a WXCDInfo structure. Actually, the highlighted WXFindLyrics method is calling the proxy method, which in turn calls a method that is part of the CD Catalogue Web Service; and if you can remember, WXCDInfo and WXCDLookUp are the types exposed by this Web Service!

10. When we build and run the above project to search for the CD Name Mini, you will see the following results returned by our CD Catalogue Web Service that we have coded in the previous section:

So you have seen how to consume a Web Service using Visual Studio .NET via the Web Reference. Actually, you can also use **WSDL.EXE**, a tool shipped along with the .NET Framework, to build the proxy class. What it actually does is create the proxy source file so that we can add it in our projects as a proxy! The following picture shows you how to create a Web Service Proxy by invoking the **WSDL.EXE** using Visual Studio .NET Command Prompt:

Other Important Classes in .NET Framework

Before we move on to look at .NET My Services, let's take a brief look at some of the important classes that are provided in the .NET Framework that you need to be aware of in the context of Web Services.

.NET Framework Class	What it can be used for
SoapException	A Web Service method might throw a SoapException, when it is known that clients will be calling using SOAP. If you have to handle a SoapException, check the Actor, Code, and Detail properties for more details regarding the Exception.
SoapHeader	SOAP headers offer a method for passing data to and from an XML Web Service method if the data is not directly related to the XML Web Service method's primary functionality. The .NET Framework provides this class to optionally add SOAP headers to the SOAP messages that we send to and receive from the Web Services. This class, in conjunction with a SoapHeaderAttribute, can be used for a **custom security** design for your Web Service.
SoapExtension	You can leverage the SoapExtension class to have a low-level access to the SOAP messages before and after the serialization. If you think of **custom encryption** for your SOAP messages for security purposes, this is the class you need to use.

.NET My Services

Microsoft .NET My Services (formerly codenamed HailStorm) is a set of Consumer-Centric Web Services. Consumer-Centric Web Services could be defined as the Web Services that are designed with a focus on user data rather than specific applications, platforms, or devices. Developers can leverage these Web Services to build consumer-oriented Internet applications for web sites, Web Services, applications and devices. The architectural specifications for .NET My Services are no different from those of normal Web Services.

However, Microsoft Passport Service handles the security aspects of .NET My Services, which is a member of the .NET My Service family itself. So if you want to use these services you need to have a valid Microsoft Passport account!

More .NET My Services

At the time of this writing .NET My Services is still in Beta stage. In fact, the latest word is that Microsoft are considering offering My Services to corporations in a traditional package form, rather than as a service. But what makes .NET My Services interesting is the set of User-Centric services that it provides. Let's take a look at some of the interesting services that are provided with .NET My Services:

Service	Description
.NET Notifications	Using this Web Service users can receive notifications from applications, web sites, and Web Services on any device, any time, anywhere.
.NET Calendar	Using this Web Service, users can store all of their calendar information in one place, so that they can access it from any device at any time.
.NET Inbox	This is an integrated messaging Web Service, which gives users access to their e-mail from any device. This means that users can check e-mail from Microsoft Hotmail on any computer or device from which they sign in to .NET My Services.
.NET Wallet	This service allows the user to store information used for purchasing items online. The advantage of this service is that you do not need to enter your personal information again and again when you go shopping on-line.

And the list goes on! What makes the future of .NET My Services promising is Microsoft's commitment to its vision of accessing information on any device at any time.

> You can find more on .NET My Services and the complete list of services at:
> http://www.microsoft.com/myservices/services/userexperiences.asp

From a developer's perspective, it is important to understand that .NET My Services uses a central meta-service named .NET Services. This service brokers the interactions between clients and the other .NET Services such as .NET Notifications or .NET Wallet. So a client application must negotiate a transaction with the central .NET Services before addressing a specific requested service like .NET Contacts or .NET Wallet.

.NET My Services also uses the Kerberos authentication protocol and encrypts all SOAP packets in order to ensure the security of user's private data. This demands the client has Kerberos protocol compatibility. Also, the client must encrypt SOAP requests and decrypt SOAP responses.

As Microsoft moves forward with the .NET My Services family, Visual Studio .NET provides tools for developers to build applications around .NET My Services seamlessly and efficiently.

The Future of Web Services

After the PC revolution in the 80s and the Internet revolution in the 90s, Web Services are taking the world by storm today. This revolution seems rather natural because Web Services are providing a solution to a long time problem – that is businesses-to-business integration and application-to-application integration. Not only that, they are also closely coupled with the ubiquitous HTTP protocol.

Microsoft has released the Global XML Web Services Architecture (GXA), which is going to be the framework for the future of Web Services. GXA is designed for a wide range of Web Service scenarios, ranging from B2B and EAI solutions to peer-to-peer applications and B2C services.

GXA addresses the issues such as security, message routing referral, etc., which Web Services currently do not address. Microsoft is providing specifications such as WS-Security, WS-License, WS-Routing, and WS-Referral as a part of GXA to address the above mentioned issues.

Summary

In this chapter we have seen what Web Services really are. We have also discussed the Web Services technology stack and core components in it, such as SOAP, WSDL, and UDDI.

We have seen how to build Web Services using the .NET Framework and Visual Studio .NET. Also we have learned that one can get granular control of Web Services specifics such as parameter encoding and style using attributes in .NET.

As we have seen in this chapter, a Web Service can be consumed from any kind of client with no restrictions of programming language, operating system, or the geographic location.

At the end we have seen where the Web Services initiative is moving to with Microsoft's GXA and .NET My Services.

Nevertheless, even though the standards are still evolving, Web Services are going to play an important role in the .NET development effort since Microsoft's .NET is heavily oriented around Web Services.

.NET

8

Where Do We Go From Here?

Make no mistake about it, .NET is not an incremental technology improvement. It will have major impacts on many programming communities:

- ❏ .NET is shock therapy to Visual Basic programmers, who must learn a language that behaves a lot more like Java.

- ❏ For the Java community .NET is a major jolt: they now have credible competition for developing the next generation of enterprise web applications.

- ❏ C++ programmers now have a far higher-level class library and framework, giving them many of the RAD tools previously reserved for VB developers.

- ❏ For developers using non-Microsoft programming languages (outside of Java), .NET offers new or expanded opportunities to become fully integrated into the Microsoft application architecture.

Microsoft promotes .NET as being all about software as services. In reality, the .NET Framework supports software as Web Services as just one of several choices for software deployment. But it obviously makes the web Services option more accessible than ever.

While progress can be exciting, the costs are sometimes overwhelming. Eventually .NET will become the standard on Microsoft platforms, and it will be difficult to avoid. Of course, your organization can continue to deploy "classic" Win32 and new .NET applications side by side, and, if history is any guide, your Win32 applications are likely to stick around until they grow obsolete for business, not technology reasons.

But does it make sense to drop everything and convert? Probably not.

So what should you do now? To put matters into perspective, this chapter quickly reviews the benefits of .NET, and the price of progress. We'll look ahead and discuss how the emergence of Microsoft .NET will impact the enterprise, software vendors, and consultants.

Because Microsoft is painting .NET as your organization's on-ramp to web services, we'll explore the role of web services and how they will fit into the grand scheme of things.

Technology Highlights

.NET is intended to make a number of routine processes, from web page generation to data retrieval, far more efficient. Its enhanced middle tier and self-reflecting features are meant to reduce coding requirements. Underlying all this, .NET introduces new component models, integrates web services, and ties in non-Microsoft languages to a previously unprecedented degree.

Just about the only things that remain intact are the IIS web server and the COM+ middle-tier services, which, in .NET, are incrementally upgraded.

More Ease, Less Ease

.NET introduces changes, both to the core technology framework and to the popular Visual Studio IDE that Microsoft has been offering for years. Let's look at the impacts individually.

Framework and Languages

The .NET component architecture introduces many new features, among them broader and deeper language interoperability, a common typing system, and various middle-tier services like exception handling and reflection that are implemented as part of the common runtime.

A major change is the new evidence-based security model. With capabilities that drill down to the method level, developers could easily get overwhelmed with security that is far more granular than what they are accustomed to, or what they might actually need.

Admittedly, working with a new common framework that is designed to be language-independent can be a shock, particularly for VB programmers used to a fairly simplistic framework and doing things their own way. .NET enforces the concept of "managed code" – something that may be quite familiar to C++ and Java programmers, but new to many VB developers. It standardizes common variable types, user-defined types, arrays, classes, error handling, and interfaces that will also be new to many in the VB world. Ironically, with .NET, VB looks a lot more like Java because it is based on managed code concepts.

As for Java itself, with C#, Microsoft claims to offer a better Java than Java. In effect, C# pits Microsoft's philosophy of flexibility vs. Java's approach of enforcing strict defaults. The best example is security: Java's "secure sandbox", where features such as use of memory pointers are prohibited, vs. C#'s approach, which allows developers to override such defaults. If this is convincing enough to interest you, Microsoft's Visual J# provides a bridge from both Java and Visual J++ (Microsoft's older Java tool) to .NET, using Java syntax that compiles against the .NET Framework instead of the Java Virtual Machine (JVM).

Of course, the operable Java question is why use .NET when the real thing is also available? The answer is that you're not just choosing a language, but an entire platform. By going to .NET, you are committing yourself to using Windows as the middle-tier platform – at least until third parties develop their own ports of .NET technology to other environments like Linux. Conversely, by selecting Java, you would be keeping your middle-tier and server-platform choices open, but committing to the Java language and framework

Tools (IDE)

It's easy to confuse .NET technology or the .NET Framework with Visual Studio .NET. In fact, Visual Studio .NET is simply an IDE (Integrated Development Environment) that can be used to develop .NET applications.

VS.NET won't be the only way to develop .NET applications. For instance, you could develop .NET applications using Notepad or other text editors, although most developers are likely to prefer the ease of using IDEs. More importantly, you could develop .NET applications using third-party tools or languages as long as they comply with Microsoft's Common Language Infrastructure (CLI).

However, owing to its huge popularity, VS.NET is likely to become the predominant tool of .NET developers. Over the years, Microsoft has used the Visual Studio bundle to gradually add more common bells and whistles between the IDEs for each of its languages, including VB, Visual C++, and until recently, Visual J++. Until now, however, the IDEs for each language were not identical, and in the case of VB and C++/J++, there were also vast differences in practices, structures, and syntax.

VS.NET will change the script by unifying the front end for all Microsoft applications, plus third-party languages and tools that support APIs that are published by Microsoft. The result is that all developers using VS.NET languages will look at the same IDE. Third-party products that support Microsoft interfaces will appear as plug-ins inside the VS.NET environment. And most importantly, because the new common runtime and changes that Microsoft has made to its languages (primarily VB), syntax, calls, and practices will mostly be the same between the Microsoft .NET languages. With these changes, development teams could communicate and collaborate far more easily.

Now let's take a look at the sweet spots and pain points in particular areas.

Shared Components

The .NET Framework does a lot to make it easier to use shared components. The highlight is the declarative programming model, where a component's metadata is automatically generated at compile time.

The obvious benefits include the virtual elimination of DLL hell, which arises from shared libraries that have been overwritten or corrupted by other programs. The CLR ensures that shared libraries are versioned, using a strong naming system, to reduce or eliminate the chance that applications call on the wrong DLLs, and crash. A side benefit is the side-by-side deployment of different versions of shared DLLs, which further reduces opportunities for conflicts and crashes.

The new process also saves coding time. Because components describe themselves, we no longer need to write Interface Definition Language code for every component or register it in the Windows Registry of every target machine. Both steps are eliminated – in many cases to be replaced with a simple XCOPY.

It is also easier to keep all the instances of a component in sync on different machines. Because .NET components automatically generate their own metadata, they can take advantage of reflection capabilities where components identify themselves, eliminating the need to manually locate and synchronize with existing libraries.

Deployment Options

As we mentioned before, Microsoft is hyping the ability to deploy software as services in the new .NET Framework. .NET's Web Services deployment wizards eliminate the tedious step of writing headers for SOAP messages, WSDL definitions, and UDDI registry listings.

This is just part of the story. When working with .NET you have several choices, including new .NET components, Windows Forms, legacy COM components for older VB or C++ applications, and of course Web Services.

The .NET Framework provides other features that simplify different aspects of deployment. For instance, a new remoting feature enables you to design an application to execute on another machine (without having to install it there). Additionally, the forms designer has now been made fully object-oriented, allowing forms to be inherited. Other features simplify presentation. Automatic browser detection features interrogate the browser version on the client, and render HTML accordingly. This feature should prove especially useful with older browsers that might not support the latest bells and whistles.

Of course, making things easy – such as automating the generation of Web Services headers – doesn't necessarily guarantee that the software can successfully be transformed into a Web Service. To be deployed as a Web Service, the software must be developed with that in mind. You won't necessarily be able to take any old Windows Forms applications and magically transform just with .NET's wizards or checkboxes. Tools only take you so far.

Less Code, Better Performance

Microsoft boasts that .NET applications will require less coding than previous VB or Visual C++ apps, and even provide some improvements over Java. In some cases, .NET builds on improvements already made in the development of COM. For instance, the emergence of the COM+ middle tier in versions 5 and 6 of the Visual Studio languages eliminated the need to manually develop various middle-tier services such as transaction pooling and caching. These improvements continue in VS.NET with the elimination of writing IDL code, and the development of visual and server-side controls, memory management, and data management.

In other cases, the improvements include new technologies, or dramatic new improvements to existing technologies, including:

❑ ADO.NET's introduction of intermediate XML data formats, expanding the possibilities for manipulating and integrating data

❑ ASP.NET's improvements, adding faster web page generation, improved stability, new server controls, "code-behind" compilation, event-handling capabilities, and the elimination of the need to know a scripting language

❑ File streaming, which .NET now extends to VB users, eliminates the need to code open/read/close steps

These enhancements each reduce coding requirements, and in many cases improve performance. But there is always a price for progress, as we discuss under *Impact on the Enterprise* below.

What Kinds of Applications Can be Developed

You can use .NET to develop several types of applications. A highlight of .NET is that it also allows you to develop Web Services applications. Thanks to standard APIs, applications that operate with the Framework's runtime can easily be deployed as Web Services, with the runtime generating all the necessary headers.

Web Services can serve several functions. First, they can be used to change the way software is made available to end users by 'deconstructing' traditional monolithic applications into individual, modular business services – either to internal end users, or with your company's business partners.

Web Services could also be used as a lowest common denominator form of enterprise application integration (EAI) inside the firewall. The beauty of Web Services is that they are platform and architecture-independent. As long as the applications support the same Web Services protocols and are semantically compatible (the logic fits), they can interoperate.

If you want to migrate code, .NET versions of roughly two dozen other languages, such as Eiffel, Python, and Perl, certified by Microsoft for compliance with the CLI already exist. However, as we note below, migration always has limitations. In this case, even if the language complies with .NET's CLI, the code must be properly engineered to support the .NET classes, data typing, and object structures.

The Impact of Standards

With .NET, Microsoft has come to terms with the standards process with a vengeance. Its philosophy could be well summarized as, "If you can't beat them, join them." Microsoft is not only embracing standards, it is even leading many of the standards initiatives. Furthermore, Microsoft has gotten some of the innards of the .NET Framework – the C# language and the Common Language Infrastructure – approved as international standards.

Of course, anyone could debate Microsoft's motives here – cynics might suggest that Microsoft is simply co-opting the process to lock in Windows platforms. Also, of course, much of .NET technology remains proprietary.

For corporate users and software vendors, the impact is that the externals of the .NET Framework will be as standard as they come. With .NET, vendors and users should feel assured that the technology will stay in the mainstream of Web Services development. However, the internal component models remain proprietary to Microsoft – meaning that features such as ADO.NET and ASP.NET will always be optimised to Windows platforms, and at best become de facto standards. In this respect, the Java technology framework is far more open, governed by a standards process that is quasi multi-vendor. Depending on your point of view, internal skills base, and platform environment, the proprietary nature of .NET may or may not make any difference.

Some Things Never Change

Although the .NET Framework shows Java's influence, it also remains very consistent to Microsoft's computing visions. .NET is language-independent, but for now Windows-based – it doesn't emphasize platform-independence half as much as Java does.

There are other differences that are consistent with Microsoft's competitive philosophies. For instance, Microsoft still believes in fat clients where appropriate. Therefore, while Java is premised on the notion of thin clients and fat servers, Microsoft continues to insist that the processing power in an application should be deployed wherever it is most suitable, and if that means on the client, then so be it. The .NET Framework strives to improve client-side deployment with measures such as remoting, side-by-side deployment (where different versions of shared resources are automatically versioned), and self-reflection. This eliminates some of the worst excesses of fat-client computing. With .NET, Microsoft wants to make it OK for organizations to run fat clients if they want to – a notion that will certainly help sell more Windows licenses.

.NET also showcases Microsoft's belief that application deployments should take maximum advantage of the features of the underlying OS which, surprise surprise, is Windows. So although all those CLI-compliant languages compile to an intermediate language (IL), this is not inefficient byte code. IL remains optimized for the Windows operating system (although some efforts are underway to port it to other platforms).

.NET's approach to security showcases another Microsoft trait, which is to give developers maximum flexibility. By default, .NET keeps us in a sandbox just like Java. But if you really want to fool with memory blocks and pointers, you can. In fact, Microsoft gives you so much flexibility in deciding security (you can manage it down to the class level), that it becomes either extremely useful or highly intimidating.

Impact on the Enterprise

.NET provides a lot of new technology to digest. For VB programmers, the move to a Java-like programming model will involve a lot of hard work.

The efforts will be rewarded with the availability of robust component development techniques – in many cases borrowed from the Java world. If implemented properly these could make the development process far more productive. While it's possible to apply principles of OO and component-based design to VB or C++, the .NET Framework enforces it because the runtime only accepts well-formed objects. If you've been preaching the virtues of object-oriented development, component architectures, and reuse, .NET gives you the chance to walk the talk.

While .NET could lead you to a future of software as services, in the present you can still use the framework and the tools to turn out familiar Windows Forms and COM components. VB.NET even allows developers to program in "classic" (VB 6) mode.

Furthermore, the ability to interchange different .NET languages theoretically translates to more effective skills utilization, especially if your group has developers with different language backgrounds.

Of course, the downside is that better technology never guarantees better programming practices. For example while Java is an object-oriented language, developers could defeat its purpose by developing event-oriented classes. The same is true with the .NET languages – developers still need to learn effective OO techniques, as well as the OO languages and syntax. In some ways, .NET gives developers tools to become more dangerous.

Culture Shock for VB Programmers

Change is never easy, and for .NET the learning curve will be significant. There are bridges to support legacy COM components, tools and shortcuts for converting VB 6 code, ASP, or ADO controls to the .NET architecture. However, just converting code, components, or controls to the new framework does not necessarily mean they will be able to take advantage of all the new services. For that matter, as we discuss in the following section, in some cases it may not pay to migrate existing applications.

Why is Microsoft forcing us into these decisions? Microsoft had to do something dramatic to provide a credible alternative to Java and J2EE. Microsoft realized that while it was nice to own the world's most popular programming language, keeping the enterprise on Windows platforms was far more mission-critical. If Microsoft was going to do whatever was necessary to make the framework a compelling alternative to Java, the answer was not to dumb down C++, C#, or any other language to VB's level of looseness (even if the notion were feasible). With the VB community already begging for features like inheritance, .NET provided the opportunity.

Some of the most visible changes include:

❑ The end of fixed-length strings, Active X documents, DAO and RDO data bindings, and non-zero-based arrays

❑ Less use of DHTML pages

❑ A more visible and controllable garbage-collection mechanism

❑ New Web Services middle-tier components that work differently from existing COM+ components

❑ Replacement of web classes with ASP.NET and VB.NET web forms

❑ Replacement of VB Forms with Windows Forms, which have different object models that are enforced throughout the framework

❑ Changes in the handling of late-bound objects

There are other impacts that transcend VB, with ADO.NET being the most prominent example. The plus side: by using XML as the intermediate data format for ADO.NET, barriers to enterprise data integration and reuse are dramatically lowered.

Should You Migrate?

Consequently, "If it ain't broke, don't fix it" is good advice – particularly when considering software migration. If your organization has working VB 6 or Visual C++ applications, it probably makes sense to leave them intact. This does mean your older applications won't take advantages of .NET's new services, but if the application was stable then it doesn't make sense to add new bells and whistles. If your applications rely on features that are not supported by .NET (ActiveX documents, DHTML pages with client-side DLLs, OLE container controls, DDE, and so on) then it makes no sense to migrate unless it's as part of other major changes.

241

If you do decide to migrate, take it one step at a time. Remember that once you convert an application to VB.NET, there is no going back.

While it's often not worth migrating, it's important to decide when to transfer development of new systems to .NET. Unless your company is about to fold or is planning to outsource future application development, your team should learn the new .NET technologies. If business constraints allow, adopt them as the standard for new development going forward. But be careful. There's a lot of new stuff to learn and your group will not master .NET overnight – there will be an unproductive period before the benefits start to appear.

Once you start, treat .NET as you would any new technology, by taking baby steps first. Start with modest applications and as your team advances get more ambitious.

In an ideal world, it's always nice to set definitive sunset dates for older technologies, and it's always nice to harmonize development on common platforms. Real life, however, is far messier. Of course, when migrating, you have to consider the state of your development team's knowledge base. But there are other factors as well, like the issue of developing standard Windows clients. If your organization plans to continue developing them, make sure that target client machines all have Windows 2000, XP, or later, and have the .NET Framework installed. Don't take anything for granted here. Most organizations tend to have various isolated enclaves that have stubbornly held on to older technologies. For instance, many retailers have kept their DOS-based point of sale systems because Windows never provided any advantages! So don't assume that .NET applications are going to deploy everywhere.

Impact on Vendors and Consultants

The .NET Framework provides a critical mass of services that rivals the J2EE Framework, while providing access to the huge mass of VB developers. Microsoft has already perfected the art of building third-party software support. With .NET, independent software vendors have a much more robust integration platform to support.

Another advantage is that Microsoft, unlike the Java community, has always accommodated third-party developers by embedding a standard, enforceable component-licensing model. This is the same model that helped spur the VBX controls market in the early 1990s, the first aftermarket for software components. By comparison, the aftermarket for Java beans or EJBs is next to nonexistent.

The fact that the .NET Framework is open to non-Microsoft languages should theoretically open the floodgates to third-party component developers further. Although the huge popularity of VB likely precludes a sizable market in other languages, a niche may open for Perl, Python, or even COBOL developers who want to market .NET components that tie-in legacy markets without the need to learn non-legacy languages.

For consultants, the newness and the radical changes promised in the .NET Framework will be a real bonanza, because the new technology bundle includes a lot to learn, creating a huge need for training and mentoring. Of course, the usual bunch of insubstantial confidence-tricksters will be out in full force, taking advantage of customer naïveté.

Software as Services: What Does it all Mean?

To comprehend Web Services, it helps to understand the saga of systems integration and the evolution of the web. Since the dawn of the age of the computer, developers have dreamed of finding a magic way to integrate information and services. Before the 1980s data and logic were largely intertwined. There was hardly even a software industry to speak of, because most applications were custom built from scratch. This made sense because computers were so expensive that few companies could afford them.

In the 1980s, opposing software architectures emerged at opposite ends of the spectrum – new mainframe and midrange corporate applications versus standalone desktop systems. In both cases the software was largely self-contained. The birth of relational databases provided the first opportunity to separate data from the business logic. When client-server architectures emerged a decade later, the hope was that data, stored on off-the-shelf database systems would open up data access across applications. In most cases, those dreams were unfulfilled because applications tended to structure their data uniquely.

Therefore, systems integration became a major enterprise cost center, as organizations often hired expensive consultants to find ways of integrating applications. Despite much effort, systems integration has remained stubbornly expensive.

Ironically, the Web's emergence onto the scene in the mid 1990s was not about databases, but about sharing documents. However, that soon changed as a result of several developments, including the introduction of enhanced web application environments from Java and the Microsoft DNA architecture, which provided database-driven web pages.

Enter Web Services

As the twenty-first century dawned, new Web Services technologies emerged, patterned around XML and promising to be the holy grail of enterprise integration. Stated simply, Web Services provide a standard way of exposing callable methods over the Internet. The data-transfer format used is XML. This model enables us to see software as a service, rather than a self-contained product.
The following scenarios are key to the success of Web Services. First, Web Services might finally lead to standards for systems integration. They could serve as a straightforward way for businesses to exchange information, or to integrate separate systems within an organisation. Second, Web Services might be used to improve B2B and B2C commerce web sites. Simple Web Services could cover routine transactions such as flight reservations or inventory replenishments. The use of web service technology would make these applications more flexible – instead of logging onto a web site to place a procurement after manually contacting the stock room and calling suppliers, a Web Service could automate the process with a set of services that first perform the inventory query, then search for qualified suppliers willing to ship the product at a certain price by a certain date, then place the order. This would use SOAP messages that request the service, WSDL messages that define the service, and if directories are used, UDDI registries that provide a list of potential providers of the requested service.

In the long run, the revolutionary vision for Web Services is that monolithic software applications will cease to exist. Instead, they will be offered as Web Services that are far easier to deploy, modify, and maintain – truly software as service.

Impact on Application Developers

The impact of Web Services on development teams could be significant. The time to benefit should be short, particularly if Web Services standards are faithfully employed. They should be able to roll out services that interoperate with each other inside the firewall, and with business partners and customers in the outside world. They could use the same technology to expose functions that are currently locked up in existing applications, and even communicate with J2EE apps.

This is a rather optimistic view – like any new technology, Web Services are works in progress. Web Services having emerged in public discourse barely 18 months ago, the degree to which major technology vendors have hopped onto the bandwagon is remarkable.

Today, we have a form of XML messaging over HTTP, a protocol for describing Web Services, and another protocol that covers registries. That leaves huge gaps in areas including service identification, security, authentication, recovery, and rollback. In short, Web Services offer none of the service level protections of the transaction-processing world. In effect, Web Services technologies are today where web applications were prior to the emergence of Java and Active X: stateless processes traveling in the void.

Admittedly, the early building blocks are just a start, but questions persist as to whether they will make web services practical. For instance, while SOAP is currently the only defined Web Service messaging standard, there are concerns regarding whether its RPC (Remote Procedure Call) nature is practicable given the Internet's latency. Furthermore, the fact that SOAP is not object-oriented could make it difficult to manage as the sheer volume of transactions increases.

Nonetheless, to dismiss Web Services as hopelessly immature would be akin to shrugging off web applications circa 1995, when all they did was serve up documents. The standards were just as immature then. There was little precedent for believing that stateless application environments could be made robust, that insecure public networks could be made safe for enterprise business, and that crude text interfaces would eventually acquire the rich visual controls of client-server system. In 1996, Microsoft was forced to do a 180-degree turn and embrace the Net. As the era of Web Services dawns, corporate and commercial software developers run the same risks if they fail to stay abreast of what could become the next major transition in enterprise application architecture.

The .NET Framework is hardly the only route to Web Services. Although it has solidified its web services support ahead of J2EE, the race is by no means over. As Web Services technologies evolve, both .NET and J2EE will have to adapt to support the new standards. And in the long run, both will coexist, tied together by Web Services. Thanks to its robust object model, middle-tier services, and multi-language support, the .NET Framework gives Java the competition it finally deserves.

The Next Step

So now that you've seen a lot about .NET, what it is, why it is, and what you can do with it, what's the next step in your path to becoming the .NET developer?

Ultimately it will depend on the type of applications that you are going to write. .NET provides a common development environment for a great range of applications, including web applications, Windows applications, Windows services, controls (web and Windows), components, Web Services and so on. From simple desktop apps to complex n-tier applications, the possibilities are almost endless.

However, there are a few basic paths to take regardless of your ultimate destination.

To start with you're going to have to learn a .NET-compliant language. Otherwise you're not going to be able to make much use of .NET at all. Although there are over two dozen potential languages to choose from in all likelihood you will need to choose from a smaller range of two or three languages; primarily Visual Basic .NET, C#, or Visual C++ .NET. We talked about the differences in the languages in Chapter 2, but the thing to remember is that whatever language you are currently familiar with you are going to have to learn some new stuff. Visual Basic developers might find the learning curve somewhat steeper than a C++ developer but everyone will have to learn something new.

You are also most likely going to want to learn how to use Visual Studio .NET. It's not essential but you'll find it makes your life a lot easier.

Once you've mastered a language the next step is really to learn the Framework itself – or at least the parts you're interested in. You won't necessarily have to learn it all, but the essential skills for .NET development are:

- ❏ **User Interface Programming skills**
  ASP.NET and Web Forms, Windows Forms, Event-driven programming

- ❏ **Data skills**
  ADO.NET, XML, and databases

- ❏ **Object-oriented programming skills**
  Analysis and design, and UML

- ❏ **Development Language skills**
  I/O, threading, Visual Studio .NET

- ❏ **.NET Platform skills**
  CLR and basic .NET architecture, Assemblies and Deployment, COM+ Services, COM Interoperability

Of course, there already exists a plethora of information on these topics, from books to training course, and from web sites to mailing lists. This book has given you a taster of what to expect, so now the next step is in your hands, finally. Bon voyage!

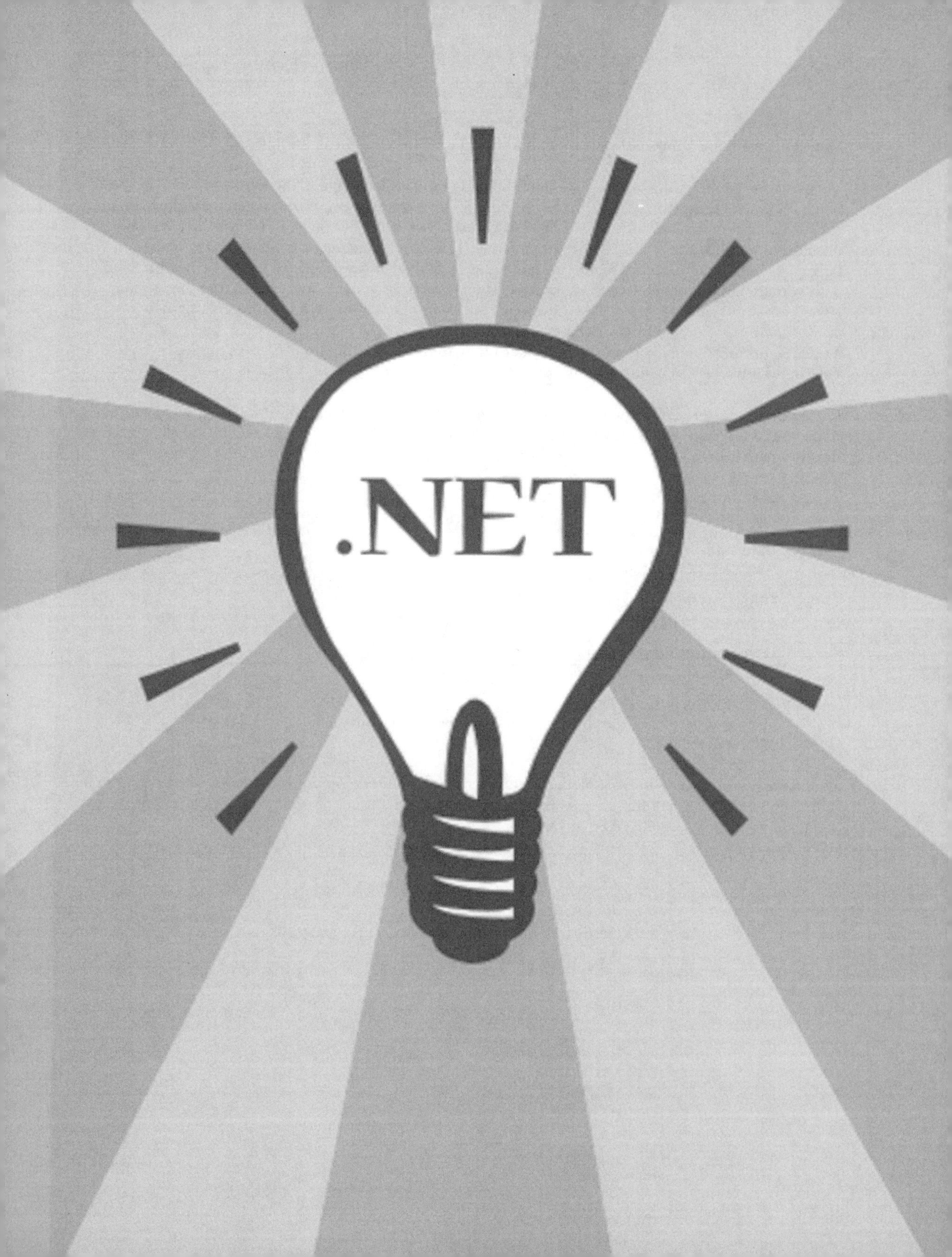
.NET

Index

A Guide to the Index

The index is arranged hierarchically, in alphabetical order.

.NET references are alphabetized as starting with a dot, with symbols (including dots) preceding the letter A.

Programmer to Programmer™

Registration Code: | 7094K00F0M742S01

Wrox writes books for you. Any suggestions, or ideas about how you want information given in your ideal book will be studied by our team.
Your comments are always valued at Wrox.

Free phone in USA 800-USE-WROX
Fax (312) 893 8001

UK Tel.: (0121) 687 4100   Fax: (0121) 687 4101

Understanding the .NET Framework – Registration Card

Name _____

Address _____

_____

_____

City _____ State/Region _____

Country _____ Postcode/Zip _____

E-Mail _____

Occupation _____

How did you hear about this book?

❑ Book review (name) _____

❑ Advertisement (name) _____

❑ Recommendation _____

❑ Catalog _____

❑ Other _____

Where did you buy this book?

❑ Bookstore (name) _____ City _____

❑ Computer store (name) _____

❑ Mail order _____

❑ Other _____

What influenced you in the purchase of this book?

❑ Cover Design ❑ Contents ❑ Other (please specify):

_____

How did you rate the overall content of this book?

❑ Excellent ❑ Good ❑ Average ❑ Poor

What did you find most useful about this book? _____

_____

What did you find least useful about this book? _____

_____

Please add any additional comments. _____

_____

What other subjects will you buy a computer book on soon?

_____

What is the best computer book you have used this year?

_____

> **Note:** This information will only be used to keep you updated about new Wrox Press titles and will not be used for any other purpose or passed to any other third party.

wrox

Programmer to Programmer™

Note: If you post the bounce back card below in the UK, please send it to:

Wrox Press Limited, Arden House, 1102 Warwick Road,
Acocks Green, Birmingham B27 6HB. UK.

Computer Book Publishers